THE ORGANIZER'S GUIDE TO ARCHITECTURE EDUCATION

The Organizer's Guide to Architecture Education serves as a timely call-to-action for transforming architecture education to meet the monumental environmental and social challenges of our time.

Written by a collective of eight educators, practitioners, and organizers and structured in three parts, the book considers organizing across four scales of architecture education and reorients architecture toward stewarding the planetary commons. It speaks to students, faculty, and administrators in architecture schools, as well as professional architects and built environment practitioners, who recognize the need to expand and decenter the discipline. Readers will gain critical understandings and skills for reimagining architectural pedagogy, practice, and relations to power structures. Empowered by this knowledge, readers will be motivated to contribute actively to and drive systemic change within the field.

Illuminated with how-to methods—from power mapping to conversation tactics—and case study precedents, the book catalyzes a collective redefinition of architecture as a vital player in building a socially just and ecologically regenerative future.

Kirsten Day (she/her) is an architect and lecturer in Architecture (Technology and Practice) at the University of Melbourne, Australia.

Peggy Deamer (she/her) is Professor Emerita, Yale School of Architecture and a founding member of the Architecture Lobby.

Andrea Dietz (she/her) is an architect-educator whose research-based practice focuses on the culture and politics of space and its representations.

Tessa Forde (she/they) is an architecture researcher, teacher, and practitioner in Aotearoa New Zealand, interested in the redeployment of architecture's tools.

Jessica Garcia Fritz (she/her) is an Assistant Professor of Architecture at the University of Minnesota, and a citizen of the Cheyenne River Sioux Tribe (Itazipco).

Palmyra Geraki (she/her) is an interdisciplinary architect, educator, and editor, interested in the tensions and opportunities present in the relationship between the individual and the collective.

Valérie (Val) Lechêne (she/they) is a systems change agent, technologist, and a trained-architect based in Brooklyn, NY, USA.

THE ORGANIZER'S GUIDE TO ARCHITECTURE EDUCATION

Kirsten Day, Peggy Deamer, Andrea Dietz, Tessa Forde, Jessica Garcia Fritz, Palmyra Geraki and Valérie Lechêne

with contributions by

Renzo Dagnino

Routledge
Taylor & Francis Group
LONDON AND NEW YORK

Designed cover image: Kirsten Day, Peggy Deamer, Andrea Dietz, Tessa Forde, Jessica Garcia Fritz, Palmyra Geraki, Valérie Lechêne and Renzo Dagnino.

First published 2024
by Routledge
4 Park Square, Milton Park, Abingdon, Oxon OX14 4RN

and by Routledge
605 Third Avenue, New York, NY 10158

Routledge is an imprint of the Taylor & Francis Group, an informa business

British Library Cataloguing-in-Publication Data
A catalogue record for this book is available from the British Library

Library of Congress Cataloging-in-Publication Data
Names: Day, Kirsten (Kirsten M.), author. | 1 Deamer, Peggy, aut | 1 Dietz, Andrea, aut
Title: The organizer's guide to architecture education / Kirsten Day, Peggy Deamer, Andrea Dietz, Tessa Forde, Jessica García Fritz, Palmyra Geraki and Valérie Lechêne ; with Renzo Dagn
Description: 1 Abingdon, Oxon : Routledge, 2 | Includes bibliographical references and in | Summary: "The Organizer's Guide to Architecture Education serves as a timely call-to-action for transforming architecture education to meet the monumental environmental and social challenges of our time. Written by a collective of eight educators, practitioners, and organizers and structured in three parts, the book considers organizing across four scales of architecture education and reorients architecture toward stewarding the planetary commons. It speaks to students, faculty, and administrators in architecture schools, as well as professional architects and built environment practitioners, who recognize the need to expand and decenter the discipline. Readers will gain critical understandings and skills for reimagining architectural pedagogy, practice, and relations to power structures. Empowered by this knowledge, readers will be motivated to contribute actively to and drive systemic change within the field. Illuminated with how-to methods-from power mapping to conversation tactics-and case study precedents, the book catalyzes a collective redefinition of architecture as a vital player in building a socially just and ecologically regenerative future"-- Provided by publis
Identifiers: LCCN 2024001635 | ISBN 9781032532844 (hardback) | ISBN 9781032532813 (paperback) | ISBN 9781003411284 (ebook)
Subjects:
Classification: LCC NA2005 .D39 2024 | DDC 720.71--dc23/eng/20240228
LC record available at https://lccn.loc.gov/2024001635

ISBN: 978-1-032-53284-4 (hbk)
ISBN: 978-1-032-53281-3 (pbk)
ISBN: 978-1-003-41128-4 (ebk)

DOI: 10.4324/9781003411284

Typeset in Sabon
by KnowledgeWorks Global Ltd.

CONTENTS

COAUTHOR BIOGRAPHIES

Kirsten Day (she/her) (ARBV FRAIA PhD) lectures in Architecture at the University of Melbourne. Her publications, workshops, and studios explore themes of future scenarios and the impact of change on the architecture profession and the human condition. Kirsten serves on committees for the Australian Institute of Architects including the National, and the Victorian Chapter Education Committees and the Victorian Equity in Accessibility Committee. She is a member of the Academia Working Group of The Architects Lobby and examiner for the Architects Registration Board of Victoria.

Peggy Deamer (she/her) is Professor Emerita of Yale School of Architecture, a founding member of the Architecture Lobby, and principle of the firm Deamer Studio. She is the editor of *Architecture and Capitalism: 1845 to the Present* and *The Architect as Worker: Immaterial Labor, the Creative Class, and the Politics of Design* and the author of *Architecture and Labor.* Her theory work explores the relationship between subjectivity, design, and labor in the current economy.

Andrea Dietz (she/her) is an interdisciplinary designer and licensed architect working at the intersection of visual culture, spatial communications and pedagogy, and representation technique and theory. She teaches in and administers the graduate program in exhibition design at the GWU Corcoran School of the Arts & Design. She is the founder of *Support Structures*, a multimedia platform for rewriting the United States' social contract with public art and architecture.

Tessa Forde (she/they) is an architecture researcher, teacher, and practitioner currently undertaking a PhD in Tāmaki Makaurau, Aotearoa New Zealand. They are a co-director of *Groupwork* Aotearoa, co-organised the *Free School of Architecture*, founded *The Night School*, and are a core member of *pre:fab platform*. Tessa's research interests center on how experimental gathering platforms provide spaces in which new realities can be imagined, performed, and deployed to disrupt and reshape the architecture discipline.

Jessica Garcia Fritz (she/her) is an Assistant Professor in the School of Architecture, the Design Justice liaison for architecture in the College of Design, an Affiliate Faculty for American Indian Studies at the University of Minnesota, and co-director of LAB-OR. As a citizen of the Cheyenne River Sioux Tribe (Itazipco), her cross-disciplinary teaching and research challenge architecture's role in nation-state building through specification writing and the extraction of material territories in indigenous lands.

Palmyra Geraki (she/her) is an interdisciplinary practicing architect, educator, and editor, interested in the tensions and opportunities present in the relationship between the individual and the collective as well as in transcalar and inter-, trans-, and multi-disciplinary approaches to knowledge and pedagogy. She is an Assistant Professor at the University of Wisconsin-Milwaukee and the founding principal of *PALMYRA*, a design practice working across disciplines, scales, and typologies.

Valérie Lechêne, a systems change agent, technologist, and trained architect in Brooklyn, NY, facilitates just social, ecological, and technological transitions. As Assistant Director of Operations and Communications at the Urban Systems Lab, New School, Val leverages geospatial data modeling to inform spatial interventions. Formerly with The Architecture Lobby, Earthshot Institute, A-Frame, and architectural firms globally, Val bridges disciplines, geographies, and sectors to decarbonize, regenerate, and repair across scales.

PROJECT ASSISTANT BIOGRAPHY

 Renzo Dagnino is an architect, studio teaching assistant, PhD candidate, and fellow researcher at UNC. He studied at the National University of Córdoba (Argentina) and at the University of Thessaly (Greece). His research interests are focused on the intersection between architecture and the political economy. He is a member of The Architecture Lobby's Academia Working Group and one of the organizers of the Architecture Beyond Capitalism School.

ACKNOWLEDGMENTS

The coauthors of this book wish to express gratitude to the many people from whom we have learned over the years and on whom we continue to rely. We are deeply appreciative of our numerous colleagues in The Architecture Lobby. Myriad participants and presenters at the Architecture Beyond Capitalism (ABC) School have contributed to the knowledge that informs our writing and the hope we have garnered for the future. We are particularly beholden to those central to organizing the first two ABC schools (2021 and 2022) who galvanized the thinking presented here: Kadambari Baxi, Frank Burridge, Aaron Cayer, Sharon Haar, Daniel Jacobs, Natalie Leonard, Tony van Raat, Priyanka Shah, and Xinyi Xie. We owe a debt the editors at Routledge—Lydia Kesell, who took a chance on seven authors, and Jake Millicheap, whose responsiveness, positive feedback, and patience skillfully coaxed the material from us. We also want to acknowledge the four anonymous reviewers of our Routledge proposal who in 2022 encouraged us to feature the existing, positive examples of organizers in architecture academia.

We thank everyone who contributed to our Case Studies; many are identified in their respective accounts, but many are not. All deserve recognition not only for their transformative activist work, but also for their participation in crafting the illuminating descriptions of their work. These individuals include Federico Garcia Lammers, Dakota Mathews Schmidt, and Shylo Hilbert, all formerly of DoArch; Felix Rodriguez, Michael Linares, and Pablo Guariola from Beta-Local; Shannon Mattern of Redesigning the Academy; Linda Clarke and Michael Edwards of BISS; Andrew

Cruse and Sandhya Kochar of Ohio State University; Miranda Critchley, Thandi Loewenson, and David Roberts of Break//Line; Jane Rendell of Bartlett Ethics/Climate Reform; Jacob Moore, Reinhold Martin, and Michelle Huynh Chu of Green Reconstruction; Yingyong Poonnopatham and the faculty and students of Arsom Silp; Scott McAulay of Anthropocene Architecture School; Deborah Gans of Gans/Dart Pratt/NJIT Studio; Amanda Yates of School of Future Environments; Gavin Robb of Gavin Robb Studio; Victoria Barnett of Design Justice Network; A.L. Hu of Dark Matter U; Eugenia Manwelyan, Adam Sennett, Tal Beery, and Catherine Despont of School of the Apocalypse; Charlotte Malterre-Barthes of RIOT; Justine Clark of Parlour; Lesley Lokko of African Futures Institute; Suzanne Hall, Thandi Loewenson, and Huda Tayob of Race, Space & Architecture; Cruz García and Nathalie Frankowsky of Loudreaders; and Sam Bennett of Clever Slice. Their generous participation made an invaluable contribution.

We want to thank Andrea Kahn, who gave us early feedback on our outline and argument. We owe immense thanks to Kadambari Baxi, who eagerly authored the inspirational preface to this book—in addition to being a staunch and steadfast ally in effecting change in architecture education. Finally, we deeply appreciate two people whose timely, emergency aid proved indispensable: Renzo Dagnino, for joining the project at a later stage to address proliferating gaps, and Dariel Cobb, for adeptly harmonizing our diverse voices into intellectual cohesion. We wish to express heartfelt gratitude to our loved ones for their unwavering support in adapting to a schedule of coordinating regular meetings across global time zones. And lastly, but profoundly, we each wish to thank our fellow coauthors for the vibrant and rewarding year and a half of collaborative research, speculation, and writing; it has been a true privilege.

PREFACE

Organizers and organizing practices are crucial to achieving vital change in the world today. *The Organizer's Guide to Architecture Education* offers a robust framework for organizing systematic change in architecture. Amplifying the power and potential of collective practices, the guide promotes ways to transform architecture education, steering it toward inclusive social, political and environmental goals. A new agenda for architecture education emerges in which everyone is, or can be, an organizer. Consider these pages as both a dispatch and a blueprint. The book's message is a call-to-action to all organizers who think, learn, teach, write, design, and dream of changing the world as we know it.

As a term or activity, organizing is most often associated with political campaigns, labor unions, or issue-based activism (i.e. on climate crises, gun control, reproductive rights, workers' rights, war and peace, etc.). In architecture, a broad understanding of organizing as a collective strategy and the roles organizers can play is uncommon. This guide aims to fill this gap. It outlines organizing principles, methods, techniques, tactics, etc., and actively prescribes coherent steps. While challenging the field's entrenched power structures, ingrained hierarchies or outdated mentalities may seem momentous, the guide's practical, action-oriented approach lays the necessary groundwork.

Mobilizing against the forces of global capitalism, the *Guide*'s co-authors argue, is essential to decenter and expand the field. They call for urgent reorientation to prioritize social and environmental concerns. More than theoretical, the Guide is sprinkled with concrete examples of academic, institutional, and professional practices and collaborations. With these insurgent and expansive examples as a reference, explicit strategies emerge for organizing a collective movement to redefine architecture education.

The *Guide* is structured in three parts. Part 1, *Organizing*, establishes "What is Power," "What is Organizing," and "What is Organizing in Architecture education" as throughlines. Part 2, *The Scales of Organizing Architecture Education*, addresses sites at four scales: *The Studio*; *The Curriculum*; *The University*; and *The Nation-State*, as critical domains of organizing. Part 3, *Toward the Planetary* redirects architecture toward the stewardship of Earth's commons, as an urgent goal for all forms of organizing. Integral to these parts are two interspersed sections that provide key resources. The first, *How-To*, outlines power mapping, empathy mapping, and conversation methods as organizing tactics. The second, *Case Studies*, assembles model precedents. International examples of classes, teachers, students, curricula, and initiatives are featured here, including summaries of their approaches to organizing and to education.

The book ends with a section titled *Coda*, on the co-authorship itself as an example of organizing in architecture education. As members of The Architecture Lobby's Academia Working Group, the guide's seven co-authors organized the online Architecture Beyond Capitalism (ABC) School, with others (I was a member). As a free educational platform, the ABC School invited participants from around the world to discuss, debate, and workshop ideas for overcoming capitalist domination in architecture. Organized horizontally—with a motto all students are teachers and all teachers are students—the school modeled a dynamic experiment in self-initiated collaborative education. Over the last three years, 500+ people from 50+ countries participated in three iterations of the school, reflections on the organizing strategies, collaborations, and outcomes of which are included here. In that sense, the ABC School project lives on through this book as a platform for organizing as an educational practice.

Change is a process. To change an entire field requires learning, unlearning, and relearning by one and all. But change also requires planned action. When such actions are plural and molecular—collective and organized—they can lead to genuine transformation. Architecture education is ready to change. The message here is simple: become an organizer. This *Guide* is for you. Read it, pass it on, get together, and organize.

Kadambari Baxi

Professor of Professional Practice in Architecture,

Barnard College, Columbia University

PART 1

Organizing

Introduction

This guide is the result of an extensive collaborative effort among seven co-authors: Kirsten Day, Peggy Deamer, Andrea Dietz, Tessa Forde, Jessica Garcia Fritz, Palmyra Geraki, and Valérie Lechêne. Together we bring experience in architecture education spanning multiple generations and locales. Our collective journey has been marked by encounters with significant shortcomings in the field of architecture, fueling our concerns about its present and future. Motivated by these experiences, we wanted to chart a pathway forward for architecture education and from there, practice, ultimately leading to the creation of this guide.

We initially came together through The Architecture Lobby's Academia Working Group (AWG), a collective dedicated to transforming architecture education and, through it, architecture practice. Over the past decade, The Architecture Lobby (TAL) has been at the forefront of this transformation, driving change in the field of architecture by advocating for the value of architecture to the public and to the professional discipline.[1] The Academia Working Group, recognizing the profound influence of academia on shaping all that is implied by "being an architect", launched a campaign to establish an online international platform, giving birth in 2020 to the Architecture Beyond Capitalism (ABC) School. We have each participated in and helped organize at least two of the ABC School's iterations.[2] The ABC School is not a mere supplement to existing education; it serves as a model for a new approach to architecture education that centers around organizing.[3]

DOI: 10.4324/9781003411284-1

We come to organizing as a theme because we recognized that we the authors, alone, are not capable of bringing necessary change to the traditional curricula, accreditation practices, power dynamics, and ideological frameworks of architecture: change must be promoted by all actors in the academic arena, who can only institute reform by *themselves* organizing. Similarly, our endeavors in TAL, the Academic Working Group, and the ABC School have taught us that organizing is essential to ensure that such work successfully and effectively serves each member of the collective, each actor who seeks reform. It has also proved integral to how we think, share, write, and move forward. Our collaborative effort with this guide serves as a microcosm of the collective movement for which we passionately advocate. It showcases the uniquely effective power of organized collaboration in producing social change.

While our shared history and involvement with TAL, the AWG, and the ABC School have undoubtedly shaped the arguments presented in this guide, this work represents the collective effort of the seven co-authors who, while influenced by and associated with TAL, do not speak for that organization. Our diverse perspectives and differing opinions have been endlessly debated; we do not all agree on everything stated in this guide, but respect for difference and faith in underlying principles are the hallmarks of collective organizing. Throughout the guide, when we employ the pronoun "we," we reference ourselves, the guide's co-authors. This approach invites readers to actively engage with our ideas, acknowledging that conflicting positions may be present while embracing the essence of organizing that underpins our co-writing process.

Fundamental to both the ABC School's efforts and the guide's arguments is the complicit relationship between architecture education and the discipline of architecture. The discipline, including the profession, is anything but neutral; it perpetuates myths of individuality, genius, and competition while instilling a belief in an aesthetic calling. Architecture education often serves as an agent that legitimizes these myths, perpetuating practices that feed back into the profession. Simultaneously, the profession exerts its influence on education, shaping what and how it teaches. Recognizing this interdependence, we contend that addressing the challenges faced by today's architecture workers necessitates a comprehensive examination of the academic system that shapes them.

This relationship has become more complex in the last fifty years due to changes that center around technology and neoliberalism. Rapid advances in technology and tools have drastically altered the material conditions of not just architecture, architecture labor, and the labor of constructing buildings, but of the world's social, cultural, economic, and political make-up. The growing hegemony of neoliberalism, which has drastically altered the conceptual space in which architecture operates—the proliferation of commercialized and luxury developments, the prioritization of profit over community needs, and the marginalization of architecture's social and cultural roles—has also changed the ideology that pervades our everyday understanding of "normal" social organization by prioritizing privatization, individualism, deregulation, and economic "efficiency." Our efforts to organize architecture might be limited in the face of these external forces, but we believe that we can only try.

The Organizer's Guide to Architecture Education is a book for students, for educators, for university workers, for practitioners, and for dwellers of the built environment at any level from any discipline. It is a resource for anyone concerned about the livelihoods and well-being of those shaping the discipline of architecture and its expressions in professional practice, as well as for anyone wanting to take action to address the needs and future of our inhabited world. It is for anyone motivated by the economic precarity of the architect's (and the academic's) career path and the underrepresentation of people of color and women within architecture's professional ranks. It is for anyone critical of the exclusivity and insularity of architecture's cognitive structures; for anyone critical of the hierarchies that both the school and the profession deploy. It is for anyone frustrated by architecture's sidelining of challenges and crises that we collectively face. It is written for people who will write to their newspapers, post to social media, and brave the comments section to protest about how architecture is (or is not) portrayed; for any educator insisting on making design crits less punitive; for a firm partner who recognizes that they are filling in gaps left unaddressed in architecture school; for any architecture student who recognizes that what they hoped would be taught is not. Anyone who acknowledges that things are not as they should be and insists on change is an organizer.

Just as we are inclusive in our appreciation of who an organizer is, we are plural in our definition of *guide*. This book is a guide to understanding how organizing can transform architecture and architecture education. It is a guide to address the convergent failings in architecture, architecture education, and our built environment. It is a guide to multiple points of entry for effecting change across architecture's scales of influence and involvement. It is a guide to speculate on a future architecture, for an expanded field, and how that might be achieved. Finally, it is a guide, via a collection of CASE STUDIES, to the growing network of organizers and organizations in architecture and architecture education that we aim to honor, support, and engage through our writing. This guide is inclusive but is by no means comprehensive. It builds on the complex project of education reform for which others have called and actively initiated.

The question arises: for what kind of architecture education do we advocate? While our seven perspectives may differ, we unanimously agree that architecture education can no longer be confined to producing the monolithic "good designer" creating architecture solely for capitalist ends, and learning only to perpetuate myths about individualism, originality, and design virtuosity. Our goal is to transcend such limited ambitions and prepare architects to operate and practice in wider worlds—beyond the boundaries of traditional architecture. We believe we must equip architects to navigate within and contribute to various fields and societal contexts. Organizing can become a transformative force that empowers architects to enact change not only within the profession, but also on a global scale.

This guide structures the exploration of organizing into three distinct parts. Part 1 establishes the foundational concepts of organizing by delving into definitions of power, and expanding the scope of organizing to encompass architecture and architecture education.

Between Part 1 and Part 2, HOW-TO'S walk through practical steps to three organizing tools on which TAL, the AWG, and the coauthors of this guide regularly rely: power mapping, empathy mapping, and conversation methods.

Part 2 forms the bulk of this guide. It examines the different scales at which organizing can be introduced into architecture education, hereafter labeled as SMALL, MEDIUM, LARGE, and EXTRA LARGE. Each category is assigned a dedicated chapter.

Chapter 1, SMALL, looks to the studio as the pedagogical unit forming the architecture worker and posits its reconfiguration to educate a new kind of architecture subject. It challenges the conventional studio emphases by redefining design as cooperative and introduces a broader array of influences, outcomes, and stakeholders. It scrutinizes the syllabi, project briefs, and crits to upend their role in reinforcing existing hierarchies and power dynamics, identifying potentials for resistance and change.

Chapter 2, MEDIUM, focuses on the architecture curriculum, questioning the split in its purpose between aesthetic sophistication, scholarly exploration and professional preparation. It reimagines the curriculum as a practice, a laboratory for reimagining the definition of architecture, the methods by which its practitioners will be taught, and the role organizing plays in both. It recognizes the importance of the interdependence of courses and their relevance to one another in the advancement of a truly holistic architecture education.

Chapter 3, LARGE, takes on the university's influence over architecture education by tertiary education's particular approach, given its position in a neoliberal economy, to "knowledge" and its supposed rewards. This offers bottom-up approaches to reorganizing knowledge boundaries and resources. It questions the university's role in contemporary society and works to redirect it to civic contribution.

Chapter 4, EXTRA LARGE, traces conditions in architecture education to impositions of the nation-state and its control of professionalism. It interrogates the nation-state as the arbiter of architecture's qualifications and professional usefulness. It exposes the limitations of the nation-state to, on one hand, include indigenous people and knowledge and on the other, address international crises. It calls attention to the need to organize beyond traditional institutional frameworks in service to broader publics and the global environment.

At the end of Part 2, CASE STUDIES highlight the organizing already happening in architecture education. The examples, divided into the topics that motivate their organizing—education/discipline, climate justice, community/urban engagement, race/space, carework/survival, and feminism/gender, demonstrate the viability of organizing in architecture and provide inspiration for ongoing and new efforts to bring about disciplinary change.

Part 3 points organizing in architecture and architecture education toward stewardship. It argues for the expansion and decentering of the practices of architecture. It presents three considerations for mobilizing architecture's evolution: respecting and making room for disparate worldviews, understanding present and past movements for change, and preparing incrementally for change.

The guide closes out with a Coda that describes the books' coauthoring process and invites others to join in collective action.

We are frustrated by the intractably slow systems of our architectural and educational institutions; the tone of the guide reflects that. At the same time, we recognize that many individual educators are moving away from traditional education and are already doing much of the work advocated for here. We articulate positions that we know are shared by others. We hope this guide catalyzes a dialogue with like-minded people who will contribute conceptual and practical positions we might have overlooked.

What Is Organizing?

Organizing is strategic, collective action. It refers to the process of arranging and structuring elements, resources, or information in a systematic and purposeful manner in order to achieve a specific goal or objective. Organizing, typically, has two main components—strategy and tactics. A strategy encompasses an organization's overarching shared vision, as well as the umbrella plan that structures a campaign. A tactic is a particular action, means, or method deployed to achieve the strategy's ends. All tactics should have some relationship to the organization's vision (strategy), and should be measured against its original (and changing) intents and purposes. Strategy is collectively decided—clear, purposeful, and big picture. Tactics are focused, nimble, repeatable, at times experimental, and contextual. We propose a third component for organizing—ritual processes. These are structures which form ways of gathering, relating, making decisions, and building community collectivity, and connections between people and place.

Organizing serves as the foundation for effective collaboration, amplifying diverse voices and empowering individuals to take meaningful action. Through organizing, solidarity and resilience are cultivated, enabling individuals and communities to pool resources and confront challenges as a united front. It systematically facilitates the creation of networks and alliances, bringing together teams with previously unknown connections. Organizing is a dual force—reflecting past actions while simultaneously projecting impactful outcomes for the future. Its successful implementation leads to a redistribution of power and decision-making.

In educational institutions, rather than teaching organizing, we propose practicing it at every scale, foregrounding learned experience rather than taught subject matter. Architects and academics aren't necessarily qualified to teach organizing, but they are the only ones qualified to organize architecture education. The curriculum should be designed so that every subject can be taught within the same framework—emphasizing collectivity, shared action, strategy, tactics, and ritual processes. The following scenarios, hypotheticals developed as a coauthoring exercise, demonstrate that organizing can be applied to any spatial subject or problem:

> In designing a chair, a student will have to develop—through research and discussion—strategy for the design process and outcome. The student must be enabled with the skills to examine the power relations of the materials, processes, and labor systems required to create the chair; to identify the resources—tools and people—needed to design and deliver the chair; to empathize with participants in and recipients of the process; and, ultimately, work through the totality of the process. The student needs time to reflect on their tactics, ritual, and relating; assess how they met or did not meet the vision; and identify emergent conditions that demanded a shift in strategy.

> Or, at a larger scale, a student group working on a sited community project will need to organize themselves as a collective; establish a shared vision and strategy for their role in the project, outline ritual processes through which they will gather, converse, and make decisions; examine

the site collectively to identify its power structures; and propose a series of initial tactics to deploy. The students then repeat this process with a community group—taking on a facilitatory role, reconsidering and strengthening the organizational approach in relation to a broader community. The students work with community from conceptualization to delivery of a mutually informed outcome.

Teaching organizing skills in school is not about setting all students up to be radical community architects (though we hope that an organized discipline increases the possibility for such work), but about giving them the skills to contextually organize and advocate in a critical, ethical, and effective way. We want to enable future professionals to ask and pursue the deep questions raised by professional tasks. Organizing depends on broad awareness, resource sharing, mutual respect, collaboration, and cooperation—and is therein an indispensable tool in driving meaningful progress in the field of architecture and beyond.

In capitalist systems, organizing is frequently synonymous with unionization, and we authors embrace that. The perceptions of unions vary widely around the world. Context dependent, they are a threat to—and target of—hegemonic power structures. Or, they are yet another model of top-down leadership, disregarding the rank and file and replicating racist and sexist practices. Or, they elicit a complex mix of positive and negative associations. Regardless, unionization remains a crucial approach to safeguarding worker rights and advocating for improved wages and working conditions.

Though unionization is a powerful organizing option, labor movements extend well beyond traditional union structures. The work of scholars like Erica Smiley and Sarita Gupta, in *The Future We Need: Organizing for a Better Democracy in the Twenty-First Century*, point both to the limitations of unionization and offer other approaches. They identify the need in collective bargaining to consider the whole person, not just the worker in the workplace. Consider this comment from Kimberly Mitchell, a union organizer and Macy's shop steward who is profiled in Smiley's and Gupta's text:

> If all you see when you meet me is that I'm a worker, you're missing the entire point. I am a whole person. I should be able to exercise control of my life in all aspects—at work, in my home, and in relationship to the big banks and the large corporations who shape so much of our society. If we fail to see people like me as whole people, then we're losing.[4]

Smiley and Gupta also promote workers who have successfully organized outside of unions, either because there was no possibility for a union at their workplace, or, as women and/or people of color, they were not heard by their union. Smiley's and Gupta's examples describe alternative labor movements, including mass refusals to work, strikes and boycotts, alliances and cooperatives, and campaigns and initiatives.

Activism, like unionization, is another term often conflated with organizing. Similarly, though, activism and organizing are not equivalents. Activism describes activity that either advocates for or impedes societal functions or positions; examples include protests, demonstrations, and media promotions. Organizing transcends activism's immediacy, or rather leverages it. Activism may serve as a springboard or tactic for organizing efforts, evolving into a potent force for transformation. It has a vital role in mobilizing public support and raising awareness about specific issues. Organizing, then, amplifies activism, situating it within a coherent and long-term strategy. Activism, in other words, is yet another organizing option; it, among community meetings and coalition building, is a potential component of organizing's intentional and methodical structures for empowering individuals and communities through sustained efforts to effect lasting change.

Ultimately, though organizing unlike activism is about power, it requires understanding existing power to build power in response. The practice of organizing holds the key to developing a uniquely valuable and resilient form of power, one that works for the multitude.

What Is Power?

There are numerous lenses through which to view power and power dynamics. Karl Marx emphasizes control over the means of production. Max Weber provides a classification of authority into traditional, charismatic, and legal rationales.[5] Hannah Arendt highlights the distinction between power and violence, grounding power in the public and political sphere.[6] Antonio Gramsci emphasizes the connection between power and the hegemony of ideas.[7] Louis Althusser delves into the performative aspect of power for both the powerful and the subjected. Michel Foucault challenges the traditional focus on institutions and individuals, asserting that power resides in complex networks governing everyday practices. Noam Chomsky draws attention to the influence of media and its manipulation of public opinion in wielding power.[8] For all the different emphases, however, these sample theories collectively raise three crucial points. First, the ruled often play a role in authorizing those in power—as power is not solely imposed upon them. Second, oppression can arise outside of this authorization, particularly when power feels threatened. And third, capitalist power relations have shaped the social framework, contributing to today's crises of inequity.

Power is manifested through ideology. Gramsci and Althusser emphasize that ideology which blinds one to one's own self-interest, permeates consciousness and the material practices of everyday life, encompassing domains usually considered private.[9] Unraveling the power vested in these subtle and pervasive apparatuses—consciousness and material practices—proves challenging due to their naturalized invisibility. Arendt's stance on violence as antithetical to power,[10] and Foucault's notion that knowledge itself is power, all point to that aspect of power that operates at the level of subjectivity.[11] Ideology, which in Marxist terms is always a negative term associated with capitalism's ability to replace self-interest with false desire, is how most willingly allow the powerful to be powerful.

To deconstruct the power dynamics entrenched within institutions, power mapping serves as a vital tool. A power map is a visual representation or diagram that illustrates the distribution of influence, authority, and other types of relationships within a specific context or organization. It identifies key stakeholders (allies, adversaries, and targets), their levels of influence, and their interconnections. This process moves beyond surface-level symptoms to uncover root causes, making the invisible and ideological dimensions of power visible. Power maps are employed in political and social movements to identify where and among whom action is best placed.[12] As architecture and architecture education have been complicit with capitalism's winner-takes-all ideology and its violent defense, power mapping becomes indispensable in our pursuit of change. In adopting power mapping within architecture and architecture education, we advocate for its expansion to encompass temporal goals and knowledge systems, integrating language, communication, and technology into the analysis of those systems. With this expanded approach, we fortify our mission to drive meaningful change in the field of architecture and beyond.

We ultimately want a more powerful profession, one characterized by "power with" and "power to" as opposed to "power over" others.[13] By organizing for inclusion rather than abuse, architects can challenge dominating, centralized power structures,[14] and propel the discipline toward cultivating a world of many worlds: the *pluriverse*.[15] The pluriverse is an enactment of collectivity characterizing organizing's *raison d'être*.

What Is Organizing in Architecture?

Architecture, both as a discipline and a practice, has proven to be resistant to organizing, displaying rigid hierarchical structures, a strong emphasis on individualism, and cutthroat competitive strategies.[16] Architecture prides itself on exceptionalism, is detached from the complexity of the world it seeks to influence, and regularly serves only those with means and privilege.[17] Its exclusive nature erects barriers for those without access to its necessary resources. The profession actively ignores the labor conditions of its workers, dismissing architectural work as a creative endeavor that is somehow not labor, while perpetuating an image of supposed self-fulfillment and prestige.[18] In undervaluing architectural work, "successful" architects often depend on pre-existing independent wealth to practice, and/or leverage profits generated through the exploitation of their architectural workers.[19] The field's underpaid and overworked practitioners lack the resources and time to engage in shaping local, regional, or federal policies. There are limited routes to built environment research, testing, or speculation because of the discipline's dependence on the private sector, those who inevitably prioritize profit over social or creative endeavors. Architecture's ideology also prompts the rhetoric of autonomy, which girds much of the discipline, and the term "architectural worker," while gaining traction,[20] remains confined to academic circles.[21] Professional organizations, such as the American Institute of Architects (AIA), the Royal Institute of British Architects (RIBA), the Architectural Institute of Canada (RAIC)[22], the Australian Institute of Architects (RAIA),[23] and the New Zealand Institute of Architects (NZIA), serve their respective countries, historically neglecting the imperative to address global challenges. Because the discipline's complacency and exceptionalism have rendered its institutions and organizations largely irrelevant, architects must make informed decisions collectively with others inside and outside the profession if they are interested in engaging global challenges.

At the same time, one could say that architects *have always been* organizers. They generate a conceptual vision, then coordinate across disciplines, schools of thought, places, concepts, and regulatory conditions in order to achieve that vision. However, obsession with the objects of architecture in its media, the "site" in which architecture as a concept is "constructed,"[24] dominates the narrative and obscures what it is that an architect can do and make. Architects have a rich engagement with culture, are able to describe culture non-verbally—which is important for civic engagement—and are already the connective tissue between disciplines, regulatory bodies, and the public. Indeed, architecture boasts unique advantages that collective organizing can harness. As a discipline, it is intricately connected to numerous related fields, blends physicality with monumentality, and interacts with diverse forms of media. However, for organizing to thrive, architecture must confront its internal problems, including exclusion, indifference to class dynamics, and labor abuse. Organizing needs to transition from the periphery to the center of the profession. Forwarding organizing as the core skill set of the architect expands opportunities for the discipline by offering a mechanism to study architecture as a framework connected to other things in the world.

To progress, architecture must lead by developing practices and structures that enable social and political change, all the while embracing cooperativism. One way or another, architects must recognize the strength of collective action. Progress lies in transcending issue-based responses and directing attention toward organizing as a foundational practice. If architects want to tackle environmental justice, affordable housing, and labor abuse in construction and design, they must organize as a whole. Organizing transforms not only the material conditions of architects but also their commitment to broader public interests and workers' rights. It calls for a comprehensive understanding of the public's needs and demands collaboration with various stakeholders to affect positive change in the built environment. Organizing must become an essential and recognized skill set within the field of architecture.

What Is Organizing in Architecture Education?

This guide advocates for the integration of organizing skills into architecture education, recognizing that such competencies are vital for architects to become effective agents of change. To achieve this transformation, architecture educators must challenge the entire educational landscape—coursework, classrooms, roles, responsibilities, standards, and systems of care—all components of which demand reevaluation and retooling. Organizing skills must permeate through various courses, curricula, and institutional hierarchies, fostering interconnections between design, technology, history/theory, and so on. Moreover, acquiring those skills must compel architects to engage with communities and suppliers often overlooked, disrupting traditional boundaries within academia, and challenging the relationship between students and their institutions. These comprehensive changes make organizing fundamental to architecture education reform.

Incorporating organizing into architecture education will not happen quickly. Architects have never been systematically taught how to teach, leading to the perpetuation of habits—both good and bad—passed down from generation to generation.[25] Hierarchies and power dynamics inherent in academic settings must be dismantled while the scope of organizing must be broadened. From architecture studios to schools of architecture, faculty governance, and the very foundations of knowledge held by universities that serve the nation-state apparatus, we seek to imbue the spirit of organizing throughout the educational process.

Notes

1 The Architecture Lobby, "TAL."
2 Burridge et al., "Beyond Capitalism?"
3 The Architects Lobby et al., "Not as Easy as ABC."
4 Smiley and Gupta, "The Future We Need."
5 Weber, Roth, and Wittich, *Economy and Society.*
6 Penta, "Hannah Arendt: On Power."
7 Prospero, "Gramsci: Political Scientist."
8 Chomsky, Mitchell, and Schoeffel, *Understanding Power.*
9 Cadeddu, *A Companion to Antonio Gramsci.* Chapter 5: The Layers of History and the Politics of Gramsci
10 Cadeddu, *A Companion to Antonio Gramsci.*
11 Foucault, *Power.*
12 Corporate structures and other powerful groups also employ similar "social graph" tools, many of which build upon social media. For further insights, see Fennema and Heemskerk, "When Theory Meets Methods."
13 Organizers often refer to the differences between "power over," "power to," "power with," and "power within" among a wide range of other characteristic descriptions of power. Based on our research, these expressions first appeared in this specific form in academic literature in a 2002 field manual providing approaches for promoting citizen participation by VeneKlasen and Miller, *A New Weave of Power, People, and Politics.* These concepts are introduced for a broad audience of organizers in the recently published PDF and online guide "It's All about Power."
14 Avelino, "Theories of Power and Social Change. Power Contestations and Their Implications for Research on Social Change and Innovation."
15 Escobar, *Designs for the Pluriverse.*
16 For example Wainwright, "Snubbed, Cheated, Erased: The Scandal of Architecture's Invisible Women."
17 Sudjic, *The Edifice Complex.*
18 See Deamer, *The Architect as Worker.*, Cortright, "*Can This Be?*, and Rudin and Pellegrino, *Out of Architecture.*"
19 Cortright, "*Can This Be?*"
20 Deamer, *The Architect as Worker.*
21 Cuff, *Architecture.*
22 Formally Royal Canadian Institute of Architects—retains R to distinguish it from the CIA
23 Formally Royal Australian Institute of Architects—retains R to distinguish it from the AIA
24 Colomina, *Privacy and Publicity.*
25 Stead, Gusheh, and Rodwell, "Well-Being in Architectural Education."

HOW-TO: POWER MAPPING

Introduction

Power mapping is a visual organizing tool for making sense of power networks and structures, revealing hidden and opaque decision-making processes, measuring the distributions of influence and authority, within a specific context or organization. It is a tool that is used by organizing groups to identify strategies for impact. Mapping power collaboratively enhances organizing discussions, minimizes blind spots, and supports collective decision-making.[1]

Power mapping informs political and social movements. In architecture education, it may be used as a pedagogical device—for students to visualize where power lies in the project scenarios around which they are designing, for faculty to plan curricular changes, or for students and faculty to understand decision-making hierarchies in the university.

Preparing for Power Mapping

As with all collaborative exercises, power mapping proceeds from collective agreements. To begin, gather a group of organizers and define roles and expectations. Will multiple people visualize a single power map or will everyone develop individual power maps that will be synthesized later? Come together to write the terms for the group activity. Build in space and time to discuss and come to consensus regarding the make-up, composition, and results of the power maps (Figure 1.1).

DOI: 10.4324/9781003411284-2

Three Horizons Template

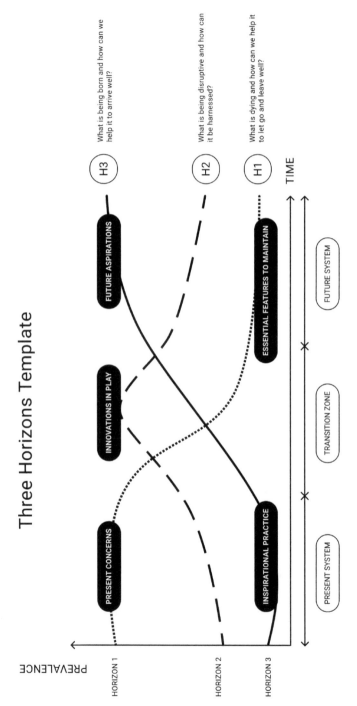

FIGURE 1.1 A Three Horizons Template provides a framework for graphically tracking changes and influences in an organizational context over time. The graph consists of three lines, or horizons, which represent different aspects: the emergence of new ideas and how to facilitate their success, the disruptive forces at play and how to leverage them, and the decline of existing practices and how to gracefully phase them out.

Step 1: Project Future Outcomes

Power mapping requires two first identifications: a subject for and the objectives of the exercise. These identifications may not always be obvious. Indeed, one of the more challenging aspects of power mapping involves anticipating how to best enter an issue. Such targeting is difficult because there is an element of predicting, or "futuring" (otherwise known as strategic foresight), that is needed. If the subject and/or objective for a power mapping scenario is not immediately clear, there are several futuring tools. These tools, generally, are frameworks for imagining multiple outcomes in order to inform a preferable future, before backcasting to determine an appropriate course of action. Fundamental to these strategies is the idea that the "future" is not a fixed, predetermined outcome, but rather a spectrum of possibilities. Various potential futures exist—some more likely than others—and choices made in the present significantly influence which future scenario will unfold.

An example of a futuring tool is detailed in Bill Sharpe's *Three Horizons* (2016).[2] The Three Horizons Framework—abbreviated 3H—documents, in a single diagram, systemic transformation and the actions needed to bring it about. 3H thinking is visualized in a two-axis chart with time on the x-axis and prevalence on the y-axis. The time axis starts in the present and looks to both the past and the future. The prevalence axis charts growth and loss of power. Three oscillating curves are drawn across the 3H chart; each curve establishes a horizon: (H1) "Business as Usual," (H2) "Disruptive Innovation," and (H3) "Emerging Future." Horizon curves, in a facilitated inquiry, are tagged with the concerns and influences associated with their rise and fall over time. 3H visualizations are not predictions, but rather aspirations. They draw out agreements and disagreements regarding an organizing movement's transformations (Figure 1.2).

Step 2: Identify the Subject and Set the Objectives

A power mapping group may work through the Three Horizons, or another futuring tool to identify likely catalysts for change—which may then be used to focus the subject and objectives of the power map. Objectives for the power map should address a set of questions to understand what is being organized. For example: Who are the stakeholders? What are the weaknesses in a system? How can something be moved through a system? Who can be approached to further the campaign (Figure 1.3)?

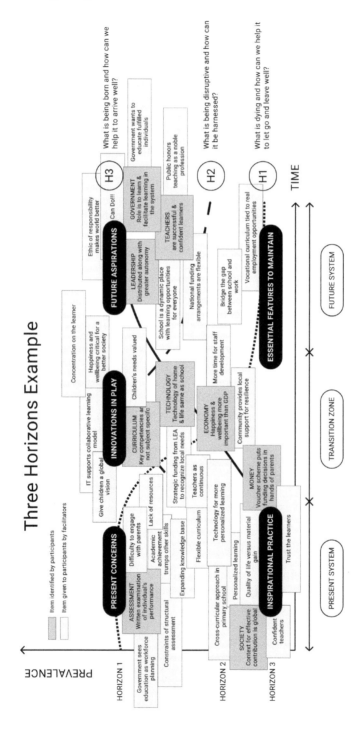

FIGURE 1.2 An organizing facilitator may pre-populate the Three Horizons Template with topical concerns and influences and associate them with points along the rise and fall of the horizon lines. Organizing participants, then, offer considerations and contexts that might inform change.

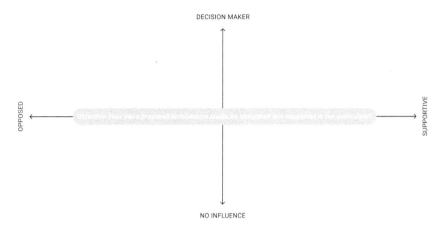

FIGURE 1.3   This is a template example of a quadrant matrix power map. In this case, the question being asked is: How can a proposed architecture studio be integrated and supported in the curriculum? The vertical axis spans, bottom to top, those with no influence to the decision-makers in the scenario. The horizontal axis spans, left to right, those who are opposed to those who are supportive.

Step 3: Establish a Visual Framework

Power maps take many different forms—from scatter-plot graphs to mind maps to timelines. Each approach has its own merits based on context and objective. Each makes visual levels and values of power in distinct ways. One of the more common power map formats is the power quadrant matrix. The power quadrant matrix comprises an x-axis and a y-axis, each with different levels and values. The x-axis, for example, may include the increasing hierarchical power of each stakeholder, while the y-axis may include the increasing or decreasing impacts of decisions.

If working digitally, choose a software that allows for the easy movement of information around the map. Likewise, if producing an analog power map, use a medium, like Post-it notes, that can be placed and replaced flexibly (Figure 1.4).

Step 4: Locate the Stakeholders

Identify the stakeholders and those impacted by decisions. Stakeholders are individuals or institutions who have an explicit role in the power structure in question. Those impacted can be part of an ally network, or an oppositional force, or collateral to the action. It is important to be inclusive of everyone within a power network. Once the human entities are named,

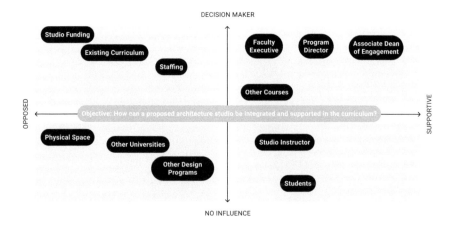

FIGURE 1.4   Organizers populate the quadrant matrix power map with a scenario's stakeholders. Stakeholders are positioned according to their level of interest and influence in the scenario's objective. Those who are most supportive and most influential are in the upper-right quadrant. Those who are supportive but have little influence are in the lower-right quadrant. Those who are opposed (or indifferent) and have no influence are in the lower-left quadrant. And those who are opposed (or indifferent) but do have influence are in the upper-left quadrant.

expand to include the non-human and the contextual. The contextual entities include natural conditions and forces, and cultural and governing logics.

Locate the stakeholders, according to their respective power role, within the visual framework. Consider levels of influence—who and what has more power, knowledge, money; levels of gain and loss; and levels of support and impediment (Figure 1.5).

Step 5: Identify the Power Holders

Once the stakeholders are laid out across the power map, the sites of power—and opportunity—are made clear. The power holders are the likely targets of any next organizing actions (Figure 1.6).

Step 6: Network the Power

Use the power map to draw out the processes for change. Contemplate how each of the stakeholders are interacting. Develop a notational key for describing different relationships between entities and label connections

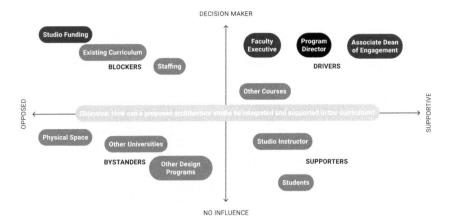

FIGURE 1.5   Once all the stakeholders are in the map, the opportunities and impediments are revealed. In this case, the Faculty Executive, the Program Director, and the Associate Dean of Engagement are identified as those with equal power to approve the new studio. Because the Program Director sits between the Faculty Executive— who is less supportive and the Associate Dean of Engagement— who is more supportive, they stand out as someone who might see both the pros and cons and make a good advocate and mobilizer. On the other side of the map, Studio Funding stands out as a significant barrier to the new course.

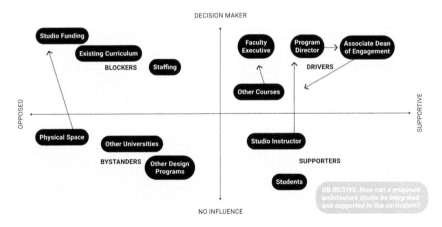

FIGURE 1.6   Organizers develop strategies for engaging a scenario by mapping the influences and protocol that relate the stakeholders to each other. These connection networks point to the information that will be key to developing a successful argument and set up sequences for collective action.

and forces as they are revealed. Nodes, or concentrations of entities and connections, that appear point to critical sites of influence and leverage.

Note: Not all influences exist simultaneously. Historical decisions and patterns (documented as patents, specifications, drawings, acts, treaties, and other forms of agreements) add to power dynamics. Thorough power mapping requires extensive research into contexts, logistics, and protocol—past, present, and future. It may take many attempts and additional investigations to complete a power map; it is only through iteration and curiosity that nuances reveal themselves.

Discuss, Integrate, and Engage the Outcomes

A finished power map reveals who and what the influences of a situation are and how those influences play out. Discuss finished power maps within a forum for future action. Center discussion on the power mapping objectives. What does the map reveal in the context of the original goal? What are the opportunities for leverage? What are the weaknesses in the system? Where can power be built? What unexpected opportunities have emerged that might change or influence the original objectives? Use the answers to identify organizing emphases and/or action items. Write the conclusions into the map and return to it as a measure of organizing progress.

Notes

1 This is a high-level how-to for power mapping. For a more in-depth guide to power mapping, see The Architecture Lobby's *Guide to Power Mapping*, which was compiled by the Green New Deal Working Group and implemented in ABC School 2021.
2 Sharpe et al., "Three Horizons."

HOW-TO: EMPATHY MAPPING

Introduction

Empathy mapping is a visual tool used in design thinking and user experience design to gain deeper insight into a target audience's feelings, thoughts, and behaviors.[1] While empathy mapping is typically done with a real or imagined end user in mind, in the context of organizing architecture education, we introduce it as a companion to power mapping.

As a companion tool to power mapping, the empathy map allows for an accompanying "feelings-based" approach to assessing stakeholder positionality and lived reality. The entities identified in a power map and those who support them or who are oppressed by them are represented by real people with their own anxieties, histories, biases, and behaviors. An empathy map is used to name human emotions and perceptions, giving organizers greater appreciation of their sphere of influence, and informing them how to best engage those implicated in the power map.

As a collaboration tool, empathy mapping allows for relationship development between those working in collaborative settings and those organizing together. Herein, empathy mapping is not deployed in abstract terms, but as a way to negotiate the real and immediate power dynamics of collaborative work. For example, in architecture education, an empathy map could be created by each member of a design studio to consider how others feel about a particular assignment. These may be shared to reveal concerns, interests, and expectations that then may be collectively addressed. Likewise, empathy maps may be used when working on situated projects with real stakeholders and communities (Figure 1.7).

DOI: 10.4324/9781003411284-3

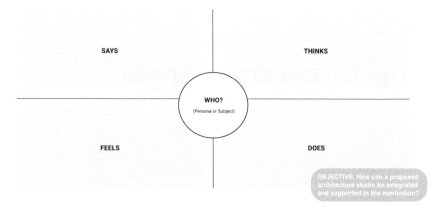

FIGURE 1.7 This is an empathy map template. It consists of a circle in the center of a quadrant graphic. The center circle is associated with the persona or subject who or that the organizer wants to understand better. Each quadrant is associated with one of four qualities: says, thinks, feels, and does.

Step 1: Lay Out the Map

An empathy map consists of four quadrants: "Says," "Thinks," "Feels," and "Does." On a piece of paper, a whiteboard, or a digital space, draw a square and divide it into four equal parts. Label each part with one of the four empathy considerations.

Step 2: Identify the Persona/Subject

Start by considering who or what it is you want to understand better. This could be a worker at a company, a place, a community member, something more-than-human, or someone you know or with whom you work. Make a note of who they are.[2]

Step 3: Gather Insights

Gather as much information about your persona/subject as you can. If you are working with a real person, you may want to ask them personal questions about their background, their experiences, and their expectations. Other information may come from data collection, surveys, and record research.

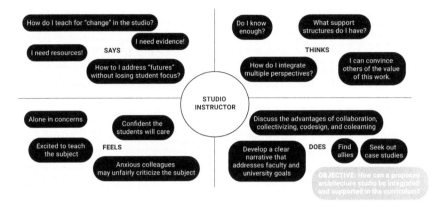

FIGURE 1.8   To develop an empathy map, work with the persona or subject to identify their perspective on the scenario in question. Populate the quadrants with their concerns, insights, abilities, and vulnerabilities.

Step 4: Fill in the Quadrants

Think about how your persona/subject may be impacted by or may respond to a particular challenge, situation, or context. Make relevant notes under each quadrant (Figure 1.8):

- Under the "Says" quadrant, write down quotes or phrases that represent what the persona/subject says or might say.
- In the "Thinks" quadrant, write out thoughts, beliefs, or considerations that the persona/subject might have.
- For the "Feels" quadrant, describe any emotions, feelings, or attitudes the persona/subject may have.
- Finally, in the "Does" quadrant, list actions, behaviors, or activities in which the persona/subject engages.

Step 5: Review and Analyze

Look for patterns, commonalities, and themes across the quadrants and/or in relation to other personas/subjects in your power map. Pay attention to challenges (anxieties, frustrations, or obstacles) or opportunities (desires, unmet needs, or skill sets) that might have emerged in the mapping. If you are working with a group, share insights to identify trends and common experiences.

Step 6: Collective Discussion

Share the empathy mapping results with relevant stakeholders or fellow organizers. Factor the empathy mapping results into your organizing strategy by tailoring appeals to and support for your personas/subjects.

Share your empathy map with your personas/subjects to aide relationship development. Describe your understanding of their reality and open space for their response; be considerate and attentive. Assess together opportunities for better collaboration. Develop a consensus strategy for moving forward and managing challenges together. It may be helpful to repeat this process regularly, or as challenges emerge in the process of organizing, learning, and working together.

Notes

1 Curedale, *Design Methods 1*, 165–68.
2 Curedale, 223–24.

HOW-TO: CONVERSATION METHODS

Introduction

The Architecture Lobby (TAL) engages in both online (for its international working groups), and in-person organizing (through local chapter meetings and for all-organization gatherings) events. The principles of its online conversation methods inform those for the live environment and vice versa. Below are descriptions of generally applicable ideals and adjustments unique to gathering either remotely or bodily with others.

Meeting Facilitation

Facilitating, or conversational caretaking, is a skill, an equity strategy, and a creative practice. As described in *The Power of Protocols*, a respected handbook on facilitation by Professor of Teaching and Learning at New York University, Joseph P. McDonald, the core task of the facilitator is not, as many believe, to "[get] the information across, [accomplish] the task, or [make] the decision," but rather to "promote participation, ensure equity, and build trust."[1]

Effective facilitators, then, rely on a series of best practices to structure inclusive meetings:[2]

- Transparency is a guiding ideal. Facilitators make strides towards all of their core tasks by revealing their intentions immediately and regularly.
- Facilitators share a complete, editable agenda as far in advance of a meeting as possible. This allows time for participants to consider the content and make suggestions for additions or edits. It confirms logistics and access.

DOI: 10.4324/9781003411284-4

- In both the written agenda and verbally, at the beginning of a meeting, the facilitator articulates the objective for the meeting and acknowledges the impacts of those objectives. They create space for others to offer insights and observations that might shift the conversation.
- The facilitator outlines the meeting norms, or rules of engagement. Alternatively or additionally, the facilitator dedicates time to the development of community agreements. Community agreements can cover anything from talking time limits to expectations for post-meeting steps.
- The facilitator organizes the meeting around explicit inclusive protocols for participation.[3] A first act is an invitation to a round of introductions (as applicable).
- Similarly, the facilitator is clear about the role of feedback and protocol through which decisions are made. Asking for volunteers to assume roles during and after the meeting encourages consensual involvement.
- Overall, the facilitator understands that they are there to steward conversation. They expect to speak for no more than twenty percent of the meeting.
- After each meeting, the facilitator provides every participant with thorough documentation of the conversation, follows up with developments from the conversation, and checks in on participants' reflections. (TAL requests volunteer minutes writers at the beginning of each meeting and shares all records in an online archive).

Facilitation is labor. TAL rotates the responsibility, asking two volunteers to facilitate on a two-week rotation. TAL also recognizes time as a resource and strives to limit all meetings to an allotted time.

Meeting Participation

Participants in meeting conversations also have a role in creating an equitable and inclusive environment. Critical to welcoming meetings are participants' conversational ability to listen. *How to Listen*, a book developed out of its author's, Oscar Trimboli's award-winning podcast, *Deep Listening*, presents listening as a learned practice. In five levels of awareness, listeners become better communicators:[4]

- Yourself, involves preparing the mind to give and pay attention.
- Content, activates the body, orienting all of the senses to the task.
- Context, seeks a backstory and observes how information is shared.
- Unsaid, picks up on the gaps between words and nonverbal cues.
- Meaning, helps those who are sharing make sense of what they are saying.

Online Meetings

TAL primarily uses Zoom for virtual meetings and is transitioning to Discord for meeting organization and communicating outside of meetings. The Academia Working Group, for example, has members that offer their institutional Zoom account for meetings. TAL also has a paid Zoom subscription that can be used on request. Discord is an open-source messaging and social media platform. Organizers are encouraged, if possible to find platforms that are accessible and affordable or free.

TAL has a community agreement for all online meetings in the form of a Zoom Etiquette statement. All participants are invited to:

- Turn on their video, if they are able to and comfortable.
- Take care of themselves: take breaks/eat/drink.
- If they need to step away, please turn off their video.
- Respect the person speaking and keep chat to "everyone" to a minimum.
- Mute their microphone when they're not speaking.
- If comfortable to do so, add their pronouns as part of their Zoom name.
- Popcorn (see below).
- Use and respect the stack (see below).

TAL also offers group discussion guidelines. All participants are invited to:

- Use and respect people's pronouns.
- Use "I" statements: don't assume they're speaking for others.
- Listen very carefully to what others are saying.
- Assume good faith and positive intent.
- Respect the spirit of the progressive stack (see below).
- Respect the workshop agenda and people's time.
- Remember that democracy and organizing are messy, and that's OK!

Popcorn

"Popcorning" is a tactic that can be used in both online and in-person meetings. It is a useful tool for inviting each person in a meeting to contribute a response to a prompt or question. For example, if a facilitator wishes to initiate group introductions:

- The facilitator introduces themself and then popcorns to a next person. They do so by saying: "I popcorn to (name of a meeting participant)."
- The new person introduces themself and then popcorns to someone who has not already shared who they are.
- This process repeats until everyone in the meeting has shared.

Stack

"Stacking" is an online conversation tool that can be used to maintain flow, avoid interruptions, and allow everyone in a call to have their say. TAL uses this technique across the organization including in working groups, public-facing online events, and for the Architecture Beyond Capitalism School.

The principles of stacking are as follows:

- A facilitator initiates a topic of conversation per an agenda.
- If a participant would like to speak they type "stack" in the chat.
- The order in which participants are called on is directly correlated to the order in which they appear in the stack.
- The facilitator should manage the stack and then calling on people sequentially.
- If a participant is asked a direct question, or has a direct answer to a question posed by another participant, they can type "direct response" into the meeting chat and it supersedes the current stack.
- Other comments in the chat should be kept to a minimum.

In some situations, particularly in larger group settings, organizers may choose to use a "progressive stack," a technique used to forefront the voices of marginalized groups. Popularized during the Occupy movement, meetings that use the progressive stack typically invite people from non-dominant groups (including women, queer folks, people of color, and very young or older people) to move up the stack. The purpose behind the technique is to counter what is perceived as a flaw in typical democratic conversation where the majority group voices are heard more prominently than minority or non-dominant groups.[5]

In-Person Meetings

The majority of the online conversation methods are directly applicable to in-person meetings. The notable exception is that of "stacking." There are, however, in-person equivalents, many that have developed through participatory and socially engaged art practices.

"The Meeting Game" is a model participatory art practice that brings stacking to life. Developed by socially engaged artist, Caroline Woolard, it asks in-person meeting participants to roll spheres across a central meeting table according to a ruleset that guides and traces a conversation. Or, in Woolard's words:

> The game visualizes the flow of dialogue, as each person starts out with the same number of spheres, and a person must roll a sphere to another

person, or "spend it," in order to speak. In this way, the spheres act as a kind of currency. People can redistribute spheres without speaking, if they wish. When played in a meeting, the game has the effect of both slowing down the flow of conversation and exchange as well as making visible who is speaking, how often, and to whom.[6]

"The Meeting Game" recognizes meetings as creative projects and directly engages the physical world in dialogue. Just as it replicates the qualities of stacking, it enhances the dynamic, making material the conversational exchange.

Notes

1 McDonald, *The Power of Protocols*, 11–12.
2 This meeting structure is a modification of one proposed by Aria Strategies LLC, "Facilitation as an Equity Strategy."
3 The School Reform Initiative offers a growing list of inclusive conversation activities and protocols as How-To guides. SRI, "Protocols."
4 Trimboli, *How to Listen*, 17.
5 Wikipedia, "Progressive Stack."
6 Woolard, "The Meeting."

PART 2
The Scales of Organizing Architecture Education

Introduction

Starting with the premise that architecture education *must* reform, Part 2 lays the historical and conceptual groundwork for identifying challenges to that goal across the scales of SMALL, studio; MEDIUM, curriculum and schools of architecture; LARGE, the university; and EXTRA LARGE, the nation-state. It also offers optimism by identifying organizing frameworks and sites of possibility at each scale, as well as including case studies that serve as proofs-of-concept for the transformative role that organizing can have in architecture education.

In adopting a structure based on progressive scales of understanding and intervention, this guide seeks to depart from—and reclaim—the architectural use value of standardized scaling systems synonymous with Rem Koolhaas' and Bruce Mau's 1995 book *S, M, L, XL*, in which "working with scale puts you in an almost godlike position."[1] In the case of *The Organizer's Guide to Architecture Education*, the language of S, M, L, and XL defines an organizing framework for mapping the specificity and interconnectedness of both existing conditions that define architecture education and strategies that can mobilize it toward systemic change. Furthermore, the scales afford an openness to interpretation that can be useful in translating the concepts presented in Part 2 to contexts that may not perfectly align with the practices described in each chapter.

In advocating for architecture education reform, this book, and Part 2 in particular, are guided by certain theoretical allegiances to educational theorists such as Paulo Freire and bell hooks. Paulo Freire teaches how

DOI: 10.4324/9781003411284-5

to resist the polarized dichotomy of the subject-expert narrator—the teacher—who deposits static and compartmentalized content into the minds of a uniform, listening, body of objects—the students. Freire's analysis of the "banking" concept of education positions the power relationships discussed in Part 1 within an educational framework, locating oppression as a force to overcome in the process of organizing.[2] bell hooks argues for the need to move past the Western metaphysical dualism that separates the cognitive, measured mind from the emotional body. Her text, *Teaching to Transgress*, supports a holistic approach to education that emphasizes collective self-actualization.[3]

There is a need to synthesize such scholarship on educational reform with architecture's pedagogical approach. In *Deviations: Designing Architecture – A Manual*, architectural pedagogists Marc Angélil and Dirk Hebel point to the importance of moving past the primacy of visual appearance, authorship, and objects delivered in a linear sequence.[4] In many ways, their argument reinforces Freire and hooks by critiquing the dominant educational frameworks that segregate content and people into exclusive categories, and trades them for a conscious form of collective knowledge production.[5]

Without focus, however, these theories cannot be acted upon. At each scale of focus, Part 2 identifies the *who*—the subject, *what*—the object(ive), and *how*—the strategies and tactics—of organizing. Ultimately, Part 2 looks for opportunities to distribute authority and share power. It values the organizer and questions categorical and syntactic logics that come to fix perception and procedure in stasis. Finally, Part 2 is conceived as an open document, a go-to for advancing organizing in architecture education in the context of ongoing and evolving education reform conversations. For those already practicing organizing or those interested in its potential, Part 2 shares a collective optimism in architecture education's responsiveness and adaptability.

Notes

1 Koolhaas, Mau, and Werlemann, *S, M, L, XL*.
2 Freire, Macedo, and Shor, *Pedagogy of the Oppressed*, 68.
3 hooks, *Teaching to Transgress*.
4 Angélil and Hebel, *Deviations*.
5 Angélil, Uziyel, and Eidgenössische Technische Hochschule Zürich, *Inchoate*.

SMALL: THE STUDIO

Introduction

The entry point for organizing architecture education is its smallest and most iconic module: the studio. On the one hand, studio is a space purportedly free from "real world" constraints. On the other hand, it is a simulacrum of that very same "real world" wherein students absorb the protocols practiced by the professionalized industry. Part 2 starts with studio because it is the first and primary place where students are socialized into the profession.[1]

The word "studio" implies both its spatial setting, linked to the professional atelier that preceded formal academic learning,[2] and the pedagogy associated with "studio culture."[3] Broadly defined, the studio refers to a group of people working together, guided by an instructor, in a typically large and adaptable setting where explorations occur through iterative making informed by feedback from both one's instructor and one's peers. Studio stands apart from other more common modes of teaching such as the lecture, the seminar, or the lab because of the extensive face-to-face interaction between faculty and students, and because of its primacy within the architecture curriculum, and the syncretic nature of its knowledge basis, processes, and skill sets.[4]

Studios often count for twice or three times as many credit hours as a typical lecture or seminar course, and rarely meet for less than eight hours per week. Sometimes, a studio unit (typically 10–20 students with one or two instructors) will operate independently, sometimes as a section within a larger cohort. Studios are generally scheduled progressively in the core curriculum, increasing in conceptual and technical complexity over time. Upper-level

DOI: 10.4324/9781003411284-6

studios, both undergraduate and graduate, are self-selected by students, often through a competitive lottery process or via priority enrollment.

Studio is where one demonstrates "design excellence" and learns to be a "good designer," both generic qualifiers which lack contextual specificity. For students working on studio design problems, design processes are rarely obvious, take a lot of time, never have a singular solution, and have opaque criteria for evaluation. And beyond the already excessive credit allocation, architecture students are expected to be present in studio far more than the suggested workload as they work through their proposed designs.[5] The curriculum suggests a student manages all their courses with equanimity, but the school rewards studio performance disproportionately. In terms of credit count, time, and resource consumption, studio doesn't simply take priority in an architecture student's education—it dominates it.

Studio is a microcosm of all the ambiguity that is architecture. Studio culture insists on passion while also prioritizing rational thinking and deductive reasoning; it insists that students act professionally while hinting that professionalism itself is dry, a threat to creativity and expansive thinking; it insists that projects be completed on time, as in a client-driven professional practice, but encourages up to the last-minute changes and elaborations. As students internalize these contradictions, the notion of architecture as "calling" trickles down from academia into the workplace, obscuring the identity of the architectural worker and perpetuating exploitative labor conditions.

Despite the difficulties that plague architecture culture in academia and beyond, studio has the potential to instill, in both student and teacher, a collective identity. Precisely because of its intensity and outsized importance as well as its immersive dynamic and nonhierarchical nature it can breed the fellowship and solidarity that forms the foundation of organizing at larger scales that studio itself.

It is important to note that this chapter's critique of traditional studio does not propose supplanting the teaching of design. Rather, it wants to (1) expand our understanding of design's purpose and impact; (2) engage the spaces, methods, and relationships that comprise studio beyond the work itself; (3) recast the architectural skill set and (4) re-envision the design student not as a struggling individual but as part of a collective. If organizing itself does not directly emerge from studio, its foundations of collaboration are laid there.

History of the Studio

The history of architecture studio can be traced back to the division between constructors and designers formalized during the Renaissance.[6] In this early model, the study of architecture primarily occurred "in the workshops or homes of the master craftsmen themselves."[7] In the second half of the seventeenth century, a new model emerged through the Académie d' Architecture,[8] and, throughout the nineteenth and twentieth centuries, its successor, the École des Beaux-Arts, which developed a centralized, government-funded, systematic architecture education that differentiated architects from other workers in the construction industry.

Central to the École's disciplinary knowledge was original composition, as opposed to adherence to historical precedents, the pre-existing directive to all architects, to which the Académie had been devoted. A teacher at the École des Beaux Arts, Jacques-Germain Soufflot argued in his design for the Panthéon that he had to space the colonnade's columns farther apart than in classical examples in order to achieve the grandeur and lightness he wanted.[9] This was not the first time that lessons of classical architecture were adjusted to accommodate new programs, but it was the first time that an adjustment to strict precedent was theoretically defended based on a mix of astronomical/mathematical/proportional lessons and humanist faith in interpreting rational aesthetic order.

As composition became a subject in and of itself, its purview and thus its principles grew in complexity. Certain teachers became famous for their ability to address pedagogical needs systematically. Jean-Nicolas-Louis Durand, who taught at the school from 1808 to 1830, was known for his *Précis des leçons d'architecture*[10] (1802–1805), which utilized grids to rationalize the composition of buildings' plans and elevations.[11] Eugène Viollet-le-Duc, who taught briefly at the École des Beaux Arts in the mid-1830s after teaching at the École Polytechnique,[12] taught new approaches to composition made possible by iron and steel construction. Pierre-François-Henri Labrouste, who taught at the École des Beaux Arts concurrently, promoted a progressive, rational, and functional approach to design that embraced iron and glass construction.[13]

The emphasis on composition did not foreground individuality, and the mark of a good student was not simply design talent. Awareness of history, the integration of theory and practice, construction as it related to ornament, and consideration of physical and social contexts were essential to design knowledge. The crowded space of the studio, while allowing individual development, was also a place of shared learning, critical discourse, and collective ideation.[14] Nevertheless, individual design virtuosity was awarded, and the shared approach to knowledge was neatly ignored.

In the École des Beaux Arts, the hallmarks of what constitute studio culture were set in place: working on drawings until the bitter end (i.e. the *charrette*, named for the horse-drawn cart that carried students still working on their drawings to the exhibition hall);[15] competition to be the best designer and reap rewards and accolades, especially the Grand Prix de

Rome; [16] and the assumption that passionate work in school would yield future exposure and employment. All these practices have been carried through to today's studio culture. Two key lessons were not passed down, however: (1) the integration of non-compositional knowledge into design, and (2) the recognition that architecture education should meet challenges specific to its time. In the era of the École des Beaux Arts, this included new programs and patronage ushered in by the Napoleonic Empire, the centralization of education to serve that empire, the correct use of new industrial materials, and the division of labor demanded by capitalism when professionalism was being invented. Instead, oblivious to vast changes in our society and culture, these nineteenth-century traditions are still practiced globally. An educational approach that responds to our present economic and social demands, globally and locally, is urgently needed.

Studio in the Present

Studio today reproduces and produces paradigms that promote architecture's exceptionalism in ways that reinforce disciplinary preciousness and marginalize the remit of both the academy and the profession.[17] The marginalization is felt by all: students, teachers, and practitioners, but especially those affected by architecture's outcomes.

For new students, studio is an intellectual leap. First-time studio students are confronted with lessons in formal and representational dexterity and disciplinary jargon that is difficult to grasp, and told to forget whatever they thought they knew about architecture. Interests that led them to study architecture—perhaps hopes for a better built environment, working with communities, learning to construct—make only a rare appearance. Those who have not been raised in environments that have exposed them to aesthetic discourse are at a particular disadvantage. Studio, in other words, flattens the strengths and skills brought by students with diverse backgrounds. The unique trajectories that these students might take to what is considered formal and representational competence cannot easily be accommodated within a fast-paced environment that embraces a sink-or-swim mentality. Indeed time management is ignored and the outsized demands of student workloads normalize unhealthy routines, conditioning students to accept similarly unhealthy routines that are quickly assumed to be the norm not just for school but for the profession.

Studio instructors also come with insecurities that can be exacerbated by the studio structure. Few are taught to teach and teach design according to individual proclivities and backgrounds. Some are hired because they were former star students at the school, some because they have been featured in culturally significant journals, some because they have subject-matter expertise. Some are part-time one-off lecturers, some year-by-year adjuncts, some full-time teachers without tenure, and some with tenure. The majority of instructors teach in the way they themselves were taught and rarely acknowledge to themselves or each other that limited pedagogy, lead to competition and establish internal unspoken hierarchies. Early-career architecture faculty typically serve at the pleasure of their more established colleagues, who then serve to uphold the image of the school; at the same time established colleagues are challenged by hipper, younger, more software-attuned studio instructors who have the students' attention.

Formed through the syllabus and the project brief, the student-faculty studio relationship is also fraught with ambiguous expectations. In a typical studio scenario, students are asked to consider how a given program—say a library—will be best arranged for a given location. The program may list required spaces, their measured areas or volumes, and the activities that occur within them, but the people who will inhabit those spaces are only implied or inferred from data-driven demographics understood at a distance; others in the neighborhood who will be affected by the new project are rarely mentioned. Likewise, the site is often understood simply as a real estate boundary, rather than a space of complex geography and contested ownership. There is limited time to ask the many critical questions that capture the complexity of a given program or site, and less time to answer them in a researched and nuanced way. The conspicuous absence of the those who are directly and indirectly involved in the production, habitation, and communal experience of architecture—the missing others—is not only important because those others deserve a voice when a student considers the "solution" to a project, it also makes the criteria of success relatively arbitrary and differing views between critic and student rampant.

Likewise the student–teacher relationship, counter to all other efforts at connection, is too often defined by grading. Because of the inherently subjective nature of design work and its reception by others, its evaluation is fraught. One of the most common experiences in higher education is the failure of expectations that unfolds at the end of each term, when faculty are inundated with emails from students who are not satisfied with their grades. The go-to address for this dilemma, instituting a rigid grading rubric supported by early and frequent evaluation, might allow faculty to offer quick and uncontested explanations to student complaints, but these strategies tend also to disincentivize risk-taking, leaving no room for productive failure. Such rigidity may exacerbate existing inequities by rewarding those already well placed to succeed in a university context. Instead of elevating the design of the constructed environment as the ever-evolving, interdependent project that it is, an effort in collective betterment shared by faculty and students alike, grading reinforces hegemonic design ideals. It also maintains unnecessary hierarchies, separating faculty from students and discouraging intergenerational learning and cooperation.

ORGANIZING—THE STUDIO

And yet there is great potential for studio to be a place for coordinated work and the foundation of organizing as a cohort. Camaraderie among both the students and the faculty, as separate entities and together, does abound in the ambiguous set of expectations. For the students, the all-consuming intensity of the studio environment creates deeply held bonds over the difficult challenges of their education and the shared pressure to perform; they take pleasure in learning from and helping each other. For teachers, teaching architecture offers opportunities to explore the more open-ended knowledges and practices of architecture, apart from pressures of professional practice and confines of practicality. Prioritizing organizing reconfigures how studio is taught and how students learn, reframing what architectural knowledge is and what it means to belong in the field of architecture. Building on the sense of camaraderie within the student cohort and among the faculty, organizing can help everyone honor their own contributions while recognizing the larger collective intelligence that is ultimately at stake. The contributions of the missing others are essential in foregrounding how and to whom that collective intelligence is being applied.

When studio is understood as a heterogeneous space for collective positions, the roles of both teacher and student change; their relationship becomes less hierarchical and more reciprocal. No longer the conveyor of truth, the teacher becomes a facilitator who embraces positionality and intersectionality and promotes student agency[18]. Lack of expertise no longer leads to knowledge insecurity, but to a shared exploration for new approaches to a problem. At the same time, the studio instructor recognizes the need to become trained in teaching, through formal and informal channels, by incorporating pedagogy into their research objectives, by sharing practices and experiences with other teachers, and by soliciting and learning from student feedback.[19] The studio instructor is also transparent about how they have come to architecture and teaching, and what they themselves hope to get out of the studio experience. Finally, the instructor is a model for what it means to be an architectural worker. This means valuing one's own time and clarifying one's availability, coordinating roles with fellow critics while openly supporting differences between them, unionizing where possible, and supporting graduate student strikes when they occur. Altogether, it means modeling worker solidarity.

For the students, remodeling studio through the lens of organizing means that studio becomes the space where the subject of the architectural worker is formed. It also implies a reorientation of that subject toward an architecture of greater agency, but also an architecture that creates space for and works with others. It means preparing students to ask uncomfortable questions and take positions, but also empathize with the positions of others so that when they engage with the scales of MEDIUM (curriculum), LARGE (the university) and EXTRA LARGE (the nation-state), they are ready to organize because it's part of what it means to be educated as an architect.

Sites of Possibility

The sites of possibility discussed below recognize that the content of studio, the interpersonal relations of studio, and the practices and spaces of studio, all contribute to the cultivation of "studio culture" and, by extension, architecture culture. Each offers opportunities for rethinking studio's role in educating a new kind of architect.

Studio Content

The content of the studio brief is the most obvious place to redirect what it means to be an architect and what architecture is meant to do. Instead of issuing imagined programs that simulate reality, faculty should look to the "real world" for problems to address—architecture education should engage with the challenges of the time, finding ways to expand the relevance of design. Similarly, site should not be taught as an abstract boundary of buildable and non-buildable areas but rather as a specific place—with unique material conditions and a potentially layered, complex, and contested history—as well as a social construct. When taught this way, site is not independent from the program and, where appropriate, it can actively inform the development of a spatial response. Considering the material conditions of the site—its geological profile, soil type, water catchment areas, histories of extraction—can serve as a foundation for informed and nuanced responses to the ecological impact of the built environment. Conversely, understanding the site as a territory upon which a collection of documents and social conventions delineate changing and often contested boundaries of ownership can help reveal the multitude of socio-economic, political, and cultural contexts that inform regulatory frameworks such as zoning and broader conversations around the notions of property and value. Power mapping can help reveal the multiple entanglements of a given site. As an analytic approach, it can inform the design process, but it should be complemented, when appropriate, by a more experiential approach, where students spend as much time as possible on and with the site, exploring its less tangible aspects sensorially.

In terms of studio output, it is important to contextualize object-oriented outcomes, establishing form as discursive rather than the manifestation of individual genius. This implies two things, both of which are foundational for understanding organizing. First, people—not simply occupants or users, but anyone directly or indirectly involved or affected—must replace the object as the primary design consideration.[20] Design could be reframed as an exploration of the possible scenarios that different design decisions might yield for those impacted by the project. Second, architecture must be understood not as a static object, but as an evolving condition; a design proposal will morph in a future that the project itself helps set in motion. Here again, designing scenarios instead of objects makes students aware of architecture's agency beyond the aesthetics of a project and over time, but it also highlights architecture's highly contingent role, both important lessons for the architect-organizer.

Studio Relationships

Focusing on people underscores the relational nature of architectural design, both internally—within the studio or the project team—and externally—within larger institutional frameworks or in relationship to clients, constructors, and the broader public. In addition to collaborating with traditional consultants—structural, mechanical, electrical, and plumbing engineers—within the context of a studio project, teachers and students can work together to identify other relationships that might activated by a project brief—with fabricators, contractors, developers, planners, labor lawyers, or policy makers. By engaging in conversations with some of these "missing others," students can better understand how the intersecting landscapes of development, finance, and political power influence the built environment. Where possible, both local and global examples of these entanglements should be explored.

The "missing others" also includes local communities. The community in which a studio project resides must be named, the relationship of the studio to that community must be made specific, and students and faculty must move beyond the community savior complex. An example of this comes from Dark Matter University, which pays locals to attend their courses, turning the relational dynamics of architectural expertise on its head.[21] When the community in question is the same community within which the school of architecture resides, the studio should acknowledge the Town and Gown dynamic between the university and its locality.[22]

To understand the communities a brief is meant to address, the teacher can introduce students to design-based outreach campaigns already connected to a neighborhood's organizations and establish connections with movements and leaders doing organizational work. One such example is the *Plum Orchard, New Orleans Studio*, a multi-semester post-Katrina studio begun in 2005 that was taught by a consortium of consulting experts, faculty, and students from Pratt Institute and New Jersey Institute of Technology in collaboration with the Association of Community Organizations for Reform (ACORN) who acted as their local partner under a US Department of Housing and urban Development Rebuilding America Partnership grant.[23]

Closer to "home," the relationship of the studio to the curriculum, the school of architecture, and the university at large should also be made explicit. The teacher should make the systems of the university transparent to students, foregrounding hierarchies and indicating where they themself are located within those hierarchies. Among other things, the teacher can describe the processes of accreditation and their impact on the syllabus, explain the administrative processes in place for grading, clarify the flows of money that affect how courses—and the school on the whole—are supported, and point to collective bargaining agreements where they exist.

Studio Practices

Situating studio within the broader pedagogical arc of an architecture program is a curricular issue (explored further in MEDIUM), but it starts in the studio, where a certain level of control can be promoted by giving students agency over their own education. Allowing students to shape their own syllabi and project briefs; collectively to define success through values-based objectives, and to establish themselves as the studio's culture empowers them as future organizers. In certain studios, students could introduce their own subjective criteria—both what they want to learn and how they want to apply their knowledge and skills to a project, suggest how they want their work reviewed and by whom, request lessons they feel are needed to meet the challenges of the brief, and organize into a collective practice through which to designate shared tasks, like research. As part of the 2022 iteration of the ABC School, a workshop titled *Student Organizing Across Syllabi and Project Briefs* asked how student organizing can affect the way syllabi, project briefs, and other documents that undergird the power dynamics of traditional studios are written.[24] Building on the 2021 organizing efforts of the Student Advisory Board (SAB) at the South Dakota State University Architecture Department, the workshop explored strategies for impactful student involvement in departmental matters, including curricular development, yielding changes that would trickle down to course syllabi and daily studio practices.[25]

Crucial to translating empowerment into organizing are practices that promote empathy and collaboration. Empathy mapping,[26] which encourages both students and their instructor to map the anxieties, interests, and positionality of one another, can make transparent the studio's diverse concerns so they can be addressed and overcome. Empathy mapping allows participants to reflect on each other's feelings about the studio environment, the brief, the university, and life beyond, creating a safe space for these issues to be discussed, and opportunities for resulting insights to infiltrate the design process. Empathy mapping also invites students to experience the teacher as a person with their own vulnerabilities. The benefits of this process are amplified when both the instructor and the students continually return to and reflect on the empathy mapping process throughout the semester.

Collaborative and collective work can also be formative as it forces students to engage with each other when something is at stake, giving them a platform to apply their organizational skills. This does not mean that all designs must be produced collaboratively or that all work must be approached through divisions of labor; even when students design individually, they can work together to propose and coordinate methods for reviewing projects internally. This may include role playing within the studio, exchanging projects so colleagues must "read" and advance the project given to them, and developing the criteria for the evaluation of a project. Shared work and collaborative work establish the concept of design contingency, the idea that architecture does not occur in a vacuum, and that its processes are heavily influenced by the presence of—indeed require—multiple participants.

Collective teaching, where multiple instructors can take turns teaching the same student cohort, is an opportunity not only for faculty to practice a shared knowledge approach to teaching, but also for students to develop their critical thinking. As multiple—potentially conflicting—perspectives come to the fore, students are forced to assess the varied feedback that they receive and make decisions about their own work. Co-teaching can also create an environment in which new or less experienced teachers can learn from the pedagogical techniques of more experienced ones and vice versa.

As studio becomes receptive to a plurality of teaching and learning approaches, it becomes clear that neither architectural knowledge nor the process of learning can be easily compartmentalized. By recognizing that design work in the studio is always in progress and always unfinished, students and teachers can reimagine the critique as a learning opportunity rather than an evaluative mechanism and an elaborate performance, leveraging its collective nature and the fresh perspectives that it brings to the fore to propel projects forward. Clever/Slice, a global space to share in-progress creative work founded in New York City as a counter to the classic critique experienced in art and design education, follows a framework known as the Critical Response Process to encourage equitable, inclusive, and focused feedback, with the aim to foster progress in the creative work. In its critique of the critique, Clever/Slice is based on two basic assumptions, first that the work presented in the space is meaningful, and that the work is in-progress. The ultimate goal is "to help people determine where their creative work needs to go next and how to get there."[27]

Rethinking the finality of the crit opens up broader questions about whether studio projects should transcend the temporal boundaries of a university term. An example of such temporal flexibility comes from the École des Beaux Arts, where, once students were admitted, they were considered mature enough to manage their own schedules, and there was no time limit for the completion of the work required to pass from second to first class, or to be admitted to the diploma examination (though no one could remain a student at the École past the age of thirty).[28] While such extreme flexibility might not be feasible within the constraints of the contemporary university, possible alternatives to current practices include projects that carry over from term to term, or students repeating the same studio as they move in and out of supporting classes that gradually widen their understanding of the field. Such iterative practices would not only allow students to learn from the organizational approaches of previous studios, but also create opportunities for vertical integration, making conversations and collaborations across skill levels within the student body possible.

Studio Spaces

The question of flexibility extends to the physical space of the studio as well. The prevalence of the open-plan layout in studio has ideological and pedagogical origins. The conventional wisdom is that studio spaces are non-hierarchical environments which encourage conversation and collaboration; just as much learning occurs through osmosis as through explicit instruction. While some of that might be true, an 2022 Association of Collegiate Schools of Architecture (ACSA) webinar titled, "Toward a More Just Design Studio: Analyzing Power Dynamics in Studio Spaces," argued that this perception doesn't take into account the possibility that open spaces can manifest and even magnify demonstrations of spatial power and tribalism.[29] Furthermore, the way the instructor positions themselves in and moves through the physical space of the studio may create imbalances in the social space of the studio—sometimes because it's hard for students to hear and other times because the proximity or visibility of certain students can subconsciously influence how the instructors perceives or interacts with them.[30] Conversely, where students choose to sit (and with whom) matters.[31] Becoming cognizant of these issues is the first step toward organizing for a better studio environment.

To facilitate an adaptable studio environment, studio spaces must be arranged to support both individual and collective production, including pin-up spaces where students can share their work with each other and their instructor.[32] Furniture can be mounted on wheels to allow flexible arrangements and student autonomy. To ensure that the space of the studio reflects the needs of the students occupying it, the desk layout can be turned into a design task, orchestrated by the teacher and/or the students collectively and revisited throughout the duration of the studio based on evolving needs. An example of this practice occurred as part of an architectural course devised in the mid-1960s by practitioner and academic Roelof Uytenbogaardt and partially implemented at the University of Cape Town.[33] Recalling his personal conversations with Uytenbogaardt about pedagogy, author Peter Buchanan describes how, as part of design research, the physical spaces of the studio, and even the cafeteria where students socialized, were constantly rearranged to encourage the students' awareness of "how their social interactions, their experience of them and the meanings they ascribed to them, were shaped by the physical environment in which the class was conducted." Such an exercise not only gives the studio occupants agency over the space where they spend so much of their time, but also provides an opportunity to test some of the basic principles of organizing—taking action with others across time. After all, designing the studio space is as much about organizing a set of places as it is about organizing a day, a week, a semester, and a cohort of people with shared experiences and goals but different individual needs and preferences.

Notes

1 Banham et al., *A Critic Writes*, 295.
2 Gutman et al., *Architecture from the Outside In*; Cuff, *Architecture*.
3 In 2005, the National Architectural Accrediting Board (NAAB) issued an additional condition for accreditation: Studio Culture, requiring each accredited program to have a written policy on the culture of its studio environment. In the "2020 Edition of the Conditions for Accreditation," the term "Studio culture" has been replaced with "Learning and Teaching Culture," defined by NAAB as "How the program fosters and ensures a positive and respectful environment that encourages optimism, respect, sharing, engagement, and innovation among its faculty, students, administration, and staff." NAAB, "Conditions for Accreditation 2020 Edition," 2. In 2018, The American Institute of Architecture Students (AIAS) and NAAB announced a partnership to promote healthier studio culture across accredited architecture programs AIAS, "AIAS and NAAB Partner to Promote Healthy Studio Culture."
4 Ockman and Williamson, *Architecture School*, 10.

5 Students are typically expected to spend approximately 3 hours per week for each credit hour Gogol, "What Are Credit Hours?"

6 Cret, "The Ecole Des Beaux-Arts and Architectural Education," 4.

7 Cret, 3.

8 As a royal institution, the Académie was disbanded in 1793 in the aftermath of the French revolution, but was resurrected in the 19th century in the form of the École des Beaux-Arts Griffin, *Rise of Academic Architectural Education.*

9 Kostof, *A History of Architecture*, 558–59.

10 Translated as "Précis of the Lectures on Architecture."

11 Kruft, *A history of architectural theory*, 273–74.

12 "Eugene Emmanuel Viollet-Le-Duc," 214–25.

13 Kruft, *A history of architectural theory*, 279–80.

14 Cret, "The Ecole Des Beaux-Arts and Architectural Education," 11.

15 Willis, "Are Charettes Old School?"

16 The Grand Prix de Rome offered prize winners the chance to study Roman antiquity and brought with it prestige and influence Cret, "The Ecole Des Beaux-Arts and Architectural Education," 6–7, 13.

17 As architecture professor Rashida Ng argues, "the boundaries of the discipline of architecture were firmly established by and for those who were educated, wealthy, upper/middle class, heterosexual, male and white." Ng, "Breaking the Chains."

18 Positionality refers to identities, experiences, values, views, and other temporal and spatial factors that shape an individual's existential perspective. Related to positionality, intersectionality is a framework for understanding how compound identities intersect in unique and complex ways with systems of power and oppression. Both concepts are discussed in more detail in Part 3.

19 An example of this comes from "On Pedagogical Transparency," an ABC 2022 session discussing the adoption of the TILT (Transparency in Learning and Teaching) framework by a number of architecture faculty at Syracuse University. As an educational project, TILT focuses on two main practices: 1) the promotion of students' conscious understanding of how they learn; and 2) enabling faculty to gather, share and promptly benefit from current data about students' learning through coordinated efforts across disciplines, institutions, and nations TILT Higher Ed, "Transparency in Learning and Teaching."

20 An exemplar of this approach, French architecture firm Lacaton & Vassal routinely place the inhabitants of the spaces they design at the center of their work. In response to a call for tenders which had assumed the demolition of the existing Tour Bois-le-Prêtre, Lacaton & Vassal's proposal to renovate the building, enlarging the units and creating better views, all while allowing the residents to remain in their units, was ultimately accepted by the authorities, who didn't have to re-house people during construction. https://www.atlasofplaces.com/architecture/tour-bois-le-pretre/

21 See CASE STUDY.

22 The Town and Gown dynamic gets discussed in greater detail in LARGE.

23 See CASE STUDY.

24 See CASE STUDY.

25 See CASE STUDY.

26 See HOW-TO.

27 See CASE STUDY.

28 Cret, "The Ecole Des Beaux-Arts and Architectural Education," 11.

29 *Toward a More Just Design Studio.*

30 *Toward a More Just Design Studio.*

31 Educator Sandy Merz III talks of "power seats" and "safe zones." Power seats, "by merit of their location," he says, "magnify a student's presence in the class," while safe zones "downplay the effects of a student's actions on the class dynamics, without compromising his or her access to content." Mertz, 'Teaching Secrets: Arranging Optimal Classroom Seating'.
32 Contemporary research into layout optimization in the workplace suggests that no single ideal physical or digital workspace architecture exists. Rather, given a particular set of circumstances and objectives, there might be a different balance between privacy and interaction that works for a given group of people. Bernstein and Waber, 'The Truth About Open Offices'.
33 Buchanan, 'The Big Rethink: Architectural Education'.

MEDIUM: THE CURRICULUM

While SMALL interrogates the potential of organizing practices in the studio, MEDIUM interrogates the question of architectural education in general. What is a curriculum and the school that sponsors it trying to achieve: a dedication to the discipline and its autonomy or future practitioners who can have impact on the environment and the built environment? By contextualizing the contemporary architecture curriculum, both historically and against external forces, this chapter posits organizing as central to a reimagined curriculum that is not static but as a laboratory for practice and as a practice in itself, responsive to the challenges of this era.

The Curriculum

A curriculum is a set of subjects, concepts, and practices that must be learned in order to meet a set of education goals within an educational institution. The architecture curriculum is an administrative balancing act. The administrative leadership of an architecture school, which is often appointed by the university, is tasked with making sure the school will be accredited and stay on budget, but also be popular, knowing that its ability to attract students rests on leveraging the imaginative and innovative aspects of a curriculum.

Curricular form, content, and delivery varies by location, by the context of the school within which it sits, and by the level of the professional degree, i.e., undergraduate or graduate. Yet even given regional and structural differences, the make-up of the contemporary curriculum of a professional architecture education is surprisingly uniform and appears to be

DOI: 10.4324/9781003411284-7

largely unquestioned. The curricular realms of knowledge comprise five broad categories of learning: design, representation, construction, history-theory, and professional practice.

Design is perhaps the most fluid of skills, centering on organizational and visual rulesets for the artful ordering and composition of space and form. Typically taught in the studio format, design studio is consistently privileged within the curriculum and is typically taught every semester.

Representation refers to the evolving skill set required for an architect to effectively communicate spatial ideas to colleagues, clients, permitting institutions, and other stakeholders through various forms of media, including drawings, models, and digital simulations.

Construction coursework supports students in developing an understanding of the technical and engineering principles necessary to the material realization of architecture by conveying the fundamentals of materials and assemblies; existing and emergent building technologies; physics and structural systems; electrical, mechanical, and plumbing systems; and environmental engineering.

History-Theory courses cover the evolution of architectural practices, movements, and ideas, providing the references and role models for architectural output and describing the terrain and values of architectural discourse. These courses help students develop a deeper understanding of the cultural, social, and political contexts in which architecture is developed, and how these contexts influence the design of buildings and urban spaces.

Professional Practice courses teach the procedural, fiscal, and legal considerations that inform the way commercial architecture is practiced. These courses also provide students with the knowledge and skills they need to enter the workforce, attain licensure, and practice as architects.

The critical limitation of these five categories is, on one hand, their distinctness from one another. Their boundaries allow particularly complex subject matter spanning between these categories—such as the history of capitalism and architecture's role within it; the realities of construction labor; modes of collective work; or the inner workings of local, regional, and national development policies—to fall through the cracks. It does not reflect the reality of what architects believe their role to be: the synthesis of diverse fields of knowledge that consider complex political, historical, social, and economic contexts in the generation of spatial form.

To examine the opportunities that the curriculum offers for organizing, and organizing for the curriculum, it is important to reexamine accreditation. Accreditation in architecture education results from a formal process of professional evaluation and recognition that ensures an institution, program, or individual meets specific quality standards. It involves the thorough assessment of educational factors including curriculum, faculty qualifications, facilities, resources, and student performance. The accreditation of architecture schools is carried out by professional organizations or agencies that specialize in delineating the competencies of architectural practice and, depending on the locale, in the licensing of future architects.[1] It is meant to serve as a quality assurance mechanism that ensures students receive a certain standard of education, one that prepares them to hold licensing power responsibly when signing off on the construction of buildings at a variety of scales.

The contemporary architecture education accreditation model emerged at the turn of the twentieth century. It started in 1897 in the United States when the state of Illinois passed legislation regulating the practice of architecture. Begun as a regional initiative, accreditation soon expanded nation-wide, formalizing with the founding of the Association of Collegiate Schools of Architecture (ACSA) in 1912. The United Kingdom followed suit when its professional organization, the Royal Institute of British Architects (RIBA), officialized its Board of Architectural Education in the Architects Registration Act of 1931. In 1940, the ACSA, along with two other professional architecture organizations in the United States, the American Institute of Architects (AIA) and the National Council of Architectural Registration Boards (NCARB), established the National Architectural Accrediting Board (NAAB) as the central authority to accredit schools of architecture across the nation. NAAB's mandate was "to create an integrated system of architecture education that would allow schools with varying resources and circumstances to develop according to their particular needs."[2] Today, NAAB still accredits professional degree paths in architecture. Some architecture schools choose not to be accredited to deliver their own nonstandard education, usually one that is more exclusively designed and/or theory-oriented.[3] In general, unaccredited degree programs can foster job precarity for their graduates. In addition, some states allow licensure without attending an accredited school. In California, one can practice architecture with ten years of work experience and be allowed to take licensure exams.[4]

European countries and the Antipodes, the application of accreditation requirements was altered by the introduction of the 1999 Bologna Accord. The Accord created a standardized system of higher education to facilitate student mobility between programs, equalizing higher education across participating nations in Europe, and to establish parity with the US master's degree. Because of this, architecture degrees in participating nations are now structured in three cycles: a bachelor's degree of three to four years, a master's degree of one to two years, and a doctoral degree. This division drastically reduced the use of the former professional undergraduate degree. The ability to move across institutions and between countries has added layers of administration to the accreditation process.[5] The shift from a five-year program to a "3+2" model has nominally shifted the delivery of accreditation requirements to the two-year professional master's degree. The Bologna Accord catalyzed conformity among higher education systems in other parts of the world, with many countries from Australasia and the Pacific region to South America adopting similar models in order to improve the quality and accessibility of higher education, and to achieve a sense of global legitimacy.[6]

Despite the Bologna agreement or the US NAAB requirements, each nation-state wants different things from its professional architects, and each school has its own pedagogical agenda motivated by expertise independent of professional standards. Indeed, almost every school wants to be known for its embrace of creativity and innovation, ideals often counter to accreditation demands. The standardization of subject areas observed across architecture curricula worldwide cannot then solely be attributed to external influences. It is just as likely to be the result of architecture's internal struggle to balance competing desires: conformity, stability, and predictability versus creativity and invention. The fuzzy boundaries of what specific skill sets can be protected in creative disciplines make them difficult to professionalize and define, and this instability results in a striving for administrative containment. Despite the pedagogical differences that help brand a particular school in a particular way, the five familiar categories persist. The more the parameters of an education and what constitutes expertise are in doubt, the more an administration strives for management logic and an appearance of certainty.

Accreditation criteria impose limitations on what and how a faculty can structure their vision of an ideal curriculum. Because accreditation requirements are difficult to change and slow to adapt to emergent challenges and new discourse, faculty are caught between compliance and the need to address current societal pressures; as a result, they are pushed into workarounds. These workarounds mean that faculty often take a tactical approach to meeting accreditation criteria by artificially weighting a particular course with accreditation requirements (allocated in a point system), or condensing the entirety of the requirements into one semester of teaching.

The Hidden Curriculum

There are other, less overt influences that impact the way a curriculum is delivered, making up a "hidden curriculum," the unofficial and under-recognized mode of ideological and pedagogical indoctrination.[7] The hidden curriculum describes the socialization that occurs in any educational setting where students are not just learning particular subject matters, but the values, norms, and beliefs of their teachers and peers and the societal practices they embody. The studio culture indoctrination described in SMALL, where it is most intimately experienced, is carried throughout in the curriculum as a whole. According to architectural sociologist Garry Stevens, "all forms of education transmit knowledge and skills," but "all forms of education also socialize students into some sort of ethos or culture."[8] For Stevens, these two functions are inseparable. Architecture education, he writes, is "a form of socialization aimed at producing a very specific *type* of person."[9]

The hidden curriculum is embedded in all the models of success put in front of a student passed on by faculty members' lecturers', and guest critics' particular tastes, behaviors, and practices—which often imply unhealthy approaches to self-care, an excessive focus on individualist design practices, and a lack of understanding of how capitalist practices intersect with the profession.[10] Those who deliver curriculum are not simply transmitting knowledge but actively contributing to the formation of individuals and their relationships to each other, to the profession and discipline, and to society at large. They model "architect" they don't just teach how to be one.

ORGANIZING—THE CURRICULUM

The curriculum should become not just a list of subjects but *a laboratory of practice*: a place to learn and understand existing practices of architecture, but also a place to test, experiment, challenge, and carve out new modes of working, relating, and being. Practice in this sense is both the protocols that shape how "architect" is performed, and the contingent experiments needed to get teaching right. Practice is theorized and played out in the curriculum through a plurality of means, methods, and forms of action that cover the modus operandi of a heterogeneous cast of actors—owners, builders, and architects. Curriculum as a practice entails a willingness to abandon old ideas and new ideas that don't pay off. It is an approach to curiosity that opens up curricula to become generative spaces that define, shift, and challenge the discipline of architecture. Curriculum as practice means redefining, reimagining, and theorizing architecture through education, rather than solely training future architects for its current form.

When practiced like this, the curriculum demands—and is ripe for—organizing. Organizing must incorporate all educational actors: students, faculty, administration, and the missing others. The lead must be taken by the faculty who can develop a curriculum that empowers students and the community. Organizing the faculty—and beyond that, the administration—requires some basic things. First, an agreement on what one is organizing toward; second, differences in faculty rank should be put aside to emphasize diversity of knowledge and the necessity of sharing that knowledge; third, the strategies and tactics for delivering an effective education should include what gets taught and by whom, and what constitutes a course and its requirements; and fourth, rituals that foster a collective identity should be established. To do this, the faculty themselves must be organized, forming the collective bonds, shared motivations, and influence necessary to deliver curricular change. It is only through the process of organizing that school power dynamics can be revealed and challenged, the university lobbied to grant better resources, systems, and working conditions, and a curriculum developed that is responsive to local and global challenges.

Sites of Possibility

Organizing at the "medium" or curricular scale of architecture education has two aims. It should make the knowledge areas of architecture education responsive to the needs of the built environment and its stewards. And it should rethink architecture education as accommodating of difference, as adaptive to change, as an ever-evolving collective conversation. It thereby imagines both an architecture curriculum changed by organizing and an architecture-specific curriculum in organizing. Organizing at the medium scale can deliver on these aims via curricular relationships, content, and the spaces of education.

Curricula and Relationships

A faculty must look inward and examine its own educational, structural, relational, and organizational practices. An in-depth study of the experience of staff and students at all levels within the school, to evaluate both where changes need to be made, and where staff and students feel seen and supported, should address the issues caused by the hidden curriculum. This must go beyond symptom analysis into cause analysis. The results of this work must be considered with objectivity—without blame or finger pointing—and with an attitude of care and collective healing. It reveals unconscious behavior, internal biases, and personal manifestations of a system that feels increasingly overwhelming and unsustainable.

At the same time, there should be full faculty support for student organizing. Faculty organizing and curricular reframing should foster the kind of environment needed for student organizing to flourish. An organized faculty provides a working model to students for how they can organize to represent their interests. Universities usually have student representatives on governance committee which faculty should support and often have funding and existing frameworks for student-led organizations. Students can organize to take control of their own education, to gain a holistic understanding of the curricular arc, and become involved in curricular decision-making. Students' trust must be earned through curricular, procedural, and communicational transparency.

A shift in how faculty see themselves—and from there, the students and the administration—is aided by the establishment of ongoing rituals that occur either inside or outside the school. These can be regular meetings where food is shared, where conceptual ideas and visions are discussed, and where experiments with styles and forms of conversation (exposing doubts and vulnerabilities) are expressed. In lieu of meetings, they can be rituals of transparency that might include weekly updates shared with all staff. They can be experimental gatherings, creating, testing, and modeling new ways in which faculty can relate to one another. All require the development of an agreement on processes for making decisions and having discussions in a space of radical democracy and acceptance of disagreement. These rituals, once established, should be as in-person and as routine as possible, ensuring continued momentum and face-to-face interaction and resolution. Actionable responsibilities should be equitably shared and continually assessed for their impact, to check if and how they are helping to build community. Joseph Henrich, a scholar of human evolutionary biology, has observed that organized ritual around a shared challenge can relieve internal tensions, or even cause an improvement in a community's overall wellbeing, simply because of the act of performing a collective ritual, and having to relate to each other, work together, and organize in order to do it.[11] The relationality encouraged by these rituals could help to make a faculty that is open, curious, and genuinely collective. This collectivity and its rituals should extend to the school as a whole.

The faculty of the architecture and design school at Pontificia Universidad Católica de Valparaíso, Chile, offers a compelling example of this, in particular through their congregating around *Ciudad Abierta* or Open City. Every Wednesday morning, the entire school travels to Open City, a sprawling, seaside dunescape. The students play a variety of sports (their participation in which is graded), while the teaching and research staff have a meeting and lunch. Two staff members are responsible for cooking and cleaning up each week, a responsibility that rotates through all staff members, no matter their position. Each week, over this lunch, the staff discuss key issues facing the school, use it as a space to welcome guests, organize events, and resolve any differences in opinion. When very big decisions must be made, the school gathers in a purpose-built agora, a large, grassed landform on a hill, designed for exchange. All decisions at the school must be made unanimously by the forty-odd faculty, and sometimes they will spend months discussing an issue before finalizing a decision. These ritual practices extend beyond the faculty and into the student body by way of "poetic acts." For example, at the start of each year, first-year students are welcomed to the school by the entire student and staff body in a ritual in the sand dunes. To pull off a successful ritual or poetic act, organizational practices can become playful, profound, and beautiful.[12]

Curricula and the University

Organizing curriculum requires understanding the history and influence of university dependencies that impact curricular elements. As discussed in LARGE and EXTRA LARGE, it remains important to consider how power relations, as imposed from above, shape a curriculum's ideology. Understanding how a school is funded, and in turn, how the school distributes its funding; a university's funding sources; and being savvy about its governance and board of directors—these all directly affect what is taught in a school of architecture and hence, where organizing for change can and should be directed.

Gathering this information requires rigorous, collective academic study. Key areas of focus could include administrative roles and hierarchies within the university, university resources, the use of the endowment and flows of capital, systems of measuring academic performance, decision-making processes, support structures, progression and remuneration systems, and admission policies regarding race, class, and economic background. For this, Power Mapping and Empathy Mapping are essential tools.[13] The results of this research are best made visual: the hierarchies, relationships, flows of money and resources, performance regulations, etc., could be rendered through a series of maps and diagrams to be shared among the academic collective. Empathy Mapping can start conversations between faculty and students and between faculty and administration about the perceived and actual challenges of a person's role within the academic system. Once this information has been gathered and processed, opportunities for leveraging more autonomy, better working conditions, and more systemic influence can be identified and actioned.

Curricula and Accreditation

Accreditation systems should be examined intentionally, critically, and transparently. It is essential that every architecture student is provided with an in-depth understanding of the different accreditation programs, their requirements, their jurisdictional structures, and their institutional histories. Teaching organizing empowers students to engage in molding these frameworks, adapting them to serve the greater good. An organized faculty could advocate for a new structure of accreditation—one that is responsive, dialogical, discursive, and attentive to emerging needs, technological shifts, and regional differences. What would it mean to advance a responsive accreditation process that protects students from exploitation and whimsy, and allows for unique reflections of place and understanding?

The accreditation process across Australia and Aotearoa New Zealand managed by the Architects Accreditation Council of Australia (AACA) is an important step forward. Revised and released in 2021 and now being implemented in architecture schools to include a much greater emphasis on Indigenous knowledge and sustainable environmental systems. The changes seek "more meaningful engagement with First Nations peoples and caring for Country" and "reform in sustainability and the role of the built environment in mitigating and adapting to the impacts of climate change."[14] But while this is an advance from the past, more local adaptability and responsiveness in the system is needed for a deeper responsiveness and resilience in the architecture profession. There is also much to learn from schools of architecture such as Cranbrook which have opted not to be accredited in order to ensure that each student identifies their own critical practice. In an ideal world, accreditation might be bypassed or reimagined completely to better support operating effectively in the world as an architect-citizen.

Teaching Organizing

While should be modeled by the faculty, include students and taught through learned experience across the curriculum, there also has to be a dedicated class where these practices are theorized, contextualized and studied. The classroom, as a space of virtual reality where the "real" world is imagined and practiced, can provide a lower stakes companion space for practicing organizing skill sets alongside sited and real-world projects. These classes could invite and include paying local community organizer groups to share their knowledge and processes with students, working through the organizing approaches that students are taking in their other classes—focusing specifically on their process rather than the intended outcome, and providing space to reflect on the challenges and successes of previous and ongoing projects.

Organizing case studies could be introduced and taught alongside their tools and processes including: ways to identify a problem or frustration; tactics for engaging with people, whether they be fellow organizers, community stakeholders, or those in positions of power; non-hierarchical conversation strategies; forming a shared collective strategy and vision; power and empathy mapping; identifying the root causes and structural underpinnings behind an issue; various tactics for building power; how to identify targets, supporters, and resources; how to formulate tactics and make demands; and how to craft a message and tell a story that catalyzes people around a vision.

Time and Sequencing

On one hand, what would happen to a curriculum if the time it unfolds is not celebrated int terms of semesters and years, but hundreds of years into the future? The projects, relationships and research students and faculty forge could take this long-term view. At Huri te Ao Hoahoanga,[15] students are encouraged to consider their design approaches over time—factoring in the time needed for meaningful community engagement processes, availability of resources, and how these might be cultivated through the project and the realization of the project far into the future. These projects are regularly connected to research projects with local iwi (Māori nations with in Aotearoa New Zealand), local councils, developers, and or community organizations. An example of a project outcome of this kind is the thesis project of Matangireia Yates-Francis who proposed a vertical papakāinga (Māori communal living) project be built over a number of decades, starting with the reforestation of the site with flaxes and timbers that would eventually be used to retrofit a skeleton structure built in the fifteenth year of the project, and assessed through a five-yearly hui (meeting), culminating at the hundredth year where it is proposed that the viability of the project into the future would be discussed.[16]

On the other, what if semester were done away with completely? The academic term is often too short for building lasting connections with missing others outside of the normal academic context. An architecture curriculum could be organized around long-term projects or research, led by faculty, and integrated across subject areas through which students learn how to practice, and how to apply their knowledge and skills to real challenges. Likewise shorter-term courses, and the content of those courses—probes—could be requested by students—giving them autonomy in their learning, and increasing their investment in a topic for which there is an immediate application. The creation of course sequences relative to project need allows for larger knowledge arcs, pairing studios with specific skill-building topics.

An architecture curriculum could incorporate co-teaching models for interdisciplinary, multi-disciplinary, and cross-disciplinary curricular interventions. It could offer classes in which students flow between instruction modules over the course of a semester, and faculty share syllabi and develop complementary approaches to the curricular thread. This method could extend to training new teachers, leveraging curricular structures. The curriculum could create opportunities to exhibit and test pedagogical techniques, and provide more equitable sharing of administrative tasks. If the curriculum is a practice, all teachers, regardless of level, are practitioners in that practice.

Curricula Content

The existing five categories of the architecture curriculum could be infiltrated by non-conventional material that broadens the notion of design. Representation should include not just images of objects but power maps representing the forces producing those objects; digital technologies must be theorized and historized; history/theory could include the history of construction and the field of architecture's deflection of environmental concerns; construction could include not just information on construction practices—including the role of unions in construction labor—but construction workers themselves; professional practice could be interrogated in all of these ways and more, exploring how practices have evolved and might change. It is critical that the architecture curriculum presents knowledge areas as interdependent and incorporate new theories and modes of thought in an integrated and transdisciplinary way. At the same time, the curriculum could recognize that many students may not use their architectural skills in traditional private practice and should accommodate their interests and goals beyond the delivery of built forms, thereby creating the foundation for a more diverse and dynamic profession. Consideration for jobs in the public sector, in advisory, consultancy, research, policy or administrative roles, etc. could also provide direction for the content and structure of the curriculum.

These changes expand the purpose and scope of architecture education to embrace a broader range of career paths beyond a traditional practice, and hence reduces job precarity for students. Likewise, the curriculum could better recognize existing concentrations in the practice of architecture, from office roles (management, marketing, technology, etc.) to project types (envelopes, systems, interiors, etc.), positioning students to understand how any one concentration contributes to the whole. An architecture curriculum should teach an organizing skill set that could be practiced across a range of disciplines and challenges. Students should be empowered with language to defend this skill set and its value in the workforce, across a multitude of disciplines.

Preparation of a thesis is the one location in the conventional curriculum where a student is explicitly required to interrogate their knowledge holistically and explore how they want to deploy that knowledge going forward. This makes the thesis a critical site of opportunity for expanding organizing practices around individual or shared projects. Its singularity also points to the need to better integrate holistic and systemic thinking throughout architecture education; students should be learning how to theorize their practice at every level of an architecture program, thus providing them with the skills necessary to produce rigorous work at the thesis level. An organizing framework incorporated across a curriculum and applied with greatest autonomy at thesis level would open the possibility of thesis to be more collective, multidisciplinary, and impactful. Thesis could be integrated into collective long-term community research projects, encouraging students to research an area of interest through an application of organizing principles; it could be sited within their community, and collectively enacted and authored. The value of thesis and its form should be assessed relative to the changing practice of the curriculum and the changing practice of architecture.

Teaching the underlying structures that produce software systems, a tool through which most architecture in the West is made today, is crucial to producing architects that are empowered with regards to their own means of production. Likewise, architecture school presents an opportunity to learn the "how" of software development—providing capacity for those students who are interested in moving beyond being the recipient of software into being an active party in its development. And most importantly technology should be harnessed for collective action, sharing information across the curriculum. Technology provides opportunities to build coalitions outside of architecture. For example, Building Information Modeling (BIM) software produced mostly by Autodesk and Graphisoft is often taught as a production tool only, when it is also a tool for collaboration between architects, engineers, builders, and other consultants. Communication tools like Discord, WhatsApp and Slack can be incredibly powerful for supporting student and faculty organizing. Digital social technologies with which students are familiar also can be embraced when utilized through a critical lens—TikTok, YouTube, and Instagram offer accessible visual mediums through which to synthesize and share ideas with a broader audience.[17] Technological shifts and emergent technology should not be ignored or avoided but examined and deployed critically in the architecture curriculum. Take, for example, Dark Matter University (DMU) (see CASE STUDY), a network of dispersed architecture educators that first came together by combining two WhatsApp groups organizing around racial justice in architecture to "work inside and outside of existing systems to challenge, inform, and reshape our present world."[18] Contributors used this platform to express shared experiences and frustrations, provide support, and promote ideas. These conversations were the catalyst to formalize collective tactics for deploying an "anti-racist model of design education and practice achieved by creating new forms of knowledge, community, institutions, practice, and design itself."[19]

As Artificial Intelligence (AI) is coming into prominence, questions around technology are particularly pressing. AI provides opportunities to develop new tools that can automate tedious and repetitive tasks: algorithms can analyze large data sets to gain insights into complex problems, make better decisions within predetermined criteria, and optimize design. AI could offer tools to democratize the design process, giving everyone the opportunity to visualize their ideas regarding shared environments. At the same time, teaching AI, as with teaching any digital tool, should be foregrounded by critical insights into its real biases, and into the legal frameworks, or lack thereof, that regulate its development and implementation. This requires careful consideration of the ethical and societal implications of AI, and the biases that might reside in its information. It calls for pluri-disciplinary coordination since every other curriculum within the university grapples with this same condition.

Curricula Spaces

The school of architecture's curriculum could experiment with the site of education. On the one hand, this means physically outside the university campus. Reaching outside academia is a practice that should be integrated across the curriculum, not just confined to studio. Community engagement is not organizing, however, organizing principles are critical to effective and meaningful community engagement. An architecture curriculum should incorporate opportunity to connect with local people and local challenges, work in concert with the ecologies of the immediate environment, learn from regional building practices, and build long-term relationships in which projects and research have a meaningful effect. The design studios organized by Chitra Wishwanath in Bengaluru, India provide a compelling example of this, where students are tasked to explore, observe, analyze, and propose opportunities for architectural and ecological intervention in the immediate neighborhood around where they live (see CASE STUDY). These goals extend beyond conventional curricular sequencing, and therefore are less about a particular set of students in a particular semester, and more about the community. How can the school be of service, and work with the community through collective action and a changing model of architecture practice over time?

For curricula to better reflect the local community and its people, feedback loops should be established that align with community needs. One way to achieve this is by integrating civic service directly into university programs. Students can gain practical knowledge about the community they serve while also providing valuable assistance. Community-based engagements require continuous evaluation and adjustments to ensure that the needs of all involved are being met. This could include regular surveys or focus groups with community members to gather feedback on what is working and what needs improvement. Ultimately, by prioritizing community engagement and institutional collaboration, curricula can be created that better reflect the needs of the people they serve. Professional practice could be better engaged by setting up architecture education with a residency model, where students are placed or apply for paid jobs in design offices as part of their learning, removing the professional burden from architecture education and freeing it up not only to evolve itself but to push the profession. The University of Waterloo's co-op education in architecture offers insight into the benefits of this practice. Starting in second year, students alternate between four months of work for architects and designers, and four-month school terms. The program allows students to "personally experience the nature and variety of the work the profession offers" and "acquire a wide array of specific skills, discipline, and experience which complements the more exploratory and speculative work in the Design Studio."[20]

On the other hand, education should embrace all that virtual, online education can offer. Education programs like the Architecture Lobby's ABC School, and PhD programs that rely on experts who cannot travel on a regular basis, are primarily—if not totally—virtual. A program that delivers a virtual education needs its own protocols, many of which have been worked out and experimented with during the pandemic.[21] These online spaces can create radical global connections and novel opportunities for knowledge exchange due to their enhanced accessibility and immediacy. These schools offer models for connectivity between curricula spaces globally, expanding the site of architectural knowledge beyond the local. Indeed media is a critical site of architecture, not just as where students look for design examples, but for how a school, its curriculum, and the discipline of architecture is conceptually constructed, branded, and disseminated. A school must therefore take this space—media—seriously, and recognize that not just the school, but architecture and its future is being created and promoted. A school and its curriculum, behaving as a practice, should theorize and publish the work of that practice, generating media that constructs the conceptual space of the discipline. This goes beyond publishing student work on a website into a critical examination of representation itself.

The organizing framework for the medium scale addresses the internal and external forces that impact curricular design, development, and delivery. By acknowledging organizing and its potential to shift curricular paradigms, practices, sequences, and spaces, as well as the bodies that regulate these paths, it is possible to create a more cohesive and united curricular community that can work toward a shared vision and mission. The framework can be applied to various aspects of the curriculum, from course design to capstone demonstrations (thesis), and can help to address underlying issues hindering collective identity, systematically improving architecture education. While the implementation of this framework may be challenging, and requires changes to overarching university structures, it offers a more holistic approach to architecture education that considers the needs of people, places, systems, and ecologies. That being said, in order to improve the effectiveness of organizing within the curriculum, it is necessary to address the larger structures and power relations within the university. These are discussed in the next chapter.

Notes

1 For us coauthors, our experiences as architecture students and educators have placed us in the presence of National Architectural Accrediting Board (NAAB) visits in the United States, and National Standard of Competency for Architects (NSCA) reviews in Australia and Aotearoa New Zealand. Other accrediting, certifying, and prescribing boards include the Architects Registration Board: Prescription of Schools in the UK, the Sistema de Acreditación Regional de Carreras Universitarias ARCU-SUR system in the Mercosur region (Uruguay, Argentina, Bolivia, Chile, and Venezuela), and the Canadian Architectural Certification Board (CACB).
2 NAAB, "History."
3 Cranbrook Academy of Art is such an example: Cranbrook's architecture program "supports individually directed studio-based research in architecture, urbanism, and related forms of spatial practice." Their model is designed to "support expansive approaches to the field of architecture within the interdisciplinary context of a graduate art academy." Cranbrook Academy of Art, 'Architecture'.
4 National Council of Architectural Registration Boards, "Licensing Requirements Tool."

5 Neuckermans, "European Architectural Education in Motion."
6 For example, see Ministry of Education and New Zealand Qualifications Authority, "New Zealand and the Bologna Process."
7 Coined by Phillip Jackson in Life in Classrooms. Jackson, *Life in Classrooms.*
8 Stevens, "Struggle in the Studio: A Bourdivin Look at Architectural Pedagogy," 105.
9 Stevens, "Struggle in the Studio: A Bourdivin Look at Architectural Pedagogy."
10 Stead, Gusheh, and Rodwell, "Well-Being in Architectural Education."
11 Henrich, *The Secret of Our Success: How Culture Is Driving Human Evolution, Domesticating Our Species, and Making Us Smarter.*
12 For more information on Ciudad Abierta see their archive here: Amereida contributors, "Open City." For more on ritual, see Henrich, *The Secret of Our Success: How Culture Is Driving Human Evolution, Domesticating Our Species, and Making Us Smarter.*
13 See HOW-TO.
14 "Architects Registration Changes 2024."
15 See CASE STUDY.
16 Yates-Francis, "TŪHONONGA: Architecture Co-Occupying with Earth and Sky."
17 The Instagram platform run by a group of anonymous admins named dank.lloyd.wright provides sardonic, critical, and political discourse on architecture practice and theory. They now have over 100,000 followers Brillon, 'Instagram Account Dank.Lloyd.Wright Aims to "Amplify Narratives That Are Excluded from Architecture's Official Consensus"'.
18 Hickman, "Dark Matter University Brings a New Model of Architectural Education to Light."
19 Hickman.
20 Waterloo School of Architecture, "Architecture: Co-Op."
21 See HOW-TO.

LARGE: THE UNIVERSITY

In SMALL and MEDIUM, organizing targets the who, what, and why of traditional architecture courses and curricula. LARGE expands the scope of organizing to the universities in which architecture education resides. At this scale, organizing builds upon the daily encounters of studio and curricular practices to position architecture among colleges, schools, departments, programs, and other aligned academic units.

Because universities evolve with cultural, political, economic, and social shifts over time, providing a singular definition of the university is challenging. For the purposes of this book, the university is defined as an institution that offers undergraduate, graduate, and doctoral studies across multiple disciplines to hundreds of students through multiple forms of delivery and funding. Universities can be public, private, polytechnical, religious, land grant, and more, and, unlike colleges and technical schools, provide advanced degrees and access to research resources that drive knowledge production.

The history of the university is vast—and cannot be comprehensively addressed in this volume—however it is critical to acknowledge that, the neoliberal ideologies that support reduced state intervention and the deregulation of labor, goods, capitalist systems, and corporate structures, permeate most universities at every level. Although the neoliberal university is global in its reach, this chapter leans into examples from the United States, due to the significant financial debt students must carry to earn an advanced degree. The neoliberal model exerts pressure on students through increased financial demands, exploits labor categories by enforcing acceptance of substandard wages, and disproportionately compensates

DOI: 10.4324/9781003411284-8

top-tier administrative personnel with exorbitant salaries. Such practices starkly deviate from the foundational mission of the university to cultivate a community of learners and scholars—diluting the essence of academic education and its societal contributions.

The hierarchical structure of university administration, particularly in neoliberal institutions, often disconnects the decision-making process from the everyday activities of students, faculty, and staff, creating challenges in achieving collective goals. However, these challenges are not insurmountable. The neoliberal university's administrative apparatus is primarily motivated by self-preservation through assessment metrics. It prescribes a system of course distribution and delivery, prioritizing efficient teaching formats and specialized knowledge production antithetical to teaching and learning practices and to the pluri-disciplinarity required by architecture education. It rarely engages with the complex realities of its immediate communities, both the one in which it resides and the population of teachers, students, and staff that comprise it.

At the same time, the university is uniquely positioned to offer significant collective resources in the form of funding, space, and access to multiple disciplines. Widening gaps in the existing neoliberal university framework opens the potential for a conceptual and functional restructuring of the university by building upon its offerings, while simultaneously integrating alternative co-learning and co-produced knowledge strategies. Although this chapter does not explicitly unfold theories of epistemology and knowledge, it does question the synonymity of knowledge production with research and the categorical separation of research, teaching, and service in the neoliberal university. Organizing in LARGE addresses these boundaries, their impact on architecture education in the university, and reimagines university connections. Specific strategies and tactics for implementing co-learning models; redistributing teaching, research, and service; collectivizing and unionizing; restructuring teaching and learning toward equitable metrics; and co-producing knowledge with students, other disciplines in the university, and the local population through shared resources, situate the sites of possibility for organizing at the university scale.

The ABC School and Allies

Organizing within and against the forces that have created the contemporary university and toward an extra- and inter-institutional alternative led to the launch of The Architecture Lobby's Architecture Beyond Capitalism (ABC) School.[1] The growing discontent among the Lobby's academic members with contemporary architecture education practices—inequity and lack of accessibility engaging with architecture education; student debt; precarious labor for students, faculty, and staff; emphasis on predominantly capital-ist modes of practice—informed the first version of the school in 2021.[2] Subsequent versions of the school focused on the studio as a key site for co-learning (2022),[3] and on building connections to make positive change in architecture practice and education (2023).[4] Organizers of the ABC School, including the seven co-authors of this book, imagined a fee-free school of architecture devoid of top-down hierarchy to facilitate learning from and with one another, and to transcend national boundaries through a global body of students, educators, and practitioners gathered in a virtual set-ting. By collectively addressing issues of precarious labor, insecure shelter, colonization, and climate precarity, the school attempted to confront the dominance of capitalism's influence over architectural pedagogy.

Like the ABC School, other extra- and inter-institutional models for fill-ing perceived gaps in university-based education exist and are detailed as case studies after Part 2. This chapter includes strategies and tactics from specific case studies, in addition to examples that inform organizing at the university scale but fall outside of architecture education. Peer 2 Peer University (P2PU) is one example. It is a non-profit, extra-institutional model offering free facilitated learning circles for educators and learners through global peer learning communities in online or in-person public spaces.[5] Although P2PU's teaching and learning strategies indirectly ad-dress architecture education, their tactics serve as a model for partnering with institutions to curate and moderate dedicated learning materials that are free, open source, and made public through facilitation. Facilitators and co-facilitators are not experts and they do not teach, but rather sup-port co-learning through the introduction of learning materials and the pacing of each meeting.

Similar to P2PU, the Free School of Architecture (FSA)[6] transformed the traditional dynamics between teacher and student. It established a tuition-free and grade-free environment for studying architecture, promot-ing experimental practices within the broader scope of the field. Specific to architecture education, the FSA also offered tactics for collectivizing when strategies are unmet. Initially started in 2016 as an independent, extra-institutional organization in Los Angeles by designer and educator Peter Zellner, the school was overturned when participants noticed the hierarchy of the teacher–student relationship remained intact. "Students" collectivized, took control of the remaining agenda, offered co-produced alternatives, and organized the final event, as well as completely reimag-ined the 2018 version of the school, independent from the founder, and lead by four women across three continents.[7]

As a final example, Dark Matter University (DMU)[8] offers an alter-native model of architecture education that operates across multiple institutions. This model is also examined as a CASE STUDY for further insight. DMU is a volunteer-operated and BIPOC-led network of members who seek to create co-produced forms of knowledge outside the university through design. Organizing tactics include coordinating studios and seminars remotely across two or more schools of architecture, partnering with communities in research/education/organizing efforts outside traditional university structures and making available in-house or co-produced installations. The common strategy among all these free educational models is to break the teacher–student dichotomy through co-learning and to transcend the university's research boundary by connecting teaching and learning to methods of co-produced knowledge. Introducing these strategies and tactics into the university setting is an organizing goal for LARGE.

While extra- and inter-institutional models demonstrate alternative modes of architecture education, they have less direct bearing on the daily lives of university workers. They also do not offer credentialed or accredited degrees. LARGE emphasizes the importance of focusing on universities as the central hub for organizing efforts because: (1) despite the availability of architectural education outside the university system, the majority of students still seek advanced, accredited, professional studies within universities; and (2) universities, which usually set the framework for architectural programs, also present opportunities to work alongside other academic departments or disciplines that have aligned interests or the desire to engage in extensive collaborative projects.

The Neoliberal University

The neoliberal university, characterized by the intersection of education with market forces, has dominated tertiary education for the last fifty years. In capitalism's current era, the concept of intellectual "excellence" is parceled and monetized within a "knowledge economy." The knowledge economy refers to an economic system in which knowledge, information, and intellectual capabilities are central drivers of economic growth and prosperity. Within this context, universities have become increasingly influenced by neoliberal economic policies and principles, enacting market-oriented reforms that commodify education and knowledge; prioritize profit generation as the primary goal of the university; emphasize competition, efficient delivery of the product of an education, and entrepreneurship and innovation; and introduce metrics and accountability procedures that attempt to assess efficiency and outcomes to produce quantifiable results. The pursuit of "excellence" in this context does not consider the substance of the education and research that the university produces beyond its capital benefit. As historian Bill Readings argues in his book, *The University in Ruins*, "excellence" is like the cash-nexus in that it has no *content*. It is hence neither true nor false, neither ignorant nor self-conscious. It may be unjust, but we cannot seek its injustice in terms of a regime of truth or of self-knowledge."[9] Despite monetary transactions, the exchange of truth, knowledge, and excellence is immaterial.

It is difficult to pinpoint the inception of the neoliberal university in the global North and West. As early as 1900, the American economist and sociologist Torstein Veblen observed that universities operated according to and in support of business principles dictated by their governing boards. Veblen noted how the university's dependence upon wealthy businessmen's support ensured the continued dominance of the ruling leisure class, rather than promoting democratic social transformation as the university administration and its donors claimed.[10] "The underlying business-like perception," Veblen wrote, "appears to be that learning is a merchant table, commodity, to be produced on a piece of freight plan, rated, bought and sold in standard units, measured, counted, and reduced to stable equivalence by impersonal mechanical tests."[11] Veblen argued that the prevalent value in American society—success by monetary terms—was reflected in the university's own metrics of success according to standards of profit and loss. Today, this modus operandi is even more explicit as neoliberal universities parcel education into units for quantifiable assessment. This assessment includes annual performance reviews, tenure and promotion processes, grades, and the distribution of scholarships and grants. Education in the neoliberal university is much less about the pursuit of knowledge, and much more about being primed for the "intellectual" professional workforce, much of which now demands a tertiary degree, either through regulated licensure, or through degree inflation. The university is in the market of training workers for the capitalist economy. Higher education scholars Sheila Slaughter and Gary Rhoades emphasize this stance by stating:

> Public colleges and universities…support corporate competitiveness through their major role in the global, knowledge-based economy. They stress their role in training advanced students for professional positions close to the technoscience core of knowledge economies, in fostering research that creates high-tech products and processes for corporations, and in preparing undergraduate and community college students to be malleable workers who will fit into (and be retrained for) new information-based jobs and workplaces.[12]

According to Slaughter and Rhoades, the assumed social role of the university to advance students' capability and worth, has "been displaced by the economic role of serving corporations' global competitiveness."[13] The neoliberal university supports competitiveness by rewarding innovation derived from specialized knowledge fields and funded research. This is further ensured through the education of future workers and controlled management of the university.

Readings further argues that "the university is becoming a transnational bureaucratic corporation, either tied to transnational instances of government such as the European Union or functioning independently, by analogy with a transnational corporation."[14] The neoliberal university not only supports and serves corporations, but also operates as one through its governance and fiscal policies. In all cases, the opaque nature of this top-down governance, and the distance between managerial roles and students, separates those at the top from the daily work concerning student education.

University operations currently reflect a corporate hierarchy, with the Board at the top. The private university's Board of Trustees, the public university's Board of Regents in the United States, and Governing Councils or Board of Directors in the United Kingdom and antipodean universities, hold authority over university interests and direction. The board maintains internal continuity and preservation of the corporation. As in all corporate operations, each management position or unit is tasked to ensure problems do not rise to the level of the board. Answering to the board, the corporation's Chief Executive Officer (CEO) and the university's President serve as visible leaders of the institution. Beyond these positions, titles change, but the roles and responsibilities are similar—Provosts, Vice Presidents, Chancellors, Vice Chancellors, Deputy and Pro Vice-Chancellors and Executive Officers answer to the President. Below them are the leaders of academic units including Deans, Associate Deans, Assistant Deans, Department Chairs, Department Heads, and Program Coordinators. Finally, the Staff, otherwise called "Faculty" in the United States, are at the bottom. This top-down list does not include academic boards, support services and staff, student unions, and external government bodies that aid the administration, nor does it include the hierarchy of staff and faculty positions such as adjunct, tenured, and part-time positions.

Because of this distancing, the excessively high pay of university administrators, much like the salaries of CEOs, runs rampant. According to the *Chronicle of Higher Education* in 2023, presidents of private universities and colleges in the United States received a median annual salary of $880,000, but as high as $8,435,657 in the case of the 2020 earnings of the President of Thomas Jefferson University in Philadelphia, Pennsylvania.[15] In the UK, University College London (UCL) pays its Vice Chancellor £589,000 (US$736,011);[16] in Australia, the University of Melbourne (a public university) pays its Vice Chancellor AU$1.5 million

(US$1.05 million).[17] To support these high salaries, university spending borrows corporate fiscal policies by decreasing labor costs at the bottom, increasing funding and profits through endowments, grants, sponsorships, and higher student enrollment, and consolidating academic units.

Non-tuition sources of funding in the form of government and private sector grants are central to profit-making, and necessitate support for programs, departments, and schools that garner the most and the largest grants. Like corporations, each university competes with others in the knowledge industry for consumers (i.e., students) by promoting the same branded come-ons—innovation, top facilities, top research—and loath operating outside the established branding. Higher-paid faculty must focus on grant-competitive research while lower-wage workers such as adjuncts and graduate teaching assistants often make up for the teaching and learning necessary to support student education. At the same time, the disciplinary units that garner large grants such as those in Science, Technology, Engineering, and Mathematics (STEM) are rewarded with expanded support through new and specialized units, labs, and services that branch from larger disciplinary units. Grant mechanisms are further fueled by global university ranking systems; the latter incentivize a hyper-competitive, metric-fixated, revenue-driven corporate model that undermines the core educational missions of universities in the quest for higher status. Ranking systems privilege university performance metrics like research output, citations, publications in elite journals, and so on. This commodifies knowledge and encourages viewing academic work mainly through a competitive, quantitative productivity lens. Rankings incentivize higher education systems to prioritize disciplines that produce profitable inventions, skilled employees for industries, and opportunities for monetizable spin-off companies.

Equating research outputs with profitable, productivity metrics evolved from early measures for societal progress in the university. An egregious example of this underlies the Land Grant university system established in the United States after the signing of the Morrill Act in 1862. In *A Third University is Possible*, la paperson (aka Wayne Yang) identifies the connection between research output, progress, and profit as a justification for stealing land:

> Morrill Act universities are also charged with the research and development of land, particularly for agribusiness. Thus the university system, especially in the westward-expanding empire of the United States, is intimately underwritten as a project of settler colonialism—the seizing of Native land, the conversion of land into capital, the further domestication of "wilderness" into productive agricultural estates, and the research mandate to procure profitable plants from around the world to colonize North American soil.[18]

Agricultural Research Stations, originally established as research facilities for the university, advocated for turning land into a form of capital, often under the pretext of serving the public interest. However, in the United States, the individuals from whom the land was taken seldom had the opportunity to attend the university. Similarly, in other countries with a history of colonization, like Australia, indigenous populations such as Aboriginal and Torres Strait Islander peoples were systematically excluded from the university system.

Likewise, contemporary universities remain physically isolated through land and property ownership from the people who reside in their urban or regional surroundings. They are financially isolated from prospective students through their prohibitive tuition costs, and from local governments by virtue of their non-profit status. Universities claim that being non-profit institutions allow them to focus on providing a high-quality education instead of worrying about making money. This obscures the fact that non-profits are exempt from paying local, regional, and federal or national taxes, meaning universities do not contribute to the public services from which they benefit. Relations with the surrounding neighborhood, town, or city in which the university resides, also referred to as "Town and Gown" relationships, are inherently fraught. In disadvantaged towns and cities facing budget constraints, residents argue that universities and colleges should contribute financially to public infrastructure such as primary schools, roads, and clean water systems. Even in wealthy communities, contestations persist. In the past few years, the city of Pittsburgh and the University of Pittsburgh Medical Center sued each other over the Center's tax-exempt status, and the city of Princeton has pressured Princeton University—which was building a $300 million arts center at the time—to put a proportional amount of money in the city's local coffers through donations.[19] When university outreach does occur, it is seen as a philanthropic gift to the public, underscoring the privileged status of the giver and the "at will" nature of the transaction. When universities engage in community outreach, for example, it positions the university as a privileged, generous benefactor rather than a party in an equitable partnership. By characterizing community outreach as discretionary charity, existing institutional privilege and power dynamics remain firmly in place, obviating the opportunity to form a collaborative partnership between equals.

Architecture in the Neoliberal University

The unique, intensive pedagogies and curricula put forth by architecture education challenge the efficiencies set by the neoliberal university. Architecture studios require low teacher to student ratios, which allow instructors to interact with each student's project and offer insights for advancing work.

The hours necessary for iterative exploration, production, and reflection by teachers and students often exceed the prescribed units of a credit hour, semester, and academic year. The physical space needed for the cold-desk model of architecture education, in which students are provided a permanent desk in the studio, allows students to keep their work and belongings at a desk and facilitates peer-to-peer reviews. The hot-desk model, in which students take their belongings at the end of each class, still requires a large amount of desk space for architectural production. Additional space and funds support the construction workshops, fabrication labs, print bureaus, and pin-up space that allow projects to materialize through collective dialogue about work. These temporal and spatial features that are so necessary for architecture's rhizomatic thinking,[20] production, and culture are viewed as expensive inefficiencies in the neoliberal university.

The conditions described above reveal architecture education's humanities-focused, Beaux Arts origins, described extensively in SMALL, with the technical structures and systems that exemplify a polytechnic education. This alliance makes architecture difficult to place within the university bureaucratically. When considering architectural pedagogy, curricula, and knowledge production, the conceptual, technical, social, historical, theoretical, and ethical negotiations of architecture necessitate inter-departmental, networked connections. Informal connections with other disciplines in the university—engineering, construction, art, humanities, landscape architecture, interior design, graphic arts, and other design disciplines—will sometimes solidify into departments, schools, and colleges that facilitate collaboration within their own boundaries, but make outside collaborations more arduous. At the same time, to deliver a professional education in which students become future licensed architects necessitates both discipline and professional independence. Discrepancies in architecture's placement within universities is an indication of the struggle to find an arena in which architecture's pedagogical, cultural, and financial value is most efficiently administered.

Tenured and tenure-track faculty are often encouraged to focus on research over teaching due to the emphasis on quantifiable grant funding. Consequently, in many universities, teaching is less valued and may not contribute as significantly to salary, promotion, or tenure decisions. This prioritization fosters an unstable power dynamic where faculty members are pitted against each other, competing for specialized seminars and non-core studios that allow them to incorporate their research into tangible, résumé-enhancing outcomes. This system effectively puts the necessary work of teaching the core of the curriculum in the hands of faculty with precarious labor contracts who are marginalized from curricular conversations. For a discipline that thrives on collective, peer-to-peer teaching and learning practices, the categorical separation between teaching and research into funded and indebted parts is antithetical to architecture education.

ORGANIZING—THE UNIVERSITY

Dismantling the neoliberal university is not the immediate goal of organizing in LARGE; exposing and blurring the boundaries in its hierarchical, top-down system to reconfigure what the university *does* offer, and how its significant resources can be redeployed for co-learning and co-knowledge production, is. Architecture's rhizomatic form of knowledge production makes it a prime model for rethinking the how, when, and where contemporary education and research through the university occurs, and what it could impact. An organized architecture faculty and curriculum demands collaboration, knowledge sharing across various disciplines, subjectivities, as well as recognition of the real-world embeddedness of the university in the daily lives of its workers and surrounding public. By necessity, it cannot remain siloed by the boundaries of studio or the curriculum. While the curriculum could become a laboratory for practice, as argued in MEDIUM, organizing at the university scale could see the university become a laboratory for project delivery: developing, and experimenting with the ways in which architects and others work and collaborate, and therefore positioning universities to design and then action how global crises are addressed.

Imagined in this way, the university would center all teaching, learning, and research around specific sited, conceptual, or speculative projects related to local, global and emergent challenges, and societal questions. Subject matter silos could be functionally dissolved (though could remain conceptually distinct), and academics could connect across disciplines and around research problems, with the goal of meaningful action—lobbying for policy change, sited community projects, material explorations etc. Student learning could be conducted on the same model, where all projects are undertaken across different disciplines around relevant local and global issues—some lower stakes and hypothetical, and some real and part of the university's research undertakings. This would be a way for architecture (and others) to reckon with their disciplinarity—what is the relevance of a skillset and knowledge in real, sited problem solving? Disciplinary relevance and what particular knowledges are important would then not be dictated by capital gains or losses, or by what the "market" demands, but by what is needed in order to solve problems and work together. This would likely forefront the importance of indigenous knowledge, social sciences, arts, psychology, humanities etc. more than the current system, as these plural knowledges feed into deeper understandings of complex issues.

An initial step for reimagining university structures is for faculty, staff, and students to analyze, interrogate, and make visible the underlying systems that impact the potential for co-learning and co-produced knowledge within their own universities. For those looking to instigate change within an architecture program, recognizing the effects of hierarchical and authoritative practices on the educational process is an essential start. Discussing these observations with potential allies and assembling across the university is a potential next step. This involves conversation strategies, such as those in the HOW-TO Section of this book, and community agreements that encourage equitable task distribution and a workflow for defining and implementing effective strategies. As described in MEDIUM, a significant necessity for organizing is understanding the power structures within which a collective operates. Power mapping, the visual organizing tool also outlined in the HOW-TO Section, helps to make visible the bureaucratic structures of a university that are top-heavy and often intentionally opaque and the administrative figure heads needed to make change.

Sites of Possibility

The university cannot exist without students, which underscore both its educational mission and its financial sustainability. In the past, most of the university funding came from the state or endowments.[21] Over the last two decades, state funding declines and growing tuition revenue have placed a heavy burden on individual students to fund public higher education, especially in the United States. Although this trend has recently started to shift back to higher state funding, students are still burdened with high tuition and fees.[22] At the same time, full-time faculty are valued for the funded grants and research they pull into the university. While research and scholarship are necessary for advancing education, a direct way to advocate for better student development in architecture education may be to center co-learning and co-produced knowledge models to better support students, faculty, and the public.

Co-Learning Models

While the university provides students with admission advisors, councilors, diversity officers, academic advisors, disability resource councilors, etc., to ease the stress of the university experience, these rarely address the structural power imbalance students encounter day-to-day with teachers. The learning strategies offered by the ABC School, Peer 2 Peer University, Free School of Architecture, and Dark Matter University—strategies in which the teacher/student binary breaks to offer a co-learning environment—serve as models. Rather than depositing knowledge and skills into students' minds, in these models, teachers become facilitators by guiding and pacing discussions throughout the course and across the curricula.

Within the architecture faculty, organizing toward co-learning models entails making visible and public all current teaching, research, and service workloads necessary to run the program for an academic year. This process should include all workers impacted by collective decisions, including adjunct faculty, staff, and graduate workers. These discussions should ask, what type of internal service, including intellectual, physical, and emotional labor, is needed to sustain the program, especially in current teaching environments? How does teaching impact research and knowledge production? How can all faculty be better supported by the university in service efforts? Although this type of reorganization and reprioritization has been argued for in ME-DIUM, in LARGE organizing must occur across disciplines and bureaucratic boundaries and consider the university's external procedures, such as tenure and promotion processes and annual reviews, to balance research, teaching, and service across the entire faculty, and among other disciplines.

While making workloads public may begin to eliminate individual deal making and unnecessary service, transparency is not a recourse for action when teaching, learning, and service become overloaded for certain ranks and positions. Unionizing across ranks through collective bargaining for all those teaching and potentially willing to co-learn is an actionable option. Although university unions do exist, they often segregate their members according to rank via a graduate student union, an adjunct faculty union, etc. Unionizing all workers who currently teach and provide service in the university, including full-time faculty, adjuncts, and graduate workers supports solidarity and collectivity between those who perform work the university cannot survive without teaching and learning. Of course, definitions of teaching may extend to work that supports co-learning, in which case, those who advise or provide counsel may also unionize together with teaching ranks. Because some faculty are deeply embedded in the status quo and may be reluctant to let go of status, organizing for co-learning models may need student-leadership along with faculty solidarity. Either way, collectivizing all who are interested in co-learning and collectivized education practices for students, faculty, and staff could advance bottom-up organizing within the university.

Equitable Metrics

Organizing equitable metrics for teaching and potential co-learning involves identifying how existing metrics are weighted in the university system, proposing alternative metrics, or eliminating them altogether. For students, the university provides frameworks for assessing student learning outcomes at the end of each course, weighing the grade according to credits, and projecting an overall grade point average. This number is carried with students from previous studies; it is a basis for admissions into graduate programs and serves as a universal and indelible mark for future job applications. For faculty, teaching metrics are weighted in the standard tenure and promotion document as well as in annual faculty reviews. In many universities, faculty teaching is assessed according to official university surveys students take at the end of each semester. These are primarily quantitative, and their timing occurs at the end of each course, while work is still being produced and students have no distance to reflect on the overall impact of the course. Completing surveys after the course means students who receive an excellent or poor assessment may be biased, leading to grade inflation and all its repercussions.

Practical metrics that assess teaching and co-learning measures begin with the elimination of quantitative methods that serve as a numerical crutch for comparing student or faculty work. Despite the differing resources to which each student or faculty member has access, they are comparatively analyzed according to a universal number or range. For students, implementing a pass/fail or a satisfactory/unsatisfactory completion system, or eliminating grades altogether, could divert focus away from the grade and toward learning practices, skills, and theories. For faculty, trading surveyed metrics from current students for integrated frameworks could enhance faculty evaluation across teaching, rather than in individual classes alone. While current letter writing practices already contribute to tenure and promotion, the process typically involves faculty from other institutions objectively evaluating the merit of the applicant's teaching, service, and research. Without assessing the resources available to the applicant, these letters are intended to assess whether the applicant could receive tenure elsewhere. Because of this, the letters typically favor research endeavors and dissemination practices common to the discipline. Integrating letters from current and former students, colleagues, and members of the public for annual reviews, tenure, and promotion is a pragmatic step. Including letters from other academic units within the internal university framework may better forefront how a faculty member balances resources and support. Framing these letters around the balance between academic freedom and academic responsibility, for example, which is the balance between the freedom to discuss relevant matters without institutional disciplinary action with the faithful performance of professional duties, begins to address effective co-learning strategies.

Concerning knowledge production, the gaps between teaching, research, and service in architecture education are narrow. The time instructors and students spend together in studio, workshops, and other areas of the curriculum; the time external reviewers donate to support discourse around student work; and the time instructors give to curating different sources, criteria, sites, and programs for each project put forth co-produced forms of knowledge, meaning knowledge cannot be claimed by an individual. Students produce multiple proposals within a given set of conditions, external reviewers position the work within the discipline and profession, and faculty can leverage this co-production by disseminating teaching methods and outcomes as pedagogical research in peer-reviewed settings, such as the Association of Collegiate Schools of Architecture (ACSA). Often, these conferences become showcases for faculty leading a given course rather than the students who produce the work or the reviewers who position it. These platforms for recognition, and the peer-review process in general, further value exceptionalism, incentivizing faculty to pursue unique and highly specialized briefs that reinforce their personal interests. There are far fewer outlets for presenting collective core-competency pedagogies—the National Conference for the Beginning Design Student (NCBDS) being an exception. (NCBDS is an institutionally unaffiliated, self-organized, peer-reviewed, interdisciplinary conference dedicated to introductory design teaching.) The student and external reviewer contributions that shape disseminated research, and how a faculty member learned from the student, should be a category for accepting proposals to conferences and as part of the tenure and promotion process. While these practical steps are necessary for the immediate present, collapsing the teaching, learning, and research categories to accommodate co-produced knowledge is desperately needed.

Financial Interventions

The prevailing fight in higher education is agitation against its prohibitive cost to students. Between 1980 and 2020 in the United States, for example, the price of attending a four-year college rose 180%,[23] growing at a rate almost eight times faster than average wages.[24] Studying architecture compounds this financial burden, with architecture graduates owing at least $10,000 more than their peers.[25] The low compensation for working in architecture, then, saddles architects with crippling debt.[26] Any real changes to this problem require organizing at the scale of the nation-state—advocating for student loan forgiveness and for reinstating and enhancing government higher education subsidies. Nonetheless, there are appeals to be made at the scale of the university.

University budgets allocate less and less funding to instruction. In the United States, that has meant a drop from 41% of the overall budget in 1980 to 29% in 2020.[27] The displaced funding is instead covering the expansion of the administration, and student and institutional support services.[28] These distributions are not inevitable. Indeed, there are growing movements to challenge the university's handling of its income. One of several institutions to experience recent strikes, graduate student workers and faculty at the University of Michigan Taubman School of Architecture organized successfully in March 2023 to demand a living wage, increased healthcare benefits, and more campus security.[29] This case, and a growing list of others, show that administrators, faculty, staff, and students have the potential to compel budgetary renegotiations—when they work collectively, across the university's borders and bounded roles.

An architecture program is a microcosm of the university. Even at this smaller scale, the distributions of its budgets are not inevitable. While arguing for improvements within an academic unit requires looking to the university as the source of a concern, there are some remediations for the costs of higher education that are feasible from within individual branches of the university. Administrators of architecture programs can push for the establishment of a budget line for basic supplies for architecture student design projects. Faculty can limit their assignments to deliverables that require limited resources, even assignments that rely exclusively on materials provided by the program. They can take a stand to, for example, campaign against no and low-pay (usually illegal) internships outside the university, or for transparency in scholarship protocol. And architecture programs, as a community, can work together in the structuring of mutual aid for general and specific purposes. The ACSA's 2023 "Convening to Advance Community College Transfer and Articulation in Architectural Education" is a positive direction for organizing across institutions. The vocational schools and trade schools that prepare students for a technical career in architecture by focusing on drafting, applied technical drawing, and modeling skills often cost less. Junior, tribal, community, and liberal arts colleges that offer coursework in architecture, often within an arts and humanities framework, typically allow students to remain close to home and their communities. Independent schools of architecture may even offer accredited degrees. Facilitating transfer credits from these institutions toward the advanced, accredited professional degrees that remain the purview of universities with widely recognized accreditation status is a necessary step toward easing debt.[30] Architecture administrators, faculty, staff, students, and graduates, similarly, are each other's best champions. The economics of architecture education are a collective project that will not be solved without everyone's active involvement.

Internal Partnerships

In the university, architecture can engage with other disciplines to create non-specialized, co-produced knowledge, and practices to address contemporary, urgent issues through integrated models of teaching, learning, service, and research. With different formats for course delivery, such as studios, workshops, lectures, and seminars, architecture education offers pedagogical and curricular models for visualizing and manifesting various forms of immaterial knowledge in the physical environment. Exchanging practices with and across departmental disciplines, creating avenues through which teaching, learning, and research are shared, can result in a holistic response to external cultural, political, economic, social, and environmental change.

Informally, these interdisciplinary exchanges may occur through shared lecture series, joint symposia, or informal pecha kuchas among faculty. More formally, interdisciplinary exchange may mean permeating separate units in order to restructure the university model. At the forefront of this strategy is a focus on budgets and budget structures. Co-teaching across disciplines, for example, is currently difficult due to departmental control over individual budget models and the loss of funding when fewer credit hours are offered, or when a faculty member teaches in another academic unit. Allocating a specific budget for inter-, trans-, and pluri-disciplinary laboratories, one that transcends grant applications to build on work that is already happening, is an approach to formalize and value specific interactions between disciplines. For architecture education, this could support architecture's project delivery methods and co-learning models, while simultaneously testing ways of collaborating to respond to real, sited challenges.

External Partnerships

Beyond the internal dynamics of the university and despite its funding models, private or public, one thing is certain: all universities reside within a physical and public infrastructure, be it a city, town, neighborhood, or an individual residence with a wi-fi connection. The separation between the physical and cultural space of the university and its immediate surroundings, otherwise known as "town and gown," alongside the lack of power that local authorities and communities have over the university's decision-making, can lead to an adversarial relationship between rooted communities and the transient population of students and faculty who populate the university. Universities are expected to be stewards of the territories they occupy. Many universities in the United States are gated, if not literally, then figuratively. The gated university presents not only a physical blockade to the resources within, but also a symbolic affront to the notion of universities as entities working for the common good. Whether a university is gated or not, they hold vast amounts of tax-exempt real estate and land. Universities, as centers of property ownership, play a significant role in establishing and maintaining the value of regional land, which in turn shapes local development and living patterns. Their influence can lead to displacement, gentrification, and, as mentioned in the context of Land Grant universities in the United States, colonization. It's imperative for universities to open up to the communities they're part of, sharing land and resources, and striving for collaboration that benefits all parties involved. There are already existing instances where such cooperative engagement is practiced. Outer Coast, a post-secondary institute located in Alaska, has shifted the three pillars of academia from teaching, research, and service, to service, labor, and self-governance. The institute restructures relationships with the community by reviving local languages and customs, and projects are driven by community needs with tangible outcomes. Locals collaborating with the institute are paid for their time and expertise. Ultimately, Outer Coast provides a model for how the university may restructure to divert more resources to the community and serve as a class mobilizer.[31]

University administration and disciplinary units must also acknowledge their own limits, mainly their isolation from daily community practices, and their potential to cause harm, especially when linking to the communities in which they reside. Partnering with institutions outside the university to break down silos and make academic work accountable to the public can support a shift toward co-produced knowledge. Universities can do this by allowing access to campus facilities and technology, sharing land, allocating resources to local issues, or joining forces with community members to advocate for legislative change around shared goals. Regardless, metrics that measure the university's relevance within the community can help institutions ameliorate their relationship with the place in which they are located.

Coordinating local knowledge exchanges, for example, in which there is genuine discourse and actionable solidarity forged among instructors, researchers, students, and community members, could remove the isolated decision-making between specialized disciplines, university administration, and the communities they occupy. Additionally, faculty, students, and administrators must participate in activities and environments beyond campus to understand the needs and perspectives of their neighbors—not as experts, but as co-learners and co-producers of knowledge acting in solidarity. Organizing around the structures that support knowledge production with plural publics rather than for the public could establish stronger connections between the university, partnering institutions, and the communities vital to investing trust in the university, and by extension architecture education.

Notes

1 ABC Architecture Beyond Capitalism School, "2021 A-B-O-U-T."
2 ABC Architecture Beyond Capitalism School.
3 The Architecture Lobby Academia Working Group, "S-T-U-D-I-O."
4 The Architecture Lobby Academia Working Group, "Future Belonging: Organizing for Global Change."
5 P2PU, "Welcome to Peer 2 Peer University, the Home of Learning Circles."
6 FSA Organizers, "ABOUT."
7 Forde, "Starting a Free School of Architecture."
8 DMU, "Creating New Forms of Knowledge, Institutions, Collectivity, Community, and Design."

 9 Readings, *The University in Ruins*.
10 Veblen, "The Higher Learning in America: A Memorandum on the Conduct of Universities by Business Men."
11 Veblen.
12 Slaughter and Rhoades, "The Neo-Liberal University," 73.
13 ibid
14 Veblen, "The Higher Learning in America: A Memorandum on the Conduct of Universities by Business Men," 3.
15 "How Much Are Private-College Presidents Paid?"
16 Shaw, "Revealed: One in Three Russell Group University Bosses Received Pay Rises Last Year."
17 Carey, "Three Victorian Vice Chancellors Paid $1 Million-plus, despite Uni Deficits."
18 See the chapter entitled, "Land: And the University is Settler Colonial". la paperson describes that the designated university land grant parcel was less a campus than a form of capital, in as much it could be traded for other, more desirable parcels elsewhere. Yang, *A Third University Is Possible*, 61.
19 McKinley, "A Town-Gown Clash Over the Costs of Public Services."
20 Deleuze and Guattari, *A Thousand Plateaus*.
21 This data comes from the 2022 State Higher Education Finance (SHEF) report, a report compiled every five years by the State Higher Education Executive Officers in the United States) "In the News."
22 ibid
23 McGurran and Hahn, "College Tuition Inflation: Compare the Cost Of College Over Time."
24 Maldonado, "Price of College Increasing Almost 8 Times Faster Than Wages."
25 Flynn, "How Is Student Debt Shaping Architecture?"
26 This data comes from the 2022 State Higher Education Finance (SHEF) report, a report compiled every five years by the State Higher Education Executive Officers in the United States) "In the News."
27 Simon, "Bureaucrats and Buildings: The Case For Why College Is So Expensive."
28 Jones Jr, "One Culprit in Rising College Costs: Administrative Expenses."
29 Walton, "Graduate Students at the University of Michigan's Taubman College Are on Strike for Better Pay."
30 ACSA, "Convening."
31 Outer Coast, "Outer Coast."

EXTRA LARGE: THE NATION-STATE

Introduction

EXTRA LARGE presents a shift toward organizing among and around the external influences and ideologies that shape architecture education. While LARGE examines university relationships, EXTRA LARGE confronts the oversight the nation-state places on architecture education through professional apparatuses. These frameworks impact professional tracks and degrees within architecture programs, particularly through accreditation, licensing, and national professional organizations such as the American Institute of Architects (AIA), the Royal Institute of British Architects (RIBA), and others. The institutional conditions, mandates, and procedures each nation-state enacts ensure that professional architecture education conforms to its economic, political, and cultural agenda. These professional organizations were first discussed in MEDIUM in terms of how professional programs must walk a fine line between conformity and creativity, which often leads to the separation of knowledge into discrete curricular categories. EXTRA LARGE focuses on the current professional paradigms that prepare students to become workers for the nation-state.

EXTRA LARGE presents motivations for and lessons from organizing the ABC School, including transcending specialized, siloed knowledge realms, and addressing conflicts between architecture as scholarship and architecture as a profession. The global reach of the school underscores a further ambition: to support architecture education critical of current nation-state-directed professionalism that inhibits collective action toward ameliorating global crises. This chapter examines organizing strategies to overcome the

DOI: 10.4324/9781003411284-9

predominance of nation-state protocols in professional architecture education by aligning with initiatives, movements, and organizations—such as those in the case studies following this chapter—that empower future architects to serve an extended ethical and societally relevant mission.

Professionalism and the Nation-State

Professions are understood in the technical sense of state-controlled licensure, not merely as a description of proper "professional" behavior or as something distinct from "blue collar" work. New York state lists thirty-six professions such as acupuncture, massage therapy, and shorthand reporting that require state licensure.[1] Likewise, professionalism is distinct from practice; professionalism is determined by the institutions that govern those who will be and are licensed—the accrediting bodies, the licensing boards, and the professional organizations. Many practitioners in occupations that require licenses don't like their professional bodies and their practices are guided by ethics, desires, and social norms that transcend and chafe against professional protocols. This is not just true for architects, but for lawyers and doctors as well; grumbling is heard in all these fields; a critique of professionalism should not be confused with a critique of practitioners, for which the authors have sympathy.[2]

The professionalization of industries such as architecture was a nineteenth century invention, the result, as Magali Sarfatti Larson has pointed out, of burgeoning liberal capitalism. At that time, its three simultaneous goals, Larson says, were to ensure a guiding, elite knowledge sector; to (ironically, at the same time) hark back to pre-capitalist ideals of craftsmanship, universal protection of the social fabric, and *noblesse oblige*; and to offer conventions of standardization, scientific and cognitive rationality, and a functional division of labor.[3] In essence, it was and remains a means of market control for a new form of expertise. Today, fair market advocates still criticize professionalism as a form of monopolization.

The nation-state is understood as the official political designation of a country as recognized by the United Nations (UN). While the nation-state apparatus is now globally ubiquitous, there are political difficulties created by the existence of nation-states—they foster false divisions that deny geographical cultural affinities; they leave some people completely or ambiguously stateless; and today they function to secure capitalist-dominated policies. The particular interest that each nation has in promoting its hegemony thwarts a comprehensive discussion of and action toward climate change, or coherent approaches to returning and stewarding stolen land.

The relationship between professions and nation-states is embedded in the country's specific forms of capitalism but in general, professionalism resides in a country's bureaucratic organizations, larger class structure, and its university system. As Magali Larson also writes,

> [T]wo sets of elements—specific bodies of technical-theoretical knowledge, and actual or potential markets for skilled services or labor—... are structurally linked. However, the linkage between these two sets of elements could only be effected in the modern university—the prototypical training institution which cumulates the production of knowledge (the research function) with the standardized production of educated workers (the transmission or teaching function). With the establishment of graded systems of public education, the university takes its place at the top of a hierarchy which both mediates and legitimizes the structure of inequality of advanced capitalist societies.[4]

Architecture in the Nation-State

Within this apparatus, nation-states promote norms of architectural citizenship that discourage identification with people, places, and situations that are unfamiliar. The architect-citizen is prodded to serve the nation-state's rules regarding what, where, and how to build—rules that prescribe what can be owned and traded, on what terms, under what conditions; and what is public or private.[5] The architect-citizen occupies a category of "learned" professionals in which individuals must acquire advanced academic knowledge and adhere to an ethical code. Learned professions include law, medicine, teaching, engineering, etc., that are distinct from occupational professions such as personal training, cosmetology, plumbing, etc., that require licensure, but in general hold no code of ethics nor require the extended education/training.[6] In this regard, architects, like lawyers and doctors, barter their prestige as well as their licensing. In law and medicine this prestige comes with financial reward, whereas in architecture the compensation rarely justifies the cost and time for licensure. Organizing at this scale is as much about lifting the veil of "prestige" that has evolved with architecture's ties to the nation-state as it is about offering alternative modes of professional practice disengaged from the nation-state.

In most nation-states, three types of organizations connect the profession of architecture to the state: those that determine which schools of architecture are accredited to produce future professionals; those that determine the qualifications for licensure; and those that regulate the activities and ethical behaviors of members of the profession. The relationship between these three entities varies from country to country, but for the most part, these organizations work together to produce "architectural professionals" that fit an agreed upon mold. Still, disagreements may arise from the misaligned interests of each entity. For example, accreditation organizations may argue for high standards that limit the number of qualified architects. At the same time, licensing organizations that obtain revenue from licensure may argue for easier access to the profession. Likewise, regulators who protect the public from incompetent architects and ensure clients receive fair value can end up at odds with professional associations that argue for the worth of architects and the importance of their role in society.

A nationalized approach to architecture professionalism yields nonstandard architectural procedures across the world, as each country produces an architect for its own ends. Take, for example, the differences between various national professional organizations. France's professional organization, *l'Ordre des architectes*, which sits in the Ministry of Culture and funnels national projects to France's qualified firms, is the protector of France's built heritage, making French architects agents of French cultural hegemony. In Germany, *Kammers*, the professional organizations of each district, are members of the German Cultural Council and are tied to an education system that is highly technical and engineering focused; architects there are trained to act as an extension of Germany's engineering prowess and technological exports. In Sweden, where there is no form of licensing and anyone can call themselves an architect, the Swedish Association of Architects (SAA) is a union incorporated into a government which prides itself on manufacturing innovation, and whose main exports are industrial products (think Volvo, Saab, Electrolux, IKEA, and H&M); its architects work within and under construction companies such as SKANSKA, and see themselves as production innovators. In China, the government is the architectural client, the accreditation apparatus, the licensing agent, and, via national Design Institutes, its professional club; all promote architecture as nation-building. Chinese architects have a degree in engineering, not architecture or architectural engineering.[7] In contrast, the architecture profession in the United States serves neither the public nor the government but rather private developers. Its professional association, the American Institute of Architects (AIA), reflects laissez-faire economic policy, and licensed architects do not need to belong to it to practice. The AIA has no relationship to governmental agencies other than through lobbying; it tracks metrics, but takes no position on project fees, wages, or architecture labor; and it caters to the largest and most powerful architecture firms that deliver the most AIA membership fees. As such, architects in the United States are seen by the public and developers alike as expensive and unnecessary add-ons to a given construction project. In all these examples, the commonality among various nations' approaches to architecture professionalism is how each serves the nation's cultural hegemony and, from there, its economic goals.[8]

Part of the inherent problem with a nationalist approach is that there are many types of enforced exclusions—of indigenous nations and confederations, of subjugated groups, of non-state entities—that disregard, repress,

and embattle the participation of certain peoples in professional architectural citizenship. In the United States, for example, the University of
Puerto Rico is assessed by NAAB, but has no representation on the NAAB
board. In NCARB's "licensing requirement tool," the five hundred seventy
four recognized American Indian Nations are likewise absent. Enrolled
US citizen-students in Puerto Rico who wish to be licensed architects in
their nation—the US—must enter an arcane process of jurisdictional reconciliation. The architecture profession in Aotearoa New Zealand, which
is dominated by Western design principles, has traditionally overlooked
Māori cultural values and traditional building practices, resulting in the
displacement and erosion of Māori architectural heritage, and limited opportunities for Māori architects and designers to contribute to the architecture profession.[9] Palestine has an official architectural organization, the
Palestinian Engineers' Association (PEA), which represents architects, civil
engineers, and other engineering disciplines in the West Bank, East Jerusa-
lem, and the Gaza Strip, but has no officially recognized national domain
of operation. This contradiction has gained even more attention due to the
recent Israel-Hamas war, as well has the elevated position of architecture
and the built environment in exacerbating settler-colonial practices.

It is not surprising then that excluded architects reassert a more meaningful
role for themselves outside of the professional apparatus, given their cultural
ontologies and the political stakes at play. Issues surrounding land ownership
and occupation, resource management, and cultural appropriation in architectural design, for example, are brought to the forefront in Aotearoa New Zealand by Māori architects, as are entirely different approaches to time, ecology,
and cosmology, which are further described in Part Three.[10] The architects of
Turtle Island (present-day North America) likewise offer holistic spatial and
temporal paradigms that highlight issues of cultural appropriation, land confis-
cation, ownership, and private property, in addition to resilience, stewardship,
and disaster preparedness. In advocating for a role in the political, geographical, and cultural arena in the Middle East, Palestinian architects engage in
issues of transient settlements, preservation, material distribution, and community engagement that confronts the profound imperialist practices which
harm the people and dictate how the land is inhabited. These stances offer
a vision for surpassing the professional nation-state symbiosis to address urgent global issues, such as climate justice, that transcend national borders.

ORGANIZING—THE NATION-STATE

Organizing architecture education at the EXTRA LARGE scale requires a
reevaluation of architecture's professional role within the nation-state apparatus. Presently, organizations that manage accreditation make efforts to

support the value of architectural knowledge independent of its professional uses. In the United States, for example, the National Architectural Accreditation Board (NAAB) has promoted the value of design exploration in and of itself, and made efforts to support the varied, non-standard ways that architecture is taught in different schools. Students of architecture programs in many cases do their best to argue for a more socially and politically engaged, less professionally prescribed, education. In the United States, student members of the American Institute of Architecture Students (AIAS) and members of the National Organization of Minority Architecture Students (NOMAS), for example, take positions that actively challenge their national bodies' complicity with market-driven forces that do not uphold the health, safety, and welfare of the public. And, for the most part, teachers do their best to teach and learn about their subject matter in the context of the discipline, not just the profession. Even those who teach Professional Practice courses are increasingly instructing students about expanded or alternative practices in the profession in addition to those that currently exist. Despite this, architecture education across various countries cannot realistically escape national professional paradigms; the ultimate connection between curriculum and accreditation and accreditation and licensing is just too strong.

This implies architects, architecture educators, and students must find a voice in global and transnational organizations that work across borders, while simultaneously organizing with people and groups residing within local neighborhoods and cities that are disenfranchised, without citizenship in the country in which they reside. Options such as reprofressionalization, deprofessionalization, and transprofessionalization remain at the core of these efforts. Despite the specifics of these approaches, all three reevaluate relationships between the nation-state and the architecture profession. This includes reevaluating licensure, contracts, and ultimately architects' relationships with others involved in constructing the built environment. Therefore, the goal of organizing architecture education at this scale is a means to an end: to confront the current impacts of the nation-state apparatus on the architecture profession for the purpose of making space for other modes of professional practice divorced from the dominance of the nation-state.

Sites of Possibility

Before offering sites of possibility, it is important to note the coauthors' disagreement regarding how to organize toward new paradigms for the profession. While we agree on the need for professional paradigms to move beyond a singular position within the nation-state apparatus, the coauthors do not all agree on the best tactic. Reprofessionalization, deprofessionalization, or transprofessionalization are all options and each, in their own way, underscores the sentiment that to enact social, cultural, political, and economic changes in architecture, the profession, and its ties to the nation-state, must first be confronted and disentangled.

Most if not all schools of architecture, especially those with an accredited degree, include at least one professional practice course. These courses typically cover stakeholder roles in architecture, project management, business practices, legal responsibilities, and professional conduct as they currently exist in the profession. For example, NAAB now includes these in Student Criteria 3.2.2 of the 2020 Conditions for Accreditation; schools tend to pack these criteria into a single professional practice course.[11] Often, this class is taught by someone active in the profession with substantive experience, but little connection to other courses and minimal participation in curricular discussions. In contrast to this, a reprofessional practice course or curriculum could look at the ethics of the relationships architects form through work and contracts, organizing against the repercussions of uniform contracts, for example, in which a guaranteed maximum price and delivery date dominate and usually undervalue the quality of architectural work. A deprofessional practice course or curriculum could discuss the current role of the architect and the limitations of licensure, the inability to discuss salary, and barriers to confronting developers' profit-driven programs. It could promote new agreements with contractors, changing who holds responsibility and liability over construction, bringing architects once again closer to the trades, and more empowered to resist short-sighted developer directives. Finally, a transprofessional practice course or curriculum could reimagine architectural knowledge and practices at a global, not national, scale and introduce a residency model[12] as a form of education that expands global citizenship. It could restore models of architectural practices that organize internationally to collectively address global crises.

Reprofessionalization

Reprofessionalization calls for a thorough reassessment of the ethical framework within which architects operate, particularly when engaging with international entities or organizations outside the architectural discipline, in order to address broader ethical and societal issues. As noted, all established professions adhere to a specific code of ethics. However, unlike the fields of medicine and law, which have ethical codes that define their duties to society at large, architecture has traditionally focused on ethical guidelines that govern behavior within the profession itself. In the United States, architecture's codes of ethics, beyond the call to serve one's clients, deal largely with architect conduct. While the AIA's 2020 code of ethics, the national model, adopts an obligation to the environment,[13] the AIA has little capacity to enforce this value; at most, it can rescind membership in the organization. Since licensed architects have no requirement to join the AIA, there is little consequence to the new provision. Individual states, then, where licensing is regulated, may or may not publish codes of ethics; those that do typically are general statements that apply to all state professionals.

Certainly architects could put pressure on their licensing bodies and professional organizations to take up more environmentally and socially aspirational commitments. But academia, in general, and professional practice classes, in particular, could act as the laboratory for these proposals, introducing and developing ethical concepts that are missing in official arenas. Instead of favoring accreditation criteria that reinforce what already exists, they could open discourse into the contradictions in architecture's codes of ethics regarding who and what architecture is supposed to serve. Professional practice classes could become the spaces to offer addresses to gaps in architecture's internal ethics, such as poor labor practices, and external ethics, including the needs of the environment or the unhoused, alike.

Another solution is to expand professional practice into a thread, sequence, or curriculum that connects professional practice to studio. Here, students would be asked to understand the relations between what they design and its procurement implications, tracking what labor forces, in which countries, are set in motion. Or, the sequence, motivated by a human rights framework, could cultivate architects' legal literacy. It could point to jurisdictional and governance structures at various scales, including the conventions and motions of the UN and its underlying multilateral institutes, such as UNESCO, that advocate for the right to housing, the right to water, the right to food, etc. Offering different global architecture practice models, ones that operate outside capitalist standards, could lead to a more ethical global professional practice paradigm. Or, the sequence could reposition the studio as a laboratory for project delivery methods, in general. In this case, the studio acts as a platform for engineering new economic models to realize architectural work beyond the commission model—in which only clients with means can participate. It could work with lending and philanthropic institutions, governmental and non-profit organizations, and community and special interest groups to envision viable pathways to support projects and research in the constructed environment that currently are unimaginable.

Deprofessionalization

Although "deprofessionalization" may sound jarring, it is important to consider what the term does and does not entail. Deprofessionalization simply means separating architectural licensure from the state apparatus and placing competency assessment elsewhere. At the core of deprofessionaliza-tion is the question, what does architecture gain from being a profession?[14]

As noted in architect and professor Peggy Deamer's text, "Deprofes-sionalisation," in which she cites the work of Magali Sarfatti-Larson, three simultaneous goals have shaped the exclusiveness of professionalism: en-suring an elite knowledge sector remains intact; maintaining the dominant *noblesse oblige* or aristocratic class; and offering conventions for stand-ardization, scientific, and cognitive rationality, as well as a functional divi-sion of labor. While these goals may have been relevant in the nineteenth century, architects must ask if continuing the status quo through a profes-sional apparatus is still necessary.

Deprofessionalization would offer several advantages. It would allow the integration of other disciplines, other expertise, and other industries into architectural practice and knowledge production. Because licensure forms boundaries to keep those untrained as architects out of the profession, it pre-vents lateral and rhizomatic associations; eliminating these boundaries would allow architecture to enter the twenty-first century of connected, systemic thinking and, thereby, have more economic flexibility. It would allow firms to legally form worker-owned cooperatives, something not allowed in most states because licensing boards want to prevent the equalizing of licensed and unlicensed workers. It would allow architectural workers to get paid over-time; architecture firms are exempt from rules that enforce minimum wage and overtime pay because they belong to a learned profession.[15] It would al-low a direct discussion of fees and wages across firms, something that is now illegal in professions due to the potential for collusion. And it could help over-come the public's negative or misguided opinions of architects—that of people in a privileged and expert class that make most major decisions for the built environment and who often prioritize their vision over that of their client.

All of this can be done with no reduction in the architect's pay or meas-ured expertise. In Sweden, where licensing does not exist and anyone can call themselves an architect, the average architect salary matches that of the rest of Europe.[16] As education rather than licensure is the proof of competency, the dismissal of professionalization, also, has led to more robust and rigorous architecture education practices.[17] Or, in the aviation industry, which inherently transcends borders, pilots are certified through national-level specialized organizations that coordinate internationally; in the United States that body is the Federal Aviation Administration.[18]

Transprofessionalization

Transprofessionalization establishes a global, holistic approach to address-ing the built environment. Underlying this model is making visible what is excluded from architecture education when the nation-state is involved in licensure. Because professional education is dictated by regulatory bodies that respond to national actors and agents, organizing must consider the distinction between knowledge in and of itself, and the structures around professional gatekeeping. Organizing across multiple or above individual national associations may mean that architects need to be called something other than "architects," which rings of aesthetic and not social and ecological expertise. Practices that concentrate on problems that are not contained by national borders—climate and migration for example—could act as a global mediators between architecture education, on the one side, and the profession, its accrediting bodies, and non-architecture communities on the other. Further embedding architecture educators in non-governmental agencies to retool and reshape these relationships—not just as a productive bridge between education and practice, but also as a catalyst for positioning architecture itself as interdisciplinary—could restore the image of architecture as a valuable practice that shapes material conditions at multiple scales. This could be enacted through professional exchanges and residencies that move beyond the typical internship model. This includes exchanges with allied disciplines and practices such as the building trades or material suppliers. A residency model, in which architects live and work elsewhere for extended periods of time, could expose architects to alternative and diverse building practices across the globe. In this way, architecture education can teach students to gain a voice in already existing, influential organizations that bypass the nation-state apparatus.

Likewise, practices that explicitly transcend their nation-state obligations to directly tackle global issues should reenter our architectural lexicon. The Congrès Internationaux d'Architecture Moderne (CIAM), and later Team X, were an alliance that gathered architects from across Europe to address the rebuilding of the continent's cities after World War II. Discussed in greater detail in Part 3, CIAM, in this context, is an important example of the faith in collective, international architecture organizing. History rightly has been harsh in its criticism of CIAM's policies, but that does not justify dismissing its efforts and ambitions.

Schools also have the potential to transcend national boundaries and connect international architects in community. Certainly, the ABC School[19] is one such example. As described in LARGE, the virtual program annually gathers architects, academics, and allies from around the world to prototype new curricular structures and content, develop new modes of co-producing, and share knowledge equitably. Another example, the African Futures Institute,[20] positions Africa as the new center of gravity for thinking through issues of urbanism, land use, housing, and climate reform and prepares students to tackle the biggest challenges facing contemporary humanity. Likewise, the Anthropocene Architecture School[21] makes clear that architecture education must primarily produce architects capable of taking on the climate crisis, not only in terms of environmental knowledge, but through collaborative alliances.

Notes

1 "New York State Licensed Professions."
2 See two articles on the distinction between "practice" as the contractual norm ("the practice of architecture") and "practice" as something one does to perfect a skill ("she practiced the piano 8 hours a day"). Last, "Of" and Deamer, "Practicing Practice."
3 Larson, *The Rise of Professionalism: Monopolies of Competence and Sheltered Markets.*
4 Larson, "Professionalism: Rise and Fall."
5 Reich, 'The Myth of the "Free Market" and How to Make the Economy Work for Us'.
6 Deamer, "Deprofessionalisation."
7 Kvan, Liu, and Jia, "The Emergence of a Profession: Development of the Profession of Architecture in China."
8 Deamer, *Architecture and Labor.*
9 Examples of this are numerous and span the entire ongoing history of colonization in Aotearoa. A more recent example is the *Urban Design Protocol* released by the government's Ministry for Environment in 2005, which was part of catalyst for the establishment of Ngā Aho, a network of Māori Design Professionals, because the protocol "failed to meaningfully engage with Māori aspirations and interests in the built environment." Ngā Aho and Takenga Mai have since partnered with a large number of design professional bodies, including in architecture to foster "connectivity between disciplines and the associated professional bodies." For a comprehensive historical analysis of Māori architecture see Brown, *Māori Architecture.*
10 Much of the resistance by Māori related to built (and beyond) environment systems has taken the form of long term occupation of land or ahi kā (literally burning fires), legal battles through the Waitangi Tribunal Treaty claims - of which the majority relate to land, and hikoi (walking protests). The five-year occupation at Ihumātao, one of the few sites in Aotearoa to have archaeological evidence of Polynesian settlement, ended successfully in 2019, preventing the slated construction of 480 houses by Fletcher Construction Group. Described as "agricultural activism," Yates argues that "each seedling planted, each harvest, each whānau fed, is a disruption in the fabric of urban colonial infrastructures and spaces." Yates-Francis, 'TŪHONONGA: Architecture Co-Occupying with Earth and Sky'.These along with significant organizing efforts by collectives have driven the implementation of Mātauranga Māori (Māori knowledge) within the architecture profession and in the academy, but critically across legislative frameworks at all levels of governance.
11 NAAB, "Conditions for Accreditation 2020 Edition."
12 In a residency model, the architecture profession would assume some of the responsibility for preparing new architects for practice. It would replace current credit models, like NCARB's Intern Development Program (IDP), in which new architecture graduates are left to their own devices to accrue measured work

experiences, as defined by a certain number of hours doing prescribed activities that the nation-state deems requisite for architectural competency. Instead, new architecture graduates, like new medical professionals, would enter practice under structured tutelage. An architecture residency model would remove many of the burdens of professionalization on architecture education. It could structure a more accessible pipeline into the profession for those who are underrepresented in the field. And, as a transnational practice, it could cultivate interconnectedness in architecture, as new graduates gain and share insights as they move around the world.

13 AIA, "2020 Code of Ethics and Professional Conduct."
14 Much of the argument here comes from Deamer, "Deprofessionalisation."
15 Deamer, "Deprofessionalisation," 188.
16 The upper-end average architect salary in Sweden is approximately $76,000 per year ERI, "Architect Salary in Sweden." Across Europe, it is approximately $75,000 per year Grozdanic, "Which Countries Pay the Highest Salaries for Architects?"
17 Deamer, "Deprofessionalisation," 190.
18 Federal Aviation Administration, "Office of International Affairs."
19 ABC Architecture Lobby, "ABC Architecture Beyond Capitalism."
20 See CASE STUDY.
21 See CASE STUDY.

CASE STUDY

Introduction

The following are case studies of studios, courses, and programs that exemplify the positions and possibilities that Part 2 has put forward. This list is not comprehensive. The ones that are here are chosen because we authors had access to them from our mutual efforts in the ABC School, or became aware of them through individual and collective research and teaching efforts. They serve as proofs-of-concept regarding this book's advocacy for the role of organizing in architecture education.

The criteria for being a case study, at whatever scale, are the following: it relates to architecture; it involves education; and it includes some aspect of organizing. The latter criterion of "organizing" meant that many courses and programs that are extremely worthwhile in their social and ethical focus could not be considered because organizing was not the thrust. This led to difficult conceptual exclusions because the boundary between "organizing" and what fosters "organizational intelligence" is blurry. The case studies that are here also are the result of an effort to have parity in the number of examples in each scale, aiming for around four per scale. But this quota was hard to adhere to, especially because many worked across multiple scales.

The multiscalarity of the case studies resulted in their categorization first according to theme, and second according to scale. This organization contradicts the stated goal in the introduction to this book to prioritize the process over the target of organizing. In accepting this contradiction,

DOI: 10.4324/9781003411284-10

the following collection of case studies sheds light on the topics that *do* turn educators to activism and organizing. Likewise, if readers come to this guide with a targeted theme in mind, this taxonomy is a guide. The case study themes are: (1) Educational/Disciplinary Horizontality; (2) Climate Justice; (3) Community/Urban Engagement; (4) Race and Space; (5) Carework/Survival; (6) Feminism/Gender; and (7) Plural Worldmaking.

The hope for sharing an incomplete archive of case studies is that it will drive others to complete it—and build a network of solidarity in the process. The ABC School offers an online Hub that is a repository for programs and courses, as well as other outlets for overturning the status quo of architecture education. The Hub can be accessed here: https://linktr.ee/arch_lobby_awg.

EDUCATIONAL/DISCIPLINARY HORIZONTALITY

(S) From Comprehensive to Inclusive Design Studio Teaching

Raison d'Etre

"From Comprehensive to Inclusive Design Studio Teaching" was a two-semester teaching experiment at The Ohio State University's Knowlton School that reimagined the traditional comprehensive design studio as an inclusive one. Conducted by Andrew Cruse and Sandhya Kochar,[1] this studio "fulfilled the stated goals for professional architectural education while acting as a productive critique of normative educational and disciplinary practices. It also opened new avenues for creative practice in the design studio." (Figure 2.1)

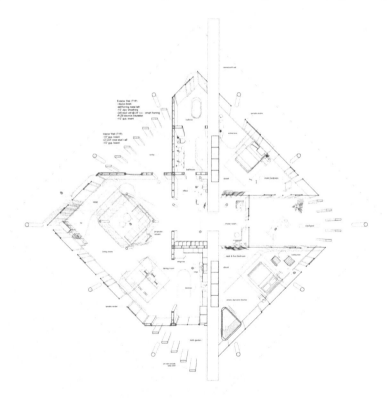

FIGURE 2.1   Andrew Cruse & Sandhya Kochar. Student work from Advanced Architectural Design Studio II at Ohio State University, Spring 2021. "A Society of Rooms." Image by Oscar Camacho-Cabera, Nun ChungBik, Caitlyn Lux, 2021.

Traditional comprehensive studios purport to replicate in school the conventions of professional practice. Yet, as Cruse and Kochar write, "in its ambition to address a wide range of largely technical issues, the comprehensive studio perpetuates a depoliticized vision of architectural design that reproduces established norms and canonical knowledge, while privileging dominant social identities."

It is from this problematic that Cruse and Kochar developed the idea of an inclusive studio to address the impact of design practices beyond the commercial models. They taught this studio for the first time in 2021, during the COVID pandemic. Given how lockdown was upending daily life—with students on Zoom at home—they chose to focus on the room as the visible protagonist of our private and public lives. The students worked through a series of design exercises and ended with a project for a "society of rooms" for a group they defined through the design process. In teaching the studio again the following year, the second in person, the instructors centered their approach on Donna Haraway's call for "making kin." The studio investigated "the relationships between different forms of kinship and forms of architecture as an alternative to the architectural program and building type." Like with the room, the studio scaffolded design exercises, starting with a single human-non-human kinship and built early work into an intentional community designed around an orchestrated set of kinships.

Approach to Education

In most of the United States, students must graduate from a professional degree program in order to sit for a registration exam and become licensed architects. The National Architectural Accrediting Board, or NAAB, accredits these professional degree programs. To gain NAAB accreditation, schools must demonstrate that their students have met a list of performance criteria that range from pre-design to professional conduct. The comprehensive studio emerged in the early 2000s as a way to satisfy many of these performance criteria in one academic experience. As commonly understood, the comprehensive design studio is an important element in a student's professional formation in that it mimics the real-world design development process within the academy. In the Ohio State instance, in the words of the authors, the inclusive studios "offer students an opportunity to use their design skills in an academic studio to reflect on the assumptions about people, places, and things embedded in normative practices … [S]tudents design new practices and approaches that embody a more diverse and inclusive set of values." Students don't just take a course that fills a NAAB requirement, but one that teaches them a critical approach to what "comprehensive" means.

While many comprehensive studios focus on the standards of normative professional practice, inclusive studio teaching frames the standards historically—as socio-technical constructs. In examining architectural practice through this lens, the inclusive studio exposes the "hidden curriculum" of many comprehensive studios. The "hidden curriculum" describes the norms, values, and beliefs that are learned but not openly acknowledged. Exposing and discussing how standards reflect implicit attitudes toward age, gender, ability, heritage, and race broadened students' understanding of their impact on building occupants and opened new design opportunities for them to explore.

The attention to convention led to a greater understanding of the role of design education in the formation of professional identity and empowered students to think about how they can shift this identity. By centering difference and cultivating students' empathetic imagination, the inclusive studio invited in the students' broad range of lived experiences and prompted ways of working alternative to the status quo. Student-led discussions de-centered the faculty as the sole authority and transferred some of the authority to the students, empowering them to direct discussions and design. Finally, the inclusive studio teaching built upon the tremendous pedagogical potential of the architecture studio to enhance the student's experience. In the words of the studio teachers, "studio pedagogy aligns with many educational best practices, including active learning, peer teaching, and the growth mindset. We believe that broadening studio teaching to explicitly address educational ideas of inclusive teaching, transparency, metacognition, and deliberate practice can improve studio-based design education. We hope that in reviewing work produced in these studios and reflecting on this experience, we can nudge the profession toward more equitable and inclusive modes of practice."

Approach to Organizing

Its Organization

Cruse and Kochar did not have to organize themselves in any particular way in order to teach the course in the manner they wanted. As they said, however, if the course had been taught closer to NAAB accreditation, they would probably have gotten administrative pushback.

Its Organizing

The organization of the inclusive studio highlights socio-technical entanglements inherent in architecture, as well as the pedagogical potential of studio-based educational practices. As such, while it did not teach organizing per se, it established the foundation by which the students see themselves as united and organized in managing their education and in preparing for their professional lives.

(M) Redesigning the Academy

Raison d'Etre

Redesigning the Academy was a 2022 graduate workshop conducted by Shannon Mattern[2] at The New School as part of the Anthropology and Design minor, although the course was open to all graduate students (Figure 2.2).

The workshop—an integration of critical university studies, educational anthropology, decolonizing movements, theories and methods of radical pedagogy, histories of alternative schools, and art and design work committed to institutional and pedagogical critique—an assessment of the state of academia in the United States in order to imagine possible alternatives.

Redesigning the Academy explored everything from pedagogies, syllabi, evaluation systems, admissions and even publishing models in order

FIGURE 2.2 A toolbox for Redesigning the Academy. Photography by Ctsu, 2018. Public Domain.

to be able to deconstruct the status quo in academic institutions. Some of the core contemporary issues that the workshop addressed were the ubiquity of managerialism and technocracy, the expansion of the administrative class and the casualized workforce, inequity, and student debt. The class also rooted these concerns within their historical contexts by asking: What are the simultaneously noble and ignoble legacies of the university's various genealogies? How have those histories shaped the present, and how *should* they inform potential future courses of action toward reform?

Approach to Education

Redesigning the Academy had the following learning objectives:

- To develop a basic understanding of the functions of and aspirations for higher education throughout its long history, and to appreciate the institution's various genealogies.
- To develop a basic understanding of how universities operate and why they work the way they do.
- To identify the academy's contemporary challenges and opportunities, and to imagine its possible future trajectories.
- To attune to the aesthetic, ethical, epistemological, and political implications of academic conventions, to consider how those conventions have been naturalized and what ideologies and ontologies they embody, and to imagine how they might be otherwise.
- To develop a capacious understanding of what constitutes scholarship, teaching, learning, and service, and to appreciate the values—and potential risks—of such generous thinking, and to appreciate why we should care about these things.
- To consider how to make principled choices within the academy and to appreciate how the capacity to make such choices is inequitably distributed.
- To recognize the power that students possess to reimagine and reshape—or raze and rebuild—the academy.
- To appreciate how potential interventions are strengthened with critical insight and historical knowledge about how the academy functions, and to acknowledge the potential of modest interventions to effect meaningful change.
- To appreciate for the opportunities and responsibilities—practical, epistemological, ontological, and political—that come with interdisciplinary research and practice.
- To cultivate supportive contexts for conceptual and methodological experimentation and inclusive collaboration, and to apply concepts and methods central in the workshop to other learning environments.

The workshop included seminar discussions, design exercises, fieldwork, and host guest speakers. It engaged collaborations through parallel projects at other institutions. Students were required to create speculative syllabi and curricula, compose manifestos and critical pitch decks, and to design other pedagogical materials and epistemological infrastructures.

Approach to Organizing

Its Organization

Shannon Mattern not only offered this workshop, but she also founded and directed the New School's Anthropology and Design graduate minor where she was charged with designing courses that served and appealed to both anthropology and design students from across Parsons. The workshop was a direct response to student discontent with the academy—and to their expressed desires to imagine how things could be different. Mattern's prior courses and program directorship encouraged student concern about their own fate and the workshop was responsive to their activism.

Its Organizing

Redesigning the Academy offered space for students to identify collectively the origins and expressions of the problems in academia today. In that capacity, it worked through a collaborative mapping activities in which students developed an organizational imaginary for changing the academy.

The workshop was structured around three exercises, each with its own approach to organizational thinking:

Object Analysis/Academic Repair Manual: This exercise "invited students to analyze an 'academic object,' liberally conceived." The students' chosen case studies ranged from snacks to application fees to learning management systems to office hours. Acknowledging the absurdity of creating a repair manual for a broken institution, the exercise was a speculative exploration of the tools for resistance and in understanding how ideological logics scale within academic structures.

Self-Syllabus: Instead of the requirement to write a traditional project proposal, students were invited to design a syllabus that could scaffold their own project development. Students were encouraged to experiment with both content and form in order to create a syllabus that addressed the following prompt: "What material format should the syllabus take so it can embody the kind of learning experience you want to cultivate for yourself?" It gave students, before they collectively protested their current education, something specific to target or suggest.

Final Project: The final project was an open assignment that could be done either individually or in a group of students in order to synthesize the workshop learning objectives. It required not a term paper that would stay within the confines of the course itself, but a public facing, public changing mechanism—an organizational chart, manifesto, a documentary, a podcast, a zine, or a pitch deck for a new, experimental para-academic school.

(M) Bartlett International Summer School (BISS)

Raison d'Etre

The Bartlett International Summer School (BISS),[3] which assembled for one week every summer from 1975 to 1995, was focused on "The Production of the Built Environment." Its mission was two-fold: (1) to overcome the conceptual and disciplinary divisions that plague architecture and overlook construction as a social, as opposed to purely technical, process; and (2) to focus, in studies of the built environment, on the importance of *production* in lieu of the functionalist/formalist dichotomy. The school was framed around the insight that labor is the driver of change in the built environment and the need to show the underlying social relations that analysis of the production process reveals (Figure 2.3).

The first four iterations of the summer school were held in London, but the BISS became increasingly international over its lifespan. It moved to many cities, including not only Brussels, Dessau, Dortmund, Geneva, Glasgow, Lyons, Moscow, Paris, Roubaix, and Venice, but also Mexico City and Sao Paolo. In these different venues, the aim was to understand the various ways that the social production process was organized under different economic and political regimes.

The BISS quickly abandoned the distinction between teachers and taught, though it retained the word "school" in its title. The themes explored over the seventeen summers were historical transformations; modes/manners of production in socialist and non-socialist countries; labor and labor processes; employment and working conditions; and production, aesthetics, and built form.

The BISS ceased to operate due to the fatigue and frustrations of participants in the face of triumphant neo-liberalism. Some of its work and participants continued their work and mutual support in the European Institute of Construction Labour Research and the International Network for Urban Research and Action[4]—the former sustaining the production and labor focus very strongly; the latter spanning broader methodologies, while self-organizing in the same way as the BISS.

THE PRODUCTION OF THE BUILT ENVIRONMENT

CAPITAL AND LAND

CAPITAL ACCUMULATION
AND THE STRUCTURE OF
THE BUILDING INDUSTRY

CONCENTRATION AND COMPETITION
IN THE BUILDING INDUSTRY

HISTORY AND ORGANISATION
OF CONSTRUCTION LABOUR

TECHNICAL CHANGE
AND FIXED CAPITAL

STATE INTERVENTION
IN URBAN DEVELOPMENT

OWNERSHIP OF LAND
AND CONSTRUCTION

PROCEEDINGS OF THE FIRST BARTLETT SUMMER SCHOOL

FIGURE 2.3 Front cover of the proceedings of the first Bartlett Summer School. Bartlett International Summer School (BISS) 1975. Image provided by BISS.

Approach to Education

The BISS sessions were attended by educators, practitioners, unionists, researchers, and students from a range of different countries, with each averaging about sixty participants. Presentations of papers were accompanied by workshops, field trips (especially to building sites), social events, and discussion. After each school, the organizers produced a volume of *Proceedings* with full texts of the talks and summarizing that year's findings. The topics pursued by the BISS were consistently Marxist in their aims: how the social relations involved in construction were organized; what this revealed about capitalism's (always contested) control of the systems of production; and how physical and mental labor were intertwined in this system.

The work of the BISS had two outlets in formal teaching: a masters' program on the Production of the Built Environment and a long-running first year undergraduate program—which had little explicit theoretical content but introduced students (not just of architecture, but also of construction and planning) to production processes through talks and visits in London and a foreign city.[5]

Approach to Organizing

Its Organization

The summer school was sponsored by the Bartlett (a faculty of University College London) in agreement with fourteen other institutions, each taking turns in organizing and hosting a school. Participants paid their own travel and accommodation costs, and no significant conference fees were charged. There were occasional grant contributions from foundations, but essentially this was an organization run on the voluntary labor of participants.

Its Organizing

The goal of the BISS was not organizing per se; it did not directly teach its participants how to organize to change either the production process of or education in the built environment. Nevertheless, its emphasis on labor, its redirecting educators to focus on the social process of producing the built environment, and its mode of organizing were lessons in labor activism. Likewise, the skills needed to produce the school and the subsequent production of the proceedings over the many years present a model of organizing for change in architectural education.

(L) DoArch SAB

Raison d'Etre

The Department of Architecture (DoArch) Student Advisory Board (SAB)[6] is a formal representative organization for architecture students to interface with faculty and administration in DoArch at South Dakota State University. DoArch, established in 2010, is the first architecture school in South Dakota and, as such, was set-up with an unusual self-supporting funding structure. This built-in vulnerability led to the SAB's activation as a hub for student organizing. In 2021, early in a DoArch restructuring—that included its flattening into a program within the School of Design—the SAB organized to demand more from the university's administration. The precipitating events, the structure of the SAB, and their organizing methods were shared in the ABC 2022 Workshop *Student Organizing Across Syllabi and Project Briefs*, conducted by former DoArch faculty member Federico Garcia Lammers, and former SAB representatives, Dakota Mathews Schmidt and Shylo Hilbert (Figure 2.4).

Approach to Education

The practices of the SAB prioritized disinvestment from traditional concentrations of power in teaching and learning through critical student representation while simultaneously challenging the hierarchies and power structures held in the university. Weekly organizing sessions that built the collective power to mobilize against opaque top-down, decision-making involved the following:

- Information exchange
  - Communicating student concerns to faculty and administration to address challenges and codesign opportunities for departmental change.
- Departmental functions
  - Participating in weekly faculty meetings to share students' concerns, while connecting them to curricular and operational discussions.
  - Creating and maintaining studio culture policy to increase student agency and collectivize departmental culture.
- Student feedback and surveys
  - Organizing student curriculum surveys to assess how the rhetorical positions of the faculty align with students' learning experiences across the curriculum.
  - Organizing forums for curricular discussions with currents students, alumni, and faculty.

FIGURE 2.4   DoArch Student Advisory Board's (SAB) six-point letter published
in the Collegian, asking South Dakota State University administrators to address architecture students' concerns. April 27, 2022.
Photography by Federico García Lammers.

- Student collective action
  - Drafting open letters to students, alumni, and media sources to explain students' organizing efforts.

In 2021, student concerns over the flattening of the department within
the School of Design and the spread of resources were communicated to university administrators via a letter drafted by the SAB. The letter highlighted
the department's funding structure, a self-support model in which founding
firms donated the initial funds to launch the department in 2010, and, after
four years, student course fees became the primary funding source. This
meant that, in addition to tuition, architecture students paid $480 per credit
hour in course fees—almost twenty times the amount students in other
School of Design disciplines paid. The letter further addressed concerns over

faculty retention, technology, and human resources, as well as lack of advocacy for the studio model in state legislative processes.

The 2022 ABC workshop was a chance to expand, explore, evaluate, and propose strategies for furthering the SAB's student organizing practices in architecture education. From its daily practices, the SAB challenged the opaque, top-down character of typical course assessment in the discipline, to support a student-led process that reshaped syllabi and began to redraw the hierarchical lines of power that are inscribed into architectural education. In its activist form, the SAB student representatives, "who had gained the chance to look under the hood,"[7] discussed and publicly mobilized to demand transparency about the financial organization of the department and the distribution of resources shaping their education.

Approach to Organizing

Its Organization

The DoArch Student Advisory Board was started in 2010 to accommodate and inform the newly organized Department of Architecture. The SAB is a departmental organization of elected student representatives from each year of the undergraduate and graduate architecture programs. The organization's purpose is to act as the link between the faculty and the student body, facilitating the exchange of information, explaining departmental functions, and gathering student feedback. The SAB acts in the best interest of the entire student body by conducting weekly meetings with each other and students and by sending a representative to participate in faculty meetings.

Its Organizing

The DoArch SAB serves as a model for both students and faculty to promote "an ethos of transparency and inclusion of students in decision-making"[8] by making a collective effort to disseminate the implications of the academic and administrative devices of the university and to propose alternatives. For DoArch, the flattening of the department into a program within the School of Design proceeded, yet students and faculty were able to maintain more control and agency over the resources their course fees funded. Other practices, such as student organizing, the mobilization of local media outlets—including the college newspaper and interviews with local news channels, empowered students and the public to hold the university accountable. For other architecture schools, the organizing strategies offered by the SAB offer an example for formalizing and balancing student engagement within the power structures that shape their education.

(L) Beta-Local

Raison d'Etre

Beta-Local[9] is a study/production program, an experimental education project, and a platform for critical discussion. It supports and promotes aesthetic thought and practice without the intention of becoming an institution in the globalized art market or academic spectrum. With the desire to support and encourage artistic production, experimentation, and research in Puerto Rico, the organization works as an incubator for the artistic community. It is a critical response to the excessive bureaucratization that characterizes cultural institutions and the recurring economic obstacles faced by cultural workers in Puerto Rico. In Puerto Rico, the state of permanent crisis, the lack of support from local institutions, the disinvestment for culture and public education by the government in Puerto Rico, the weakness and/or highly bureaucratic nature of its institutions—all require Beta-Local to fill an essential cultural void (Figure 2.5).

FIGURE 2.5   Critical seminar program formerly known as "La Práctica" (the practice), now "El Laboratorio" (the lab). Photography by Beta Local, 2019.

Beta-Local insists on artistic practice and aesthetic thought as essential to social and political life. Immersed in the local reality of San Juan and the characteristics of its present moment, it is dedicated to supporting and promoting cultural practices. As they say, "We believe that cultural production is a collective exercise and that it is our duty to look after it, not only for the material product of that culture, but for those who produce it, our people."

Beta-Local recognizes the urgency of supporting the plurality of local artistic manifestations and their strategies of social and political involvement. To respond, the organization offers a space for direct critical discussions by diverse artists and non-artists interested in changing the current social and political conditions and a place to foster a strong and healthy artistic community. It emerged from an effort to formalize direct daily dialogue and to facilitate public meetings that were happening in private at artists' and curators' homes. The most important role of Beta-Local is to support artists in making work anchored in aesthetic thought and artistic practices of Puerto Rico. Its example of homegrown community self-help has fostered a growing movement that promotes paths to self-sufficiency. When knowledge is shared, culture manifests itself.

Approach to Education

Not a school per se, Beta-Local nevertheless has programs offered in a space that functions as a community center in which learning is offered and shared. While its agenda is artmaking, it focuses on creating links across disciplines and finding connections between artistic practices and other ways of thinking and doing.

The work of Beta-Local is channeled through its three main programs:

El Laboratorio (formerly known as La Práctica), a nine-month production-based program, is a critical seminar for cultural workers of different disciplines. It is designed for those interested in creating new conditions from which to produce in and beyond established art and culture circuits. It now aims to build on the life work of artists to promote generational bridges and continuity of their legacy through new production practices generated through open dialogue and participation.

The Harbor is an international residency program aimed at developing long and strong collaborative relationships with artists, curators, and thinkers based outside of Puerto Rico. It works by invitation only. This program is currently shifting to a more local approach, offering residents of the archipelago much needed time and space to rethink their production practices.

La Iván Illich is an open school through which anyone can propose a class that they want to take or teach via workshops, talks, study groups, and others. Beta-Local's public programming brings together a wide range of thinkers and practitioners, placing arts and culture in dialogue with varying fields of knowledge and perspectives. As a study and production program, an experimental education project and a platform for critical discussion, it is immersed in the local reality of San Juan and the characteristics of its present moment.

Approach to Organizing

Its Organization

Beta-Local, founded in 2009, is a non-profit organization, a working group, and a physical space based in Old San Juan, Puerto Rico. Since its founding, the organization has been led by a team of three co-directors. The organization is shifting to give a more prominent role in programming affairs to a broader deliberative body that will better reflect the priorities and pace of the programs.

Its Organizing

While not teaching organizing skills per se, Beta-Local provides a space for contact and exchange between artists and other publics that otherwise would not interact. The space works as a catalyst for new situations and other collaborations, thereby offering a framework in which organizing flourishes. The user-generated elements of some of the programs, as well as the interest in education and exchange, open the space to a wide range of audiences not necessarily connected to the art world. As such, they extend their network beyond the immediate neighbors of Old San Juan to other people interested in various structures of intellectual and/or knowledge production and exchange. It is not collective bargaining, but it is collective action for change.

All in all, those who manage and represent Beta-Local and those who attend (whether they are taking courses or not), are involved in an association that depends on organizing—organizing the programs, the use of the space, the individual responsibilities, dissemination of material, and the growth of its association. One could not participate in Beta-Local without learning about organizing.

(L) Break//Line

Raison d'Etre

Break//Line is a "revolt" structure rooted in the Bartlett School of Architecture. Organized by a contingent of staff and students, it arose in opposition to the myriad forms of hostile environment in UK higher education and pervasive government policies of hostility toward people deemed to be undesirable immigrants to the United Kingdom. They understand that this hostility goes hand-in-hand with the ever greater encroachment of capital and "the idea that the built environment should be determined by the logic of the market."[10] As a "revolt," it takes no consistent form, cohering irregularly as a studio, or an incubator, or a residency, or a sound system. Its unifying motivation is to resist the impositions of capitalism and the spatial representations, practices, and experiences of hostile environments in higher education. By bringing these hostilities to the fore, it enacts a different kind of politics, and provides space for an imaginary of how things may be constructed otherwise (Figure 2.6).

Approach to Education

Break//Line plays out as interruptions to the architecture education status quo. They put forth experimental pedagogies that both occupy and supplement the existing curriculum.

FIGURE 2.6 BREAK//LINE teachout as part of University and College Union strike, then the longest ever strike in UK higher-education history. Photography by David Roberts – Break//Line, 2018.

Its process begins in the issuing of circumstantial challenges to architecture education's canon and ideologies:

- It rejects capitalism as inevitable and forwards degrowth as a vital architectural project.
- It decries the discriminations built-into architecture education and practice.
- It calls out the systemic dismissal of the ideas and work of the global majority.
- It confronts the isolationist and individualizing working and teaching practices commonplace in architectural education.
- It seeks a dismantling of the barriers to and a cultivating of support for radical architectural research and practice.

They organize and agitate against outsourcing, precarious employment practices, unsafe workloads, failing pay, the gender and race pay gap, pension cuts, and for education as a public good, accessible and affordable for all.

Break//Line's classroom interventions include efforts in de- and transinstitutionalization and course cooption. It has sought to nurture spaces of collaboration across courses and creative resistance within and beyond the institution. It has opened the curriculum to student direction, empowering a total rethink of capstone research and procedure. And it has taken inspiration from Christina Sharpe's framing of "wake-work," or the notion of sitting in the problem, as central to all teaching and learning.

Break//Line uses publications, workshops, and institutional disobedience to get beyond the university's structures. Through its online presence, it is collecting educational resources, both internally generated and invited content that includes essays, games, films, and mix-tapes. Its workshops either test educational material or relationships or they respond to contemporaneous events. They offer alternatives to architecture education's knowns, as exemplified by instruction in speculative futuring, getting to know a place from afar, and feminist practices. And they develop as needs arise, in particular, to organize a public hearing, to develop an advocacy campaign, and to participate in and support academic labor strikes.

Approach to Organizing

Its Organization

In 2018, when the Bartlett staff and student members of Break//Line were on the picket line striking against precarious employment/teaching practices—unsafe workloads, falling pay, the gender and race pay gap, pension cuts, and for education as a public good, accessible and affordable for all—the Bartlett Faculty of the Built Environment advertised a new position of Vice Dean Equality, Diversity & Inclusion, the first such senior appointment at a UCL faculty.

Break//Line cooked up plans to intervene in this new position by instigating a network of student-staff "active intermediaries"—a concept adopted from Beth Perry's work[11] which critiques the capacity of organizations to absorb and embed critical feedback in real time as initiatives are put in place. They brought together existing student- and staff-led groups and projects across the faculty, first by establishing non-hierarchical, collaborative, open fora and second by conceiving of new cross-faculty initiatives, and third by maintaining regular communication with the Vice Dean.

Its Organizing

From the picket line to classroom to peer-reviewed article, Break//Line has sought to deinstitutionalize and reimagine spaces within the academy, involving all those who make up an institution—from security guards to events officers to undergraduate students and alumni—to build non-hierarchical, collaborative, open fora for critical appraisal and new cross-faculty initiatives. As such, Break//Line both draws architecture education directly into organizing and is guided by and to the knowledges on which organizing relies and toward which it works.

During the period of initial protest, they mobilized public hearings. For example, they initiated Deportation Disks, a public hearing of experiences of people deported from the United Kingdom through recordings taken by the researcher Luke De Noronha. Taking place on the first floor of the faculty, situated near the administrative offices, and responding to a memo sent to staff notifying them of their personal liability for monitoring foreign students' attendance, this public hearing aimed to create an aural environment of the experience of the spatial disruption of deportation.

During the most intense period of strikes, the space of the picket line was pivotal. They were supported by the University and Colleges Union (UCU) and Independent Workers' Union of Great Britain (IWGB).

During the pandemic, rather than host events and interventions within the space of the institution, Break//Line curated a series of online publications and a symposium to analyze the varying manifestations of hostile environments in higher education. Titled "UNBUILDING," the work resulted in the curation of original commissioned pieces of scholarship, each tackling a different form of hostility including trans and binary gender discriminations, racism, structurally embedded institutional barriers, and oppressive legislation—understanding the university's complicity as an arm of the state's violent, racist bordering practices, and enacting and celebrating alternatives, always and already present.

(L) Practising Ethics

Raison d'Etre

Practising Ethics[12] aimed to develop a practice of ethics for built environment researchers and practitioners "navigating [the] connection between universal principles and particular processes." It brought together specialists from across the Bartlett and University College London, other universities internationally, and external organizations, all "with collective expertise in action-based, humanities, participatory, practice-led, social science, and science methods. The *Practising Ethics* project was a collaboration between the Bartlett Ethics Commission (2015–2022),[13] a Bartlett faculty-funded project cultivating an understanding of the sensitivities of ethical issues in built environment research and professional practice and Knowledge in Action for Urban Equality (KNOW) (2017–22),[14] an ESRC-funded Bartlett project seeking to deliver urban equality via transformative research (Figure 2.7).

Practising Ethics was led by Professor Jane Rendell, Director of Ethics for the Bartlett School of Architecture, and Dr David Roberts, Bartlett Ethics Commission Fellow. Together with Dr Yael Padan, Research Associate on KNOW, they co-curated an open access educational toolkit, co-produced by over thirty contributors, to emphasize the relationship between ethics and the built environment. The toolkit "includes a lexicon of ethical principles, guidelines on how to negotiate ethical issues in practice, reading lists of ethics publications, overviews of ethics protocols, and case studies including reflections on the hotspots, touchstones, keystones, blind spots, moonshots and milestones of ethical processes."

Approach to Education

Clearly not a "program" residing in a departmental curriculum, *Practicing Ethics* shows that knowledge production doesn't stop in the classroom; it can be generated through university administration, and can be top-down as well as bottom up. Inspired by the "whole institution approach" from UNESCO Education for Sustainable Development response,[15] *Practising Ethics* works through four inter-related modes: what? or ethical practice as a topic in the curriculum; how? or the methods through which ethics is taught, learnt, researched, and practiced; where? or the sites and institutional structures that contextualize ethical practice; and whom? or those with whom we practice ethics.

#4 Staging Research

Practising ethics guides to built environment research
David Roberts

When planning
1. Is it unethical to remain silent?
2. Do I have the right to share this material?
3. Who will I work with?
4. Will it be safe?

When setting up
5. Have I analysed site and situation?
6. Are there barriers to access?
7. Should I provide contextual information?

Before displaying
8. How will I engage audiences?
9. Should I document the event?
10. Who will keep the work?

#8 Co-writing Research

Practising ethics guides to built environment research
Alejandro Vallejo and Catalina Ortiz

When writing
1. How will we address disciplinary definitions of 'authorship' and writing conventions?
2. What kind of labour and contribution will count as 'writing' or 'authorship' and allow a researcher to be listed as co-author?
3. Are the data in the public domain, and how can we protect it?
4. What kinds of referencing systems will we use?
5. How will we support and care for co-writers during the writing process, and how will they respect us and each other?
6. Who will lead the process intellectually, and who will manage the practical elements?
7. How can different forms of knowing and technological routes that may arise?
8. How will we plan for and commit to the task of writing the research output in terms of timescale and deadlines?
9. What kinds of referencing systems will we use?
10. What processes will we use for giving each other feedback?

#3 Co-producing Knowledge

Practising ethics guides to built environment research
Yael Padan

When planning
1. What kind of relationships will we build between the co-producing partners, and how can we ensure everyone gains from the research?
2. How will we distribute the work to be done—fieldwork, analysis, interpretation, management, and whose knowledge counts?
3. How do I handle difference, problems and disagreements when our team, and ethical issues that come up?

When transferring
4. Are our decision making processes collaborative, open and transparent?
5. When issues arise are we able to change our modes of collaboration and research plans?
6. Are we using appropriate formats within our project, open to discovering these, and finding ways of avoiding their reproduction?

When producing & communicating
7. Are we able to collaborate with each other about our findings to whom are they collaboratively and linguistically appropriate?

#7 Analysing Secondary Data

Practising ethics guides to built environment research
Tania Guerrero Rios & Jens Kandt

When planning
1. What data would be best to answer my research question & do these data already exist?
2. Do I fully understand the purpose, methods, and context within which the candidate data sets have been produced?
3. Are the data in the public domain, and would data subjects expect the type of analysis I am planning?

When conducting
4. Have I selected the appropriate methods to answer my research question with these data?
5. Have I documented all the steps of my analysis, including any data cleaning, filtering, and how I have safeguarded the confidentiality and anonymity of data subjects?

When producing & communicating
6. Are my illustrating outputs clearly presented and appropriate for the audience?
7. Is it possible to identify individuals, households or organisations from my outputs?
8. Am I allowed to share data outputs for further analysis with public repositories?
9. Do I know for how long I may retain the data and how to delete them securely when appropriate?

#2 Asking Questions

Practising ethics guides to built environment research
Yael Padan

When planning
1. How do I choose and approach my interviewees?
2. Have I found out enough about the local social/cultural/political context?
3. How do I ensure my interviewees understand the purpose of our interview?
4. If my questions make my interviewees uncomfortable, what can I do?
5. How will I store and manage the information I gather?

While interviewing
6. How am I treating my interviewees?
7. Can I sense tensions/sensibilities/expectations?
8. Am I making anyone feel uncomfortable?

Before writing
9. Have I stored my data securely?
10. Have I made sure that information in the interview with my interviewee?
11. Will I share my interpretations with my interviewees?

#6 Researching Internationally

Practising ethics guides to built environment research
Emmanuel Osuteye

When planning
1. Why have I chosen to work in this particular context or abroad?
2. Where exactly is my chosen field and what do I know about it?
3. Who will I work with and how does collaboration begin?

When conducting
4. How do I ensure maintaining mutual benefits and value for all research partners?
5. What are the shared roles and responsibilities and what are the research models for this research?
6. How do I navigate and gain a deeper understanding of the field?
7. How do I ensure compliance to institutional ethical requirements while in the field?
8. How will I deal with the practicalities of remoteness, and remote working?

When producing & communicating
9. What are the range of outputs planned and who is the audience?
10. Will I understands come home?
11. Am I not empty representation of collective effort?
12. How have I sought and used feedback prior to dissemination?

#5 Researching Risk & Wellbeing

Practising ethics guides to built environment research
Ariana Markowitz

When planning
1. Will I cause harm?
2. Will I need a support system?
3. Will I be able and willing to improve existing practices on the ground for keeping safe?

While researching
4. Am I maximising the benefits and minimising the harms that my research might cause?
5. Am I feeling supported?
6. Am I devoting time to activities besides my research?

After finishing
7. Have I checked in with my research participants to let them know how it went?
8. Have I adopted my support system?
9. Have I learned ways of building distressing or conflicting information?

#1 Making Images

Practising ethics guides to built environment research
David Roberts

When planning
1. Will it be possible to identify someone from my image?
2. Will I ask for consent to take images of others?
3. Will I need permission to make images of this site and situation?
4. Will I collaborate with others to make images?

While recording
5. Am I making anyone feel uncomfortable?
6. Am I mindful of local tensions and cultural sensitivities?
7. Am I alert to the history and power of this medium?

Before displaying
8. Have I invited the subjects or owners of the images to have a say in their use?
9. Have I considered how audiences might make alternative interpretations?
10. Have I protected information that might compromise dignity or safety?

FIGURE 2.7 Practising Ethics guides to built environment research 2021. Image provided by David Roberts.

Aligning with a number of collaborators in the United Kingdom and internationally, the project devised and hosted numerous workshops, conferences, and events, identifying specific issues pertaining to the built environment and "guid[ing] the practice of ethics in teaching, research and enterprise in the built environment." It responded to ethical issues on the ground, collaborating with external partners, other disciplines, and institutions, for example in: "Reactivating the Social Condenser," (with anthropologist Michal Murawski);[16] "Speech ExtrActions—Testimony, Evidence and Witness in Response to the Mining Industry,"[17] (with ecologist Diana Salazar, the Colombian Solidarity Campaign, and the London Mining Network); "Judgement Calls," (in collaboration with the Slade School of Fine Art, Kings College London, and the Australian-based iDARE);[18] and "Rich Seams/Dark Pools," (which involved UCL management and professional services, as well as academics and students). All these conversations focused on specific ethical concerns, but also developed a shared set of ethical principles and research guides "drawn from institutional codes and protocols, various branches of theory and philosophy, as well as lived experience."

Approach to Organizing

Its Organization

The work began with "ethical hotspots" that Jane Rendell and David Roberts had experienced in their own research. Rendell then applied for Bartlett funding for a year-long project to examine ethics in built environment research, in which Roberts produced a mapping of ethical issues in Bartlett research practice. This developed into the Bartlett Ethics Working Group, in which representatives from across the faculty engaged with UCL's review of ethics procedures. This developed into the Bartlett Ethics Commission, for which Roberts produced a study of the ethical codes that govern around sixty built environment professions,[19] and prototyped ethical guidance to help students and staff deliberate ethical dilemmas.[20]

The Commission collaborated with "The Ethics of Research Practice," as part of KNOW, where Padan and Rendell ran workshops with partners in Havana, Dar es Salaam, and Kampala, to ask the question: "What does ethics mean to you?" Padan examined the Western-centric bias of the three institutional ethical principles of "confidentiality," "informed consent," and "benefit not harm," exploring how they stem from enlightenment thinking that privileges the individual over the collective.[21] With KNOW partners, Rendell and Padan drew on feminist, care, and decolonial ethics, conceptualizing ethics as a shared lived practice[22] that operates between specific situations or "hotspots" and universal principles or "touchstones."[23]

Its Organizing

Practising Ethics did not aim to teach "about" ethics, but to advance its practice. The resulting toolkit provides those working in the university with activist knowledge,[24] and assumes that it is only by working together that all educators and administrators will figure out and promote a new ethical approach to producing and maintaining a livable planet.

Notes

1 CASE STUDY write-up was developed via and quotes come from exchanges with Cruse and Kochar between Nov. 18–26, 2023.
2 CASE STUDY write-up was developed via and quotes come from exchanges with Mattern between Nov. 18–26, 2023.
3 CASE STUDY write-up was developed via and quotes come from exchanges with Rendell between Nov. 18–26, 2023.
4 INURA, "About INURA."
5 Edwards, Campkin, and Arbaci, "Exploring Roles and Relationships in the Production of the Built Environment."
6 Case Study write-up was developed via exchanges with Garcia Fritz between Nov. 18–26, 2023.
7 *Student Organizing Across Syllabi and Project Briefs.*
8 *Student Organizing Across Syllabi and Project Briefs.*
9 CASE STUDY write-up was developed via and quotes come from exchanges with Beta-Local between Nov. 18–26, 2023.
10 CASE STUDY write-up was developed via and quotes come from exchanges with Break//Line between Nov. 18-26, 2023. https://breakline.studio/.
11 May, Perry, and Hodson, "Active Intermediaries for Effective Knowledge Exchange."
12 CASE STUDY write-up was developed via and quotes come from exchanges with Rendell between Nov. 18–26, 2023.
13 UCL, "Ethics in the Built Environment."
14 KNOW, "KNOW: Knowledge in Action for Urban Equity."
15 UNESCO, "What You Need to Know about Education for Sustainable Development."
16 Murawski and Rendell, "The Social Condenser.'
17 The Bartlett Development Planning Unity, "Speech Extractions Witness, Testimony, Evidence in Response to the Mining Industry."
18 University of Melbourne, "iDARE: Innovation, Design, Art, Ethics."
19 Roberts, "Reflect Critically and Act Fearlessly: A Survey of Ethical Codes, Guidance and Access in Built Environment Practice."
20 Roberts et al., "Practising Ethics."
21 Padan, "Researching Architecture and Urban Inequality."
22 Padan et al., 'A "minifest" as the Promise of Collective Voice'.
23 Rendell, "Hotspots and Touchstones."
24 Roberts, "Why Now."

CLIMATE JUSTICE

(S) The Plum Orchard, New Orleans Studio

Raison d'Etre

The multi-semester post-Katrina studio—the Plum Orchard, New Orleans Studio—was taught by a consortium of consulting experts, faculty, and students from Pratt Institute and New Jersey Institute of Technology (NJIT) and led by Deborah Gans,[1] Ron Shiffman, Vicki Wiener, James Dart, Darius Sollohub and Denise Hoffman Brandt. The faculty learned about Plum Orchard through the Association of Community Organizations for Reform (ACORN), who acted as their local partner under a US Department of Housing and Urban Development Rebuilding America Partnership grant. The grant was intended to bolster the capacity of the local community to rebuild what was there and establish protocols for future sustainable development. Working with a group of Plum Orchard residents organized by ACORN, they reimagined both the individual yard and the shared landscape of the block (Figure 2.8).

Begun as a studio in the Fall of 2005, it continued as coursework in the Spring and Fall of 2006 and, in a more limited way, through the Spring 2007. James Dart and Deborah Gans then continued the project as architects for ACORN until 2009, with the help of former students who joined their offices.

The studio's first move was to produce a brochure addressed to residents in the middle of rebuilding that directed them to local services, directions for cleaning and demolition, and a list of environmentally sound and flood-resistant building materials and methods. The second move was the mapping, socioeconomic modeling, and environmental analysis necessary to envision and propose a Model Block—the covenant for which was that "no individual should reclaim a territory alone, that the neighborhood is the smallest sustainable unit, and that a cluster of at least three houses should be the fundamental unit of the neighborhood." In this, the Model Block is understood as a water management landscape that continues well beyond the block and joins it with the extended area of the city.

At the conclusion of the grant in Fall 2006 and course work in Spring 2007, many of the strategies and tactics that the consortium developed for water management and some of the specific desires of the neighborhood were incorporated into the official Lambert/Danzey Neighborhood Rebuilding Plan for District Nine. ACORN hired James Dart of the New York City firm DARCH and Deborah Gans as architects for a city-sponsored project slated to create as many as four hundred prefabricated houses on

FIGURE 2.8   Housing fair organized by ACORN (Association for the Community Organizations for Reform Now) in the spring of 2006. Plum Orchard New Orleans Project: The boards presented are Gans Studio students retrofits of existing houses in Plum Orchard that had been damaged by Hurricane Katrina. While they reimagine particular houses, they collectively propose architectural ideas and methods that could be applied to many similar suburban homes. Photography by James Dart, 2006.

adjudicated sites. In consultation with residents, they developed five different prefab house typologies. While Dart and Gans worked closely with manufactures, the reality was that none of the prospective buyers of the houses with whom they were working were able to secure enough financing to build the model house.

Approach to Education

The Fall 2005 studio consisted of surveys, oral histories, and brochures. The Spring 2006 seminar consisted of retrofits and visioning sessions. The Fall 2006 seminar consisted of further ideation and infrastructural analysis, landscape remediation, and modeling. In the Spring 2007 seminar, faculty and students presented their work publicly and infrastructure planning students continued their efforts to influence the larger district post-Katrina plan that was framed at that time. From the Fall of 2007 through

2009, Dart and Gans continued to work with ACORN along with two students who joined their firms upon graduating.

So many aspects of this studio make it a model for studio education. The consortium of experts, faculty, and students worked collaboratively; they worked in cooperation with the residents of the community; the studio involved mixed institutions—Pratt and NJIT; it connected with governmental policies and grants; it didn't separate environmental from architectural proposals; its outputs were not merely designs, but brochures, analyses, and policies; and it was conducted over multiple semesters. It is a model for Paulo Freire's anti-banking of education: students applied their learning in real time.

Approach to Organizing

Its Organization

To receive the HUD COPC grant, the teachers created a very detailed work plan of how each institution would participate and what they would bring to the table. Pratt Center was the lead on the grant. They wrote it and administered it. At the time, Pratt Center had a dual identity—as a distinct entity that worked as a community-based planners funded by grants, and as an extension of the Graduate Department of Planning and the Environment.

Its Organizing

The studio is an example of organizing at many different levels: studio critics organizing to push for an unusual collaboration among institutions; critics teaching students how to coordinate and organize with the community residents; critics and students together organizing to insert themselves in local and federal policy exchange. At the same time, Gans noted that the more significant organizing lesson was the limited effect of this type of community engagement when the appropriate political and governmental actors were not on board. She applied this lesson in her subsequent post-Sandy Sheepshead Bay studio in 2012.

(M) Huri Te Ao – School of Future Environments

Raison d'Etre

Huri te Ao, or the School of Future Environments,[2] is a transdisciplinary school founded in 2020 in Aotearoa New Zealand within the Auckland University of Technology. The school integrates research and teaching across the disciplines of Hoahoanga-Architecture, Creative Technologies, and Built Environment Engineering exploring strategies, transitions, and transformations for regenerative or future-focused environments (Figure 2.9).

FIGURE 2.9   Kaupapa Mo Hoahoanga (Regenerative Architecture Manifesto): Designing Regenerative Environments for Living Systems Wellbeing. The poster outlines the Kaupapa, or strategy of Huri Te Ao, which is deployed across its research projects, knowledge sharing, and collective action (2022). Image provided by Huri Te Ao—School of Future Environments.

The school is itself conceived as a future-focused "collaborative project to co-create an outward-facing civic research platform for sharing ecologically positive design thinking across diverse communities of practice."

The Hoahoanga Huri te Ao—the architecture program—is structured around indigenous ways of knowing (Mātauranga Māori), transdisciplinary and collaborative systems, and regenerative design as a means to explore new-old ways of thinking about transformational logics and placed-based actions. The current institutional frameworks underpinning the conception, design, construction, habitation, and management of the built environments impacting ecological crises—climate change, biodiversity loss, environmental degradation, and global-scale social inequity—are inadequate to the challenge. To date, the program believes changes in built-environment education have been largely limited to a socio-technical approach, focusing on the metrics of energy consumption, efficiency, and production. Hoahoanga Huri te Ao, instead, examines the eco-ontological foundations positioning living systems well-being. The school and its Kaupapa (strategy/ethos) aims to overhaul the existing structures within the built environment disciplines in order to tackle environmental crises anew.

Approach to Education

The primary teaching objective of Hoahoanga Huri te Ao is to empower students to assume an active role as catalysts for change by equipping them with the ability to collaboratively facilitate regenerative transformations alongside local communities. Rooted in a transformative pedagogical approach and characterized by its emphasis on a place-based, ecologically centered education, the school aims to furnish the students with the knowledge and skills needed to transform, often collectively and with diverse stakeholders, ecological strategies.

The program employs a number of pedagogical tools to co-create its tactics with students, teachers, and practitioners. Key among these are:

- The Kaupapa, the manifesto for change: The Kaupapa identifies the overarching orientation and critical areas of pedagogical focus. The manifesto emphasizes the design of regenerative environments and the need to learn from living systems in a way that is supportive of indigenous practices. It emphasizes a transition from extraction to regeneration; from linear take-make-waste economies to circular; and from carbon-based to zero-carbon energy technologies.
- The Te Ara Ako, the curriculum map: The Te Ara Ako assists staff in creating a connected curriculum and helps students track their

regenerative learning journey. It visually depicts the written manifesto, making it a graphic curriculum map that charts progression from year one, focusing on Whakapapa (ontologies of and strategies for relational living-systems); to year two, oriented around Mauri Ora (complex and holistic wellbeing that is social, cultural and ecological); to year three, addressing Ki Tua (futurity and intergenerational exchanges); to years 4 and 5, focusing on regenerative research.

Each course in a semester is designed to connect the design studio to annual conceptual platforms.

The Nga Tohu Mauri or the Living Systems Wellbeing (LSW) Compass, a curriculum change tool, is a graphic device grounded in Te Ao Māori (Māori cosmology and context) and other relational and regenerative modalities. The tool offers a graphic means for students to "navigate and integrate ecological relationships at different scales and levels of complexity" while identifying key actions for living systems wellbeing. The Nga Tohu Mauri Ora—LSW Compass "integrates bio-regenerative, nature-positive actions within a matrix of other human-centered actions for place-specific community wellbeing." As an interactive diagram, "it is an analysis and action tool that outlines key necessary transitions in built environment structure and systems."

Approach to Organizing

Its Organization

The course was designed by Amanda Yates, Nick Sargent, Andrew Burgess, and Priscilla Besen with engagement with Ngā Aho (the Māori designers network). After it was finessed, it went to Aotearoa New Zealand's Committee on University Academic Programs (CUAP) for approval. CUAP considers academic matters across the university system, including the exercise of program approval and moderation procedures and encourages the universities to develop courses that facilitate the transfer of students between programs and institutions.[3] Yates, who was the Head of Department of Architecture and Creative Technologies from 2019 to 2021, was able to hire two new staff at the beginning of 2020, neither of whom were expert in the field, nor Māori, so they had to co-create the tools to build regenerative knowledge and indigenous Mahitahi-collaborative approaches.

Its Organizing

Huri te Ao—School of Future Environments relies on partnerships and community allies in its call for socially and culturally ethical strategies for ontological and strategic change. It relies on Indigenous-led or partnered collaborations. As such, the students are both shown and taught collective and inclusive approaches to community participation.

Likewise, students within the course are asked to co-create the specifics of the curriculum, its charts, and its maps. They learn techniques for collecting their disparate voices and, thereby, recognize their power in the program. This power equips them with the ability to collaboratively facilitate regenerative transformations alongside local communities both in school and in their post-graduation professional life.

(M) Green Reconstruction

Raison d'Etre

Green Reconstruction is an initiative at The Buell Center of Columbia University that proposes a curricular toolkit for the built environment. The toolkit is a collaborative, in progress, work that deals with the relationship between academic curricula and societal change. In that sense, it aims to address and tackle three intersectional crises of today: the climate crisis, the mutual care crisis, and the crisis of racial oppression. Green Reconstruction operates within two axes in relationship with curricula: the ecological transformation and material distribution-reconstruction axes (Figure 2.10).

By acknowledging that the simple resolution of site-specific conflicts in the built environment barely captures the scope and scale of the underlying problems that cause them, Green Reconstruction is guided by the question: "What is a curriculum and what impact does it have on how to heed the warning, as fossil-fueled climate change forces overexposed populations onto front lines redrawn before our very eyes?"

The toolkit of Green Reconstruction proposes taking a holistic approach and a critical examination of this state of crisis to explore and address some of its key dynamics: privatization, de-democratization; racist expression, racially organized dispossession; climate denial, profit-driven embrace of a fossil-fueled future.

The Green Reconstruction network and toolkit operates both inside and outside of the curricular space. Although the focus is placed on the professional education in the built environment, with an emphasis on architecture, landscape architecture, and urban planning, it also operates within the professional community in order to challenge the construction and maintenance of the broader status quo. This perspective promotes that both scholars and practitioners as needed in order to supply the technical equipment or "tools" with which to make things change.

In that way, the aim of the project is ultimately to provoke and create a collaborative curricular transformation on a United States national scale

What connects us?

green reconstruction

green reconstruction

green reconstruction

ion green reconstruction

To stop changing the climate, we need to change our infrastructure, together.

FIGURE 2.10   What connects us? To stop changing the climate, we need to change our infrastructure, together 2021. Image provided by Green Reconstruction and Steve Hillebrand.

in order to change the material conditions of the built environment as well as the societal relationships between the subjects that dwell in it to achieve a more sustainable and equitable future.

Approach to Education

Green Reconstruction proposes a collective learning perspective. In the words of Green Construction's authors,

> Change is learned. On the streets and in the public sphere, imagination, knowledge, and know-how go hand in hand. At a time of mounting social and ecological turmoil, planning and designing a just, equitable built environment requires professional focus anchored in intellectual ambition.[4]

The Green Reconstruction toolkit is "a dossier of assessments and suggestions regarding how we learn [that] offers pre-curricular back doors into long-established pedagogical practices, through which new strategies might be introduced." Divided between a planning-oriented description of cities and an architecture-oriented visual survey of city fabrics, it offers sample course content "that raises questions that must be addressed for anything like Green Reconstruction to be conceivable." At the end, a brief conclusion puts the sample material in context and looks to future challenges.

Approach to Organizing

Its Organization

Green Reconstruction is based and organized around Columbia University's Temple Hoyne Buell Center for the Study of American Architecture. In 2020, they organized the "Green Reconstruction Curricular Workshop" comprising students, scholars, and practitioners from the built environment. Its goal was to explore and document professional and pre-professional curricula at all Association of Collegiate Schools of Architecture (ACSA), American Society of Landscape Architects (ASLA), and American Planning Association (APA) member institutions to imagine what a genuinely system-wide response to the current crises must entail.

Its Organizing

The model for the workshop was an online gathering as a public assembly of colleagues in architecture, landscape architecture, and urban planning from across the USA. It borrowed its configuration from previous experiences at the Center and was organized around a "two-part structure, adapted to Zoom, of smaller, thematically organized breakout groups followed by a larger plenary session."

They collected information drawn from surveys of over a thousand professional, pre-professional, and post-professional programs in the built environment across the United States. From 2020 through 2021, as an ongoing and collaborative project, teams of both graduate research assistants and adjunct associate research scholars at the Buell Center, compiled, organized, and analyzed information on 1,115 academic programs at professional schools of the built environment across the United States.

As part of their mission and as a way to create a working body of applicable knowledge, they also have released digitally and in print their "Green Reconstruction: A Curricular Toolkit for the Built Environment" publication—that is available for free on their website.

(L) Arsom Silp

Raison d'Etre

Arsom Silp Institute of the Arts[5] is a not-for-profit higher education organization located in Bangkok, Thailand. A spin-off of the Roong Aroon School, Arsom Silp was established to bridge a preexisting holistic childhood learning program to the needs of the region. Offering three interdependent areas of study—holistic education, architecture for community and environment, and social entrepreneurship—it centers architecture as the channel for building a knowledgeable citizenry, relationships with people and place, and culture. Arsom Silp sees itself as a change agent, a pedagogical platform for thinking beyond the market economy, and a laboratory for restoring balance with the natural world—with architecture as its means (Figure 2.11).

Arsom Silp models a departure from competitive learning and hypothetical instruction. Motivated by making a difference, it recognizes its work as two-fold: part human and part ecological. It comprehensively relies on participatory processes and is committed to the support of everyone's mental, physical, and spiritual well-being. All of its projects are

FIGURE 2.11   Theeraphon Niyom and team, Arsom Silp Community and Environment Architect at their studio, Rabindhorn Building. Image supplied by Arsom Silp.

real-world, architectural addresses of local issues or research into econom-
ical and sustainable building assemblies and practices.

Approach to Education

Arsom Silp is an institution for which architecture is a unifying ideology.
It is structured as an educational architecture and landscape firm. It offers
both undergraduate and graduate degrees. Its campus is a realization of its
architectural principles and processes. And architecture is a shared interest
of its multiple educational programs.

Arsom Silp's architecture education is project-based. Members of the
community, the private sector, and the government bring projects to the
Arsom Silp firm. These projects, then, are both the subjects of professional
work and of student learning. Faculty, staff, and students all have roles
in their stewardship; those with more experience serve as facilitators and
managers and those with less experience learn by hands-on doing. Everyone is recognized as a valued contributor, and everyone is understood to
have unique knowledge.

Arsom Silp manages all projects through a rigorous participatory process. It considers its members, outside builders and vendors, topical experts
(from doctors to ecologists to politicians), and community representatives
as equal partners and actively involves everyone in decision-making by
consensus. Herein, architects are perceived as coordinators, negotiators,
and friends. Clients agree to collaborative working. Design is understood
as the creation or strengthening of bonds between people and place. And
architecture is an embodied agreement of this method. Arsom Silp projects
range from architectural designs, to conservation efforts, to community,
and urban developments.

Arsom Silp's five-year undergraduate education is forty percent discursive coursework and sixty percent immersive fieldwork. Course requirements include Contemplative Practices, Nature Appreciation, Holistic
Health Care, Appropriate Technology, and Community Engagement. In
the first year of field study, students develop artisanal skills through small-
scale design-builds. In the second, third, and fourth years of field study,
they are embedded in one of the firm's projects. Each project is assigned an
Arsom Silp project architect, a facilitating faculty, and up to eight students.
Students are part of a project from beginning to end, including research,
conceptualization, design development, construction documentation, and
construction administration. In the fourth and fifth years of field study,
students pursue a thesis by selecting a community, training in listening and
communications, and proposing a responsive design. Arsom Silp's graduate degree condenses the undergraduate experience into two-plus years.

Recently, the school has begun offering classes and workshops for the neighboring community.

Arsom Silp, the campus, is the outcome and a living reflection of its architecture program's principles and process. Sited on 1,100 square meters of land (approximately a quarter acre), the school was designed and built by faculty, staff, and students. It models the community's shared goals of living alongside nature, prioritizing space for exchanging ideas and knowledge, providing for private and public needs, and advancing the regional aesthetic and trades. The project preserves eighty percent of the green space as a tree nursery and the buildings are fifty percent balconies and terraces. Arranged as a village, it offers spaces for gathering, a communal kitchen, and individual quarters. Arsom Silp faculty, staff, and students live together and collectively maintain the buildings and landscape. All construction is passive and the campus handles the majority of its recycling and waste on-site.

Despite its unique pedagogy, Arsom Silp satisfies the Thai national accreditation requirements. It does so by combining and splitting criteria across its coursework and retrospectively converting assignments to standard assessment measures. Its graduates qualify as architects.

Approach to Organizing

Its Organization

Arsom Silp was established in 2006 by Theeraphon Niyom, a renowned Thai architect who rethought his interests according to Buddhist philosophy. It runs as a not-for-profit architecture firm that uses project fees to support its educational and community service purposes. Its personnel include a director, professional architects, teaching architects, support staff, and students. Everyone lives and works in community, sharing authority and responsibilities.

Its Organizing

Organizing informs Arsom Silp's mission, operations, and projects. Arsom Silp was organized to catalyze the transformation of Thailand's cities and communities by implementing sustainable building practices and reconnecting its people to each other and to nature. It teaches organizing, like it teaches all things, by doing. Ritual practices structure the school's governance; faculty, staff, and students gather for daily meditations and weekly check-ins, at the end of each term to reflect and anticipate, and annually for deep dialogue. And the school's participatory design process, in which projects are designed in consideration with and representative of community, exemplifies the potentials of organizing for architecture.

(L) University College London Divestment Campaign

Raison d'Etre

This is not a school, a program, or a course. It is a campaign, one that originated in The Bartlett School of Architecture that aimed to stop research on sustainability being funded by a charitable donation from the Australian mining company, *BHP Billiton*, and for the university to divest from fossil fuels. As a result, the university altered its procedures for accepting gifts and donations to include environmental, social, and governance due diligence; and following votes in a public debate (24 March 2015), and UCL's Academic Board (10 February 2015), both in favor of divestment, UCL divested from fossil fuels in 2019 (Figure 2.12).

In January 2013, Jane Rendell[6] questioned the decision of her employer, UCL, to accept $10 million of funding from the Anglo-Australian multinational mining and petroleum company BHP Billiton to create an

FIGURE 2.12 University Anti-Mining Campaign. Broken Hill (Silver City), Australia (2015). Image provided by Jane Rendell.

International Energy Policy Institute in Adelaide, and the Institute for Sustainable Resources in London at the Bartlett Faculty of the Built Environment.[7] The partnership was initially set up in a time of enforced austerity economics in the public sector and higher education in the United Kingdom, taking place after the introduction of £9,000-per-year fees for undergraduate students, and the charitable donation expanded research capacity by funding PhD scholarships over a five-year period.

As part of a risk management exercise undertaken across UCL, as a Vice Dean of Research, Rendell was asked to conduct a risk register to assess the risks of research expansion. Rendell argued that by allowing BHP Billiton to buy legitimacy for the continued mining of fossil fuels, UCL was taking a risk with its reputation for independent research into sustainability. She judged the risk of potential damage to UCL's academic reputation significant enough to purchase a report by RepRisk on BHP Billiton.[8] The findings indicated that BHP Billiton was breaching principles of the United Nations Global Compact concerning human rights and the environment.

As Vice Dean of Research, Rendell was in a position to criticize the Bartlett–BHP alliance. The fact that *BHP Billiton* decided not to renew their charitable donations to the school is an indication of the campaign's success. This, along with subsequent actions calling out UCL's complicity in carbon-producing policies, has led to changes in institutional behavior.

Approach to Education

This campaign, successful and important as it is, would probably not qualify as a CASE STUDY in this book if Rendell had not linked the campaign to new forms of architectural and educational output. This output is less course-work pedagogy than lessons on the subjectivity of architects and architecture educators. Rendell emphasizes that the writing of criticism is a form of situated practice, and her "site-writing" around this experience includes two registers—*bios*, a set of diary entries noting personal anxieties and hopes related to her institutional role at UCL; and *logos*, an attempt to relate these issues to the development of her own intellectual work and concepts concerning ethics.[9] Subsequently she has emphasized the importance of combining sole-authored and co-produced work in the practice of ethics in the institution.[10]

Based on this experience, Rendell gives public talks that question the governance structures of the neoliberal contemporary university and its marketization of education. The first, at the University of South Australia (Adelaide), in November 2013, delivered under Chatham House rules, was a conference keynote for *Critique*.[11] Many other public talks have followed, as well as creative works, such as "Silver: A Courthouse Drama," performed as part of *Lost Rocks* in Tasmania with actors' scripts as composed out of the Rep Risk report and other media coverage,[12] of the Mariana Dam disaster of 5 November 2015, in which BHP were implicated.[13]

Approach to Organizing

Its Organization

While this campaign started with the effort of an individual, its success was due to its collaboration with colleagues, NGOs such as the London Mining Network, and the student activist group Fossil Free. The campaign also involved working with the UCU (University and Colleges Union) to press for, and achieve, democratic changes to UCL's governance procedures.

Its Organizing

Again, this campaign did not teach organizing in any conventional sense, but Rendell has delivered talks and related workshops on the topic of institutional ethical practice to many architecture and related programs in the United Kingdom and internationally. This pedagogical input and its related site-writing, lectures, and performances shed light on the multiple ways in which architecture educators individually and collectively *perform* activism.

This campaign is an important inclusion at the scale of LARGE and in the Climate Justice category because it indicates the value of architecture professors putting themselves on university level committees. It also is important due to the impact Rendell has had on architecture educators with her ongoing critique of architecture as a male-dominated, instrumentalized profession as well as her conviction that instituting change begins with aesthetically powered self-reflection.

(XL) The Anthropocene Architecture School (AAS)

Raison d'Etre

The Anthropocene Architecture School (AAS) is an education infrastructure, founded in response to the (architecture) education system's "deafening non-response to 2018's IPCC Special Report on 1.5°C, and its ongoing inertia in the face of the climate crisis and ecological collapse."[14] It began

FIGURE 2.13   A giant playthrough of Climania (https://climaniathegame.com/), a board game that the AAS supported the development of, featured at Unlearning Powerlessness in Central St. Martins' Lethaby Gallery during Architecture is Climate (07–19 March 2023). Image provided by Simeon Shtebunaev.

with a provocative theatrical protest during the 2019 Architecture Fringe Open Program where it declared that "Architectural education as it is being taught, is obsolete in the face of climate breakdown." It received no challenge and knew it had struck a chord (Figure 2.13).

Initially, the AAS shared and prioritized the energy of the 2019 Extinction Rebellion and youth climate strikers, striving to raise consciousness in the built environment about the climate crisis. Over the following two years, it moved beyond consciousness-raising and became one of architecture's earliest champions of climate literacy evidence-based and opportunities-orientated explorations.[15] It has invited participants to action while cultivating an awareness of the socio-economic and political forces shaping architectural practice. It has situated its activities to protest "a modernity built upon, and sustained by, sacrificial lands, lives, and communities." Rooting its activities in agency, spatial justice, and the radical imagination, it envisions a just transition, that does not stop at borders, for all people through change to climate policy, and cultural transformations.

If sustainability knowledge is to be deployed and mainstreamed, AAS believes, it must be linked to economic and political realities. Actions of adaptation, construction, demolition, dispossession, gentrification, and maintenance, they understand, do not take place within vacuums; they are shaped by powers that control energy systems, fossil fuel politics, labor capacity, and resource availability.

Approach to Education

The AAS connects the realities of the climate crisis to architecture's entanglement with it, counterbalanced by "stories of the possible." Workshop participants learn sustainable design while consciously unlearning unhelpful cultural assumptions, assumptions not only about climate beliefs and neoliberal rhetoric but also about traditional architecture schools and the assumed role of the architect. Regarding shifts in climate assumptions, it doesn't merely impart statistics but "distills actionable steps, replicates lessons, and shares resources." A library of reading, listening, and watching materials, can be accessed on Instagram.

Regarding shifts in assumptions about architects and architecture, AAS believe that architecture education cannot separate the realities of power and "the experiences of regenerative design, practice, and technical experience." In its workshops, participants do not just analyze the network in which climate change operates, but "consciously imagine what their future could feel like if that abundance of technologies, and wisdom, that we do have, was deployed at the pace and the scale that the climate crisis requires."

Since 2019, workshop formats have included the transdisciplinary Crisis Studios—where tutor teams introduce themselves to students, who then initiate learning dialogues, climate literacy sessions—for the public, students, and educators, Climate Emergency Ready City hackathons at the Edinburgh Fringe, XR's Rebel Rising Festival, and Scotland's first People's Assembly on Climate and Housing Justice. In 2023, it shifted its approach in order to pluralize insights and voices generated through panel and workshop formats by centering collective intelligence and lived experiences and co-program events with cultural organizations to reach beyond architecture and construction silos.

Approach to Organizing

Its Organization

Scott McAulay is the school's coordinator. Others inside and outside architecture are invited to collaborate and enter into reciprocal relations, "refusing to perpetuate exclusionary cultures of free labor in architecture, only giving time compassionately to community causes, and, when possible, student groups." It operates on a gig-to-gig basis—relying on one-off sponsorships via crowdfunding toward upcoming projects with peers.

Its Organizing

The AAS is a catalyst within an ecosystem of activist and community groups, arts and neighborhood climate transition organizations, festivals, tenants and trade unions, sustainability groups, and architectural institutions. As an organizing principle, the AAS remains agile and adaptable, consciously cultivating collaborative, reciprocal relationships within its ecology.

Notes

1 CASE STUDY write-up was developed via and quotes come from exchanges with Gans between Nov. 18-26, 2023.
2 CASE STUDY write-up was developed via and quotes come from exchanges with Yates between Nov. 18-26, 2023.
3 Universities NZ—e Pōkai Tara, "Committee on University Academic Programmes (CUAP)."
4 Temple Hoyne Buell Center for the Study of American Architecture. "Green Reconstruction: A Curricular Toolkit for the Built Environment."
5 CASE STUDY write-up is based on a conversation with faculty and students of Arsom Silp on Nov. 8, 2023. https://en.arsomsilp.ac.th/.
6 CASE STUDY write-up was developed via and quotes come from exchanges with Rendell between Nov. 18-26, 2023.
7 UCL News, "BHP Billiton and UCL Launch Natural Resources Initiative."
8 Rendell, "Critical Spatial Practice as Parrhesia," 13 December 2016; RepRisk, "ESG with a Risk Lens and Transparency."
9 Rendell, "Giving an Account of Oneself."
10 Rendell et al., "'Selvedges/Self-Edges;" Rendell, 'Seven Studies for "A Holding"'; Rendell, "Site-Writing as Holding."
11 Rendell, 'Configuring Critique (or "the Art of Not Being Governed Quite so Much")'; Rendell, "Critical Spatial Practice as Parrhesia," 13 December 2016; Rendell, "Home-Work Displacements."
12 Rendell, "Silver"; Rendell, "Silver: A Courthouse Drama."
13 Staff writer, "Brazil Authorities Expect Mariana Dam Disaster Deal to Close in December."
14 CASE STUDY write-up was developed via and quotes come from exchanges with MacAuley between Nov. 18–26, 2023. https://linktr.ee/Anthropocene ArchitectureSchool.
15 Climate Literacy is "the contextual, pragmatic understanding of the implications of climate breakdown upon any given activity, its own contributions towards those implications, and recognition of where it has the potential to positively respond." This guide from the RESTORE project focuses on the built environment offering educators, students and practitioners' insight. Martin Brown and Battisti, "RESTORD 2030: A Regenerative Guides for Educators Students and Practitioners."

COMMUNITY/URBAN ENGAGEMENT

(S) From the Ground Up: Building Solidarity in Somerville

Raison d'Etre

Ground Floor and *Common Ground* are two advanced studio courses at the Rhode Island School of Design (RISD) Architecture that W. Gavin Robb[1] conducted in the Spring semesters of 2022 and 2023. The studios started from the premise that all architecture is political, that all politics are local, and that community power is built, not given. In this, the studios formed a sequence of interrogations focusing on themes of community power and resistance against predatory forces of capital. *From the Ground Up: Building Solidarity in Somerville* was a workshop conducted as part of the 2023 program of The Architecture Lobby Architecture Beyond Capitalism ABC School that explored the nuances and ramifications of this work within and outside of the discipline of architectural education (Figure 2.14).

Through research, on the one hand, and speculative design proposals, on the other, the studio participants explored the city as a network of stakeholders, interests, and power rather than a geometric or geographic object. Students researched and interviewed community organizers, housing advocates, non-profit service organizations, city officials, and policymakers at the state and local level. Working with the city as a non-privileged stakeholder, the research captured city- and region-wide issues while focusing specifically on a city-owned site at Gilman Square, adjacent to a new public transit stop leading to Boston, Massachusetts.

Approach to Education

The research studios, *Ground Floor* and *Common Ground*, tried to take an approach to architecture education that contrasts with typical studios, where research often ignores the complex political realities facing community development and the researchers are ignorant of their own positionality. In this instance, the studios were organized in two parts:

First, the student cohort co-wrote a 170-page research toolkit for future action. In pairs and small groups, students interviewed key stakeholders in Somerville working toward housing justice, observed and critiqued a city-run community meeting, and convened two public panel discussions. This complex network of housing advocates, local residents, community organizers, nonprofit leaders, city councilors, Massachusetts state representatives, and city officials provided a key foundation for identifying needs, conflicts, contradictions, and aspirations about the built environment. Students also conducted more quantitative research, working collectively

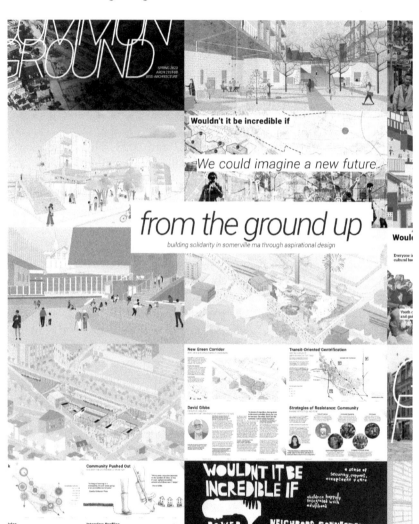

FIGURE 2.14 From the Ground Up: Building Solidarity in Somerville MA through Aspirational Design. RISD student cohort, 2022-2023. Collage by W Gavin Robb, 2023.

to investigate historical and ongoing mechanisms of displacement, gentrification, political power, corporate real estate holdings, and zoning regulations designed to promote equitable development. This research provided a complex set of inputs to feed design speculation.

Second, through architectural representations, the students depicted their answer to these questions: How can this site build permanent resistance? Can the site become a permanent anchor of stability and community against the forces of capital? Can design build community? Can spatial structures cultivate solidarity and resistance? Robb says the projects were "aspirational, joyful, and unfinished" and "drew out a "collective celebration of a liberatory future.""

Approach to Organizing

Its Organization

This RISD studio mixed fourth-year B.Arch students with second-year M.Arch students. The school was supportive of this work, but it entailed coordination with RISD's Center for Community Partnership—which led to changes in the original structure of the studio's interaction with the city. As Robb describes, "[At] the Center, there was concern that we'd be abetting gentrification and displacement and were cutting out significant portions of the community and privileging the enablers. This forced [us] to radically retool some of the methodologies... We didn't end up working with the Center for Community Partnerships at RISD."

In the studio itself, a rhizomatic working methodology promoted teamwork among students and aimed to teach them to design from a participatory and collaborative perspective, by both cultivating professional skill sets and relational practices with the community.

Its Organizing

The studios tried to catalyze a public accountability structure and a solidarity network of advocates and activists working together toward spatial justice. The students recognized that their designs were political and understood that designers are responsible and accountable to communities that are subject to the violence of capitalist development. This engagement shaped the students as people and professionals for whom organizational relations are fundamental.

The work of these studios was co-authored and is licensed for use in this publication by: Abena Danquah, Abigail Zola, Andrew Song, Chae Yeon Woo, Elijah Trice, Emily Lo, Fiona Libby, Jack Kostyshen, Jack Schildge, Jenny Zhang, John Lewtas, Kai Andrews, Lauren Blonde, Lauren Cochran, Lily Gucfa, Mackenzie Luke, Nancy Nichols, Phillip Schroeder, Ruyue (July) Qi, Shane Su, Tia Miller, Uthman Olowa, Victoria Goodisman, Viola Tan, W Gavin Robb, Yupeng (Terry) Chen, and Yuqi Tang.

(L) Design Studio for Social Intervention (DS4SI)

Raison d'Etre

The Design Studio for Social Intervention (DS4SI)[2] partners with communities, artists, and social justice practitioners in the Boston area to imagine, demonstrate, and collectively rebuild places to be more just and vibrant. In their words, they are "situated at the intersections of design thinking and practice, social justice and activism, public art and social practice, and civic/popular engagement" and they "design and test social interventions with and on behalf of marginalized populations, controversies, and ways of life (Figure 2.15)."

DS4SI's work is exemplified by one recent effort, "Re-arranging the Neighborhood to Reimagine the City," which organizers describe as "a transformative conversation series that aims to stimulate our imaginations and creativity around what our neighborhoods and cities could be, as well as how we can collectively contribute to the shaping of our shared places. Each event invites residents, practitioners, scholars, students, organizers, and curious minds to muse with our guests about how we might delve into this work at both the scale of the neighborhood and the city."[3]

DS4SI's partners are "a constellation of activists, artists, academics, designers, dreamers, tricksters, organizations, and foundations." Their outputs are social interventions, newly imagined public infrastructures—like

FIGURE 2.15   Celebration at the Design Gym of the 3-year anniversary of DS4SI book, "Ideas – Arrangements - Effects: Systems Design and Social Justice." Photograph by Marvin Germaine "Shotxmarv," 2023.

their Public Kitchens and Dance Courts, numerous writings, civic engagement, creativity labs, and events.

DS4SI is committed to spatial and aesthetic justice. They regularly work with organizers who are fighting for racial justice, education justice, climate justice, transit justice, housing justice, and more.

Approach to Education

DS4SI recently opened what they're calling a "Design Gym," with hours five days a week in the Upham's Corner neighborhood of Boston where they're located. This new civic space "creates the conditions for BIPOC neighbors, artists, youth, organizers, merchants, and more, to imagine the physical, social, and aesthetic arrangements of their lives."

In their words, "The Design Gym is a new community infrastructure, a mashup, a place to work out new ideas, stretch the muscles of imagination, meet neighborhood artists and organizers, imagine and prototype new solutions, learn design techniques, and collectively rebuild our communities to be more just and vibrant."

All offerings at the Design Gym are free and open to all. Classes range from maker classes (sewing, videography, woodworking, painting, etc.) to design classes (civic design, participatory action research, prototyping, etc.), to book groups, to providing space for other artists to teach. They offer "Open Gym" hours for people who are working on ideas or projects and want support with the design process. And, they have a resident chef to encourage participants to linger and talk or browse their "Radical Library".

Approach to Organizing

Its Organization

The studio has a fiscal sponsor, TSNE, which holds its nonprofit status. It is primarily funded through grants, as well as by doing fee-for-service work for municipalities, organizations, and foundations. It has a four-person advisory board, a total of ten to twelve full and part-time staff, and many local artists and thought-leaders who are commissioned to lead events, teach classes, and collaborate on design projects.

Its Organizing

DS4SI believes that ideas are embedded in arrangements, which in turn produce effects. This framework, captured in their 2020 book entitled *Ideas—Arrangements—Effects: Systems Thinking and Social Justice*, is at the heart of their organizing. They believe that arrangements are a powerful and overlooked terrain for creating change. In turn, they develop and teach techniques for sensing, intervening in, and re-imagining the arrangements of everyday life.

The fact that DS4SI is a studio model rather than a school or a community center forwards gathering that is participatory and organizing as a bottom-up construct. In addition, DS4SI is committed to both teaching and doing their own collaborative design work. They are always modeling organizing, as well as teaching new ways to do it and new ideas about who can use design as part of their organizing practice.

(XL) Design Justice Network (DJN)

Raison d'Etre

The Design Justice Network (DJN)[4] "dream[s] of worlds in which design is truly led by the experiences and brilliance of those who are marginalized by interlocking systems of oppression." They know that "the people who are most adversely affected by design decisions—about visual culture, new technologies, the planning of our communities, or the structure of our political and economic systems—tend to have the least influence on those decisions and how they are made." As such, DJN's mission is to empower community groups that already exist regarding their access to design, doing so through sharing stories and critical reflection (Figure 2.16).

Shaping a definition of "design justice" as distinguished from "design for social impact" or "design for good"—which they say can perpetuate existing systems of injustice. DJN wants to "redesign design."

The group is held together by adherence to the following ten principles:

1 Use design to sustain, heal, and empower our communities, as well as to seek liberation from exploitative and oppressive systems.
2 Center the voices of those who are directly impacted by the outcomes of the design process.
3 Prioritize design's impact on the community over the intentions of the designer.
4 View change as emergent from an accountable, accessible, and collaborative process, rather than as a point at the end of a process.
5 See the role of the designer as a facilitator rather than an expert.
6 Believe that everyone is an expert based on their own lived experience, and that everyone has unique and brilliant contributions to bring to a design process.
7 Share design knowledge and tools with their communities.

FIGURE 2.16 Allied Media Conference in Detroit, 2018. The Design Justice Steering Committee (of 2018), with participants of the 2018 Design Justice Network track, after the final workshop held by DJN. Photograph by Design Justice Network, 2018.

8 Work toward sustainable, community-led-and-controlled outcomes.
9 Work toward non-exploitative solutions that reconnect people to the earth and to each other.
10 Before seeking new design solutions, look for what is already working at the community level. Honor and uplift traditional, indigenous, and local knowledge and practices.

Approach to Education

Not primarily an educational institution, DJN rather rallies and empowers the communities in which the network is embedded. In this, knowledge sharing is central to its mission. Member storytelling is a major aspect of this, but so are workshops and labs that teach tools for speculative thinking, mapping, data access and sharing, and technological proficiency. Their workshops and labs "prototype ideas using analog and digital tools to begin building the future." Indeed, the group has learned that the more resource-deprived an area is, the more there is to learn about what a future might look like. As they say, "The most effective strategies for us are the ones that work in situations of scarce resources and intersecting systems of oppression because those solutions tend to be the most holistic and sustainable."

Approach to Organizing

Its Organization

DJN began in 2014 when the Allied Media Conference created space for "the Future Design Lab" to "explore alternative visions of the future and begin making them into reality." In 2015, people gathered in a session called "Generating Shared Principles for Design Justice" at the Allied Media Conference in Detroit, and work on the principles began. The Design Justice Network was established in 2016. Its principles were collectively written and edited, with the final version completed in 2018. In 2019–2020, the structure of the group as a dues-paying membership organization was established. The basis of its organization is their signatories who can engage more deeply within the network, serve on the steering committee, volunteer to facilitate a working group, and/or organize local nodes.

Its Organizing

While DJN may not teach organizing in isolation from its envisioning-the-future mandate, it is clear that skills with technology, data, shared storytelling, community narratives, design principles are forms of collective knowledge production meant to galvanize a community to direct their concerns around specific demands. As DJN says, "the strongest solutions happen through the process, not in a moment at the end of the process," implying that the teaching of organizing might best be embedded in the process by which the group gathers its members and sets about listening and formulating their thoughts and hopes. They also are inspired by the AORTA Cooperative's Guide to anti-oppressive facilitation for democratic process.[5]

Many resources are available on the DJN website, from audio and video, activities and various translations of the Design Justice Principles.

Notes

1 CASE STUDY write-up is based on Robb's September 2023 ABC School presentation and written exchanges with Robb between Nov. 18–26, 2023.
2 CASE STUDY write-up was developed via and quotes come from exchanges with DS4SI between Nov. 18–26, 2023.
3 Design Studio for Social Intervention. "What Does it Mean to Live in a Neighborhood?"
4 CASE STUDY write-up was developed via and quotes come from exchanges with DJN between Nov. 18–26, 2023. https://designjustice.org/.
5 AORTA, "Anti-Oppressive Facilitation for Democratic Process."

RACE AND SPACE

(S, M, L) Dark Matter U (DMU)

Raison d'Etre

Dark Matter U (DMU)[1] is a democratic network that aims to create anti-racist models of design education. It is guided by the following Manifesto (Figure 2.17):

> We cannot survive and thrive without immediate changes toward an anti-racist model of design education and practice. Existing systems have not been able to transform away from centering and advancing whiteness, through their reliance on an implied dominant and racialized subject and audience. The impacts of that centering are widespread and can be felt in the inequities that global extraction, racial capitalism, and colonialism have created. The earth and the majority of its people have suffered tremendous harm as a result. Collective liberation cannot only occur within the confines of individual institutions.

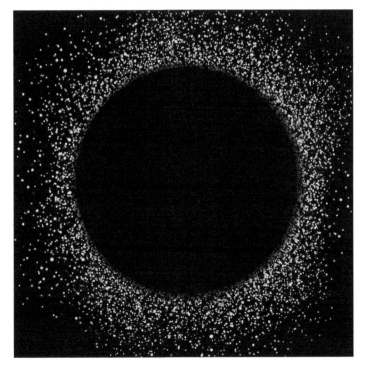

FIGURE 2.17 Dark Matter U (DMU) logo. Image by Dark Matter U, 2020.

Dark Matter U's goals are to create:

1 New forms of knowledge and knowledge production through radical anti-racist forms of communal knowledge and spatial practice that are grounded in lived experience.
2 New forms of institutions within a rhizomatic, counter-hierarchical network that facilitates equitable resource distribution.
3 New forms of collectivity and practice that democratize models of practice, education, and labor at all phases of production.
4 New forms of community and culture that expand the circle of those contributing to anti-racist design pedagogy and practice.
5 New forms of design that open the possibilities and methodologies for designing the built environment.

DMU's network operates inside and outside existing systems "to challenge, inform, and reshape our present world toward a better future." In their "aim to challenge dogma and effect meaningful change," they span multiple locations, ideologies, and opportunities.

Approach to Education

DMU supplies an education that covers varied types of dissemination, audience, and content. DMU courses are co-taught by two or more instructors; students and teachers are asked to share from their own perspectives; its courses are found in traditional academies and outside academia in the community; it reconsiders standard studio and seminar content and understands both as a mix of research, design, and engagement; and it brings together students from multiple institutions in one course.

DMU uses four modes of exposition: (1) Studios and seminars: coordinating studios and seminars remotely across two or more schools of architecture; (2) Partnerships and fellowships: engaging communities in research/education/organizing efforts outside traditional university structures; (3) Workshops and teach-ins: "selling" seminar courses that DMU has developed in-house to various institutions; and (4) Exhibitions: making available in-house or co-produced installations.

In this array, DMU provides numerous case studies, many of which operate in more than one scale. Some are listed below:

Gowanus Neighborhood Design Fellowship, "Foundations of Design Justice." This six-month course, offered in summer 2021 in partnership with the Van Alen Institute, an urban-oriented non-profit, was not a studio in the normal sense, but a model of what studio content, teaching, and participants could and should be.[2] It gathered residents of Gowanus,

Brooklyn, NY, to "consider ways design and art can make Gowanus a more equitable, inclusive place," but the design work was done by non-traditional "students"—in this case, twelve Neighborhood Design Fellows, residents who were paid to go to "class" facilitated by DMU members, Nupur Chaudhury, Jerome Haferd, and A.L. Hu. The brief given was to work toward "the future they imagine for their community" and then share what they learn with local officials and the wider community.

The curriculum was transposed from a collaboratively developed syllabus for DMU's Foundations of Design Justice course taught at multiple academic institutions in winter and spring 2021. One specific result of the efforts was a co-developed pamphlet that outlined issues and existing conditions of the underutilized Gowanus Houses Community Center, which was shared at Van Alen's annual block party that year. In the Fall of 2021 and the Spring of 2022, collaboration with the Fellows continued through a design studio at the University at Buffalo, "Our Space and Design With," in which Fellows were invited as guest speakers, collaborators, and critics for various design projects cited in Gowanus. Students' proposals responded to their engagement with the fellows and worked through complex realities of multiple voices, scales, and fields of expertise. Taking on a familiar approach to some of the work, the Van Alen Fellows developed a narrative and vision for the community members advocating for their space.

This is a model for organizing at the SMALL scale not only because it turns the missing others, the community, into students in the class but also because it takes the studio out of the institutional classroom; it is a model for MEDIUM, because it conflates design with research, and both with developing organizational skills. It is a model for LARGE, because the studio is jointly offered with a non-profit and operates outside of traditional academia.

Carleton/Kent State Studio, "Collective Bodies." When asked to teach a studio at Carleton University in Ottawa, Canada, DMU did an internal call for potential instructors. Four members raised their hands—Jelisa Blumberg, Curry J. Hackett, Jenn Low, and Quilian Riano—forming two pairs, with each pair taking one of two six-week modules. The first module, "For–With: An Individual Practice Towards Collective Expression," examined the spatial qualities of Black collective performance; the second, "Cooperative Futures," examined collectivization as exemplified by Black cooperative entrepreneurship in Cleveland, Ohio. Though developed for and with Carleton, it also was taught alongside Riano's curriculum at Cleveland's Kent State University.

This course model operated at multiple scales. At the SMALL scale, it championed the design of activism, research, and diagramming, while offering an alternative to the "single-critic" format. At the MEDIUM scale, it jettisoned traditional, siloed categories of expertise. At the LARGE scale, the model showed the importance of consulting educators outside traditional pedagogical and administrative categories and a singular institution.

Tuskeegee, Seminar Module—First Year Introductory Class, "Careers in Architecture and Construction." This course, set up with faculty and alumni from Tuskeegee, together with five DMU members, was based on the varied experiences of the five DMU teachers in the architectural space. This is a model for MEDIUM for its co-coordination, its teaching from lived experience, and its re-conception of what knowledge is considered "foundational."

University of Utah and Florida A&M; University of Michigan and SUNY Buffalo; Drexel University—Seminar Modules, "Foundations of Design Justice." An evolving series developed by brainstorming among DMU members that has developed a "live" co-written syllabus and organized guest lecturers, it offers five modules: Intro to Design Justice; Community Work and Power Building; Infrastructure and Neighborhood; Housing; and Workforce and Equity Development. These courses model new forms of knowledge production through radical anti-racist forms of communal knowledge and spatial practice that are grounded in lived experience, as well as through the co-development of its teaching and its focused intent on educating for structural pedagogical change. They also seek to empower students by operating under community agreements between both students and instructors.

Columbia GSAPP Seminar, "Power Tools." This seminar taught power mapping to understand how discriminatory spatial policies are organized; it taught design tools to combat such policies and their spatial outcomes. Deliverables were designs, not papers. This is a model for MEDIUM for teaching organizing as a curricular topic, and for the conflation of design with research, theory, and history.

Yale and Howard University; Columbia GSAPP and Tuskeegee University—Cross-Listed Seminars, "Fugitive Practices." These cross-listed courses teach "fugitive practices" and forms of urban difference and change, doing so via analyses of black cultural performances. These model MEDIUM for the same reasons listed above.

DMU Roster Affiliated Courses: These are courses that are already taught at existing architecture schools or are in development by DMU members. After approval by the general DMU membership to be registered as a DMU standard offering, the courses are made available to schools of architecture desirous of BIPOC material. Some of these courses ask students to design their own program. This is an appropriate model for MEDIUM as an unusual approach to generating a curriculum or invading an existing one. It also is appropriate for LARGE for setting up courses that could themselves constitute a parallel non-accredited school.

Approach to Organizing

Its Organization

Dark Matter U is a democratic, distributed network consisting of a volunteer-led, BIPOC group of 200+ members that started in July 2020. They are organized around a central, self-determined core group that consists of people co-leading areas related to People (growing membership), Content (curriculum), and Opportunity (grants and relationships with other organizations). In addition to this Core, there is Support, comprised of those focusing their efforts on specific projects; Advisory, consisting of those who have reduced capacity, but are still looking to stay engaged. Beyond Core and Support is the Network Roster, those who teach, have taught, or are interested in teaching or engaging with academic institutions in some way.

Its Organizing

The five pedagogical aims of DMU—new forms of knowledge and knowledge production; new forms of institutions within a rhizomatic, counter-hierarchical network; new forms of collectivity and practice that democratize models of practice, education, and labor; new forms of community that expand anti-racist design pedagogy and practice; and new forms of design—are achieved through a commitment to organizing. Most of the seminars and studios teach tools for organizing, be it power mapping, fugitive practices, structures for cooperativization, or protests.

At a meta-level, the DMU organization is a demonstration of the principles they are teaching and sharing: working together is better than working alone; organization is how change is made. The varied ways that DMU intersects with existing institutions means that they regularly confront institutional traditions that resist shared material, shared teaching, coordinating between institutions, distinct schedules, and distinct modes of evaluation. These challenges are only overcome through rigorous internal organizational principles and structures.

(M) Race, Space, and Architecture (RSA)

Raison d'Etre

Race, Space & Architecture (RSA)[3] is an open-access, web-based curriculum. At the project's core is an understanding of racialization as a simultaneous process of violent displacement—of person, land, future—and emplacement through citizenship status, territory, built objects, and knowledge forms (Figure 2.18).

FIGURE 2.18 Race, Space & Architecture: An Open-access Curriculum. Six Frames: Circulating. Image by Race, Space and Architecture, 2020.

A project that relies on spatial references from around the world, it asks what a curriculum on interdependent space-making and race-making might look like. The curriculum "recognizes a lineage of racialized hierarchies endemic to capitalist systems and cultural life that extend from colonialism to coloniality, slavery to incarceration, liberalism to subordination, and sovereignty to populism." It questions both the subject of "race" and the subject of architecture. It looks at how individuals are rendered as laborer, domestic worker, or immigrant in legal and cultural terms, in comparison with how the architectures of camp, compound, and detention center solidify the symbolic and lived forms of these positions.

The curriculum conveys how struggles for social justice are galvanized through space in the convening powers of the margins, and in the arrangements of material and practices that together stake a place. Dance halls, streets, and spiritual interiors are counter architectures in which circuits of connection, processes of validation, and alternative ways of inhabiting the world are established. Equally, it is compelled by the possibilities of drawing on wide geographies and histories to explore particular arrangements of political and economic power, and everyday practices and spatial typologies.

The goal of the curriculum is to invite different audiences into varied website explorations. In a portal on "engagements," for example, the website invites potential contributors to reflect on their own spatial practices, or a portal on "soundings" gathers a selection of readings and text responses. These soundings draw in varied voices, and have provided a mode to expand the sites, literature, and geographies not included in the initial phase of the curriculum. The curriculum is an intentionally evolving work in progress.

Approach to Education

RSA is a platform of constellations: projects, ideas, writings, and provocations that have and continue to inspire its work. RSA is a hostess of engagements. It aims for lively thought—embracing the fuzzy edges of ideas-in-formation and the crafting of weird ruptures that bring to the fore that which ordinarily lies beyond. In that sense, it is a handing over of invited contributions and originally commissioned pieces that engage with the work of the project and offer something new in return.

In the RSA curriculum, architecture is a way of imagining, building, and validating a world. Architecture is bricks and mortar, the accumulation of built forms, and the practices that produce these. It also is a professionalized institution existing as a highly mediated form of knowledge-making that interacts with speculators, planning authorities, and local communities for its pay checks, compliance, and legitimation. RSA challenges these institutions.

The curriculum is organized through frames that describe specific processes of power and racialization and the spaces and built forms in and through which they are sustained and transgressed. The curriculum's six frames each capture an ongoing process of racial ordering that is both spatial and material: centralizing, circulating, domesticating, extracting, immobilizing, and incarcerating. This structure allows for the placement of different geographies side by side, for connecting processes and exploring relations between apparently dissimilar architectures. Multimedia content within reinforces the richly creative ways in which "race,", space, and architecture are present in poetry, stories, and moving images—and thereby enable seeing differently.

Each frame is populated by links to groupings, projects, and images that help to reveal the textures and formal dimensions of race-making as it unfolds in space and architecture. Some of the links are to projects about the rampant dispossession of people from spaces and buildings in which they form lives and livelihoods. Others lead to insights about activism, and how protest emerges and is sustained in and through buildings and spaces. Others still lead to sites that illuminate different ways of reimagining human connection and disconnection, providing a vocabulary of different ways of thinking, learning, and acting.

None of the frames or lists are in any way definitive, complete, or precise. They are collections and selections of material that intentionally are varied in geography, discipline, and form; they intend to provide an engaging and varied entry point into ways of thinking about "race," space, and architecture. In this way RSA hopes to reconstitute the notion of an archive as a messy, incomplete collection, and selection of materials, that is enriched by a variety of forms of knowledge and reference points drawn from across the planet.

Approach to Organizing

Its Organization and Its Organizing

RSA is curated by Huda Tayob, Thandi Loewenson, and Suzi Hall. All the work involved in imagining and initiating the RSA curriculum happened over regular, extended conversations. Care, in this sense, is dialogic. In the beginning, these conversations were sustained by developing a shared repertoire—discussing texts, watching films, and looking at images together. This helped to dissolve some of the hierarchies that are prevalent in academia, foregrounding more centrally the curators' respective life experiences, and allowing for different kinds of co-authorship. The trio also curated a few workshops that accommodated conversations across disciplines, as well as among varied publics. This resulted in a document for download as a work-in-progress, a way of fleshing out the frames, prior to the formation of the website.[4] The website itself became something of a convening tool, where different parts of the project expanded over time.

The work remains unfinished, and there is no certainty for going forward around the maintenance or release of the project.

Notes

1 CASE STUDY write-up was developed via and quotes come from exchanges with Dark Matter U between Nov. 18–26, 2023. https://darkmatteru.org/.
2 Van Alen funded the students with a *Neighborhood Design Fellowship: Gowanus* supporting a six-month program for the (upto) 12 Gowanus residents—designers and non-designers alike.
3 CASE STUDY write-up was developed via and quotes come from exchanges with RSA between Nov. 18–26, 2023. https://racespacearchitecture.org/index.html.
4 Tayob and Hall, *Race, Space and Architecture.*

CAREWORK/SURVIVAL

(S) Clever/Slice

Raison d'Etre

Clever/Slice[1] is a global space founded in New York City to share in-progress creative work as a way to counter the classic critique experienced in art and design education.[2] The group gathers monthly either in-person or online following a framework known as the *Critical Response Process*. This approach is specifically designed to encourage equitable, inclusive, and focused feedback, with the aim to foster progress in creative work (Figure 2.19).

Clever/Slice adopts an inclusive stance, welcoming a diverse array of media, scopes, and scales as well as individuals from all over the world with diverse backgrounds in the belief that diversity catalyzed through productive feedback can improve the creative output of participants.

FIGURE 2.19   Clever/Slice Session 51, Brooklyn NY: Together, we cozied up in Prospect Heights with pizza and heard about Anam and Dylan's fascinating and beautiful collaboration with ManyMany. They shared the story of their project highlighting their circular design and clever communication process with women in Pakistan. Photograph by Clever/Slice, 2023.

When they gather in-person in New York City, they do so at the presenter's home or studio (complete with pizza); when they gather virtually, they do so over Zoom. This dual approach facilitates global participation, extending an invitation to creative minds worldwide to join a collaborative and nurturing platform.

It could be asserted that design education and critique are inseparable, as the latter serves as the cornerstone upon which the former is constructed. The critique, in the academic context, represents the evaluative mechanism through which student work is rigorously assessed. In this sense, design education is correlated with the ubiquitous practice of critique, a concept that often invokes a sense of trauma among students.

Despite the pervasive role of critique in design education, the context in which this practice unfolds remains an underexplored facet. Regrettably, it is infrequent for educators to contemplate the very questions posed to students regarding their creative work when it comes to the critique itself. That's the core reason why this initiative proposes an informal setting that deconstructs the traditional approach to critique through the Critical Response Process.

Approach to Education

Clever/Slice is based on two basic assumptions, first that the work presented in the space is meaningful, and that the work is in-progress. The goal is to help people ascertain the direction of their creative work and what is required to facilitate movement forward.

After examining the history of the critique, Clever/Slice was created to counter the academy.[3] Unlike critiques in school, which often shuts down learning, "critique can be changed to promote learning, to inspire students to do more and better work, and to teach them how to present and speak about their work with more clarity. It is also an opportunity for critics to question and evaluate the way in which they judge and respond to design work."[4]

The first twenty minutes of the sessions are dedicated to a communal meal of pizza and introductions. Following that, a session starts with slides of the Clever/Slice manifesto that shares the values and intentions of the session. After reading the manifesto, the steps for the Critical Response Process are explained, along with the role of the facilitator. Finally, Clever/Slice participants share their in-progress work through a segment called a "Hot Slice." They have seven to ten minutes to present. Once the presentation is complete, the Critical Response Process begins with "Statements of Meaning"—participants state what was meaningful, evocative, interesting, exciting, or striking in the work they have just witnessed. This is followed by "Artist Questions"—the presenter poses a few questions to the group and asks for and receives answers. The third step is "Neutral Questions"—participants ask questions without an embedded opinion to the presenter, and they respond. The final step is "Permissioned Opinions"—the participants, now with a strong understanding of how the presenter would like to push their work forward, give meaningful suggestions for the project.

According to the organizers, Sam Bennett and Will Fryer, "it is time to take back the crit" because they claim that we must "reconsider the context in which critique occurs, when it occurs, and explore critique as a communicative context of its own, one which can be reshaped for the better."[5]

Approach to Organizing

Its Organization

Sam Bennett and Will Fryer started Clever/Slice in 2018, alternating organizing and facilitating. Since 2019, Bennett has been doing it on her own. The group is completely free and volunteer driven. Clever/Slice has a mailing list on MailChimp, promotes on Instagram, and manages tickets through Eventbrite. Whoever hosts orders the pizza and suggests a $5 donation. While it is highly organized, it has no official organizational or business designation; it is not, for example, a non-profit. At the monthly meetings, hosting rotates while Bennett organizes and facilitates.

Its Organizing

Clever/Slice sessions are two hours long and are limited to twelve participants. At the sessions, three pivotal changes to the critique are made. First, they use Liz Lerman and John Borstel's four-step "Critical Response Process" or CRP, which "strategically sequences feedback so that all parties are actively and equally communicating."[6] The second change is that only unfinished work is presented at the sessions. Lastly, the review of the work is done in a domestic interior. Bennett and Fryer believe that this change in setting, from an established institution to home, results in a drastic shift in the critique process and thereby makes the community, not the artist, creative.

(s, m) RIOT

Raison d'Etre

RIOT[7] is a research and design laboratory associated with the Institute of Architecture at the Swiss Federal Institute of Technology Lausanne (EPFL). It gathers students and educators around its pedagogical intent: to encourage projects that stop building, house everyone, change the value system, halt extraction, revolutionize construction, fix the office, reform the school, "don't dig", and take care (Figure 2.20).

Construction is one of the main drivers of global warming and of environmental and social damage. Yet, we need homes, schools. Suspending new building activity, with Lausanne as a case study, the studio seeks to work out alternatives and pave the way toward an insurgent design practice.

Stop Building!
A Moratorium on New Construction – The Case of Lausanne

Studio BA6 (Malterre-Barthes), Studio MA2 (Malterre-Barthes)
Meet on IS-Academia and @riot_epfl

FIGURE 2.20 Stop building! A Global Moratorium on New Construction, the case of Lausanne. Image by Charlotte Malterre-Barthes/RIOT/ Leonard Streich, 2023.

Believing that design disciplines must pivot and wholeheartedly face the current social and climatic urgencies by rewiring themselves toward mitigating and repairing the harm, the research and design laboratory RIOT (Research and Innovation On architecture, urban design and Territory) utilizes tactics and strategies to radicalize the field—*by design.*[8]

RIOT is dedicated to changing the discipline of architecture via its educational apparatus. "To paraphrase Fred Moten, decolonizing, depatriarchalizing, and decarbonizing the university may not be possible; still, these decolonial, emancipatory, and non-extractive works are to be conducted within the institution."[9]

There are two aspects to the RIOT program relevant to organizing architecture education. The first is its commitment to changing the pedagogy and curriculum of architecture education as exemplified by their "Framework for Curriculum Repair," developed with Dubravka Sekulić, which encompasses the following principles: situatedness; prioritizing reuse; interrogating material flows; challenging individual authorship; challenging hierarchies, but accepting responsibilities; challenging property; recognizing labor; adopting an anticolonial way of seeing; complicating "neutrality"; critically engaging with images; entangling with other species; intergenerational thinking; and interrogating the idea of home and house.

The second is a commitment to stop new construction, as exemplified by the option studio offered by one of its members, Charlotte Malterre-Barthes, at Harvard GSD in the Spring of 2022. The Harvard GSD studio was entitled "Moratorium on New Construction." It was controversial, mocked on social media by some: How could an architecture studio not promote building? RIOT asks: How is degrowth not architecture?

Approach to Education

This is RIOT's approach to education: "Teaching is unlearning as much as learning and relearning. RIOT is set to contribute to a new spatial social contract centering on racial, social, and environmental justice—primarily through and within the studio. Advocating for a true curriculum revolution, we strive to change power relations in architecture and urban design while understanding that the education of designers is but one way to foster change."[10] It is a pedagogy based on research on the political economy and its agents, "from real-estate mechanisms to housing policies and sustainability norms."

The Harvard" Moratorium on New Construction" studio was unusual for recognizing that unbuilding is a form of design, as well as understanding the studio to be equal part research and experimental production. It replaced standard progression with more autonomous episodes: Legal Instruments; I Prefer Not To; Situated Knowledges (with sites selected by students, i.e., Mumbai, Houston); A Moratorium; and Unsettling Possibilities, the final projects.

A new iteration of the studio, "Stop Building: The Case of Lausanne," took place in Spring 2024 at EPFL. These studios fit into a "moratorium" pedagogical cycle with the agenda of teaching architecture "without building" and conducting systemic critiques of the construction sector—from the university to the office and the construction site.

The studio is one aspect of RIOT's pedagogical reform. They also offer seminars, workshops, research, field work, and doctoral projects. They produce publications, talks, and exhibitions and workshops in addition to their more traditional courses.

Approach to Organizing

Its Organization

RIOT is the work of Charlotte Malterre-Barthes appointed in 2022, with Antoine Iweins, Nagy Makhlouf, Tamara Pelège, Kathlyn Kao, and Summer Islam.

Its Organizing

RIOT sits within EPFL, but its pedagogy and embodiments reach across different institutions. It primarily identifies as a space for re-organizing architecture education to change a discipline in dire need of transformation. It sees itself as a commons, and as such, understands itself as a project experimenting in organizing both itself and the world it wants to produce. RIOT—by nature of its name, is also a space of dissent, and as such, supports student associations and groups that conduct political work within and outside of the school (i.e. Drag-lab, Drag-UE, L'Atelier, Parity Front, Furtive Studios).

(L) School of the Apocalypse (SoA)

Raison d'Etre

School of Apocalypse (SoA)[11] was a silo-agnostic education project rooted in artistic institutions that asked—in light of technological acceleration, ecological collapse, and cultural revolution—how do we survive? How do we live now (Figure 2.21)?

[S]o many people feel like we are approaching some sort of boundary, or paradigm shift, whether ecological, technological or cultural/spiritual, and we wanted to ask why. We wanted to interrogate whether this sense of impending doom—or revelation—was really such a new feeling, and if so what experiences and conditions were connected to it.

SoA organizers observed that "The tools of survival always seem to be defined in terms of violence or defense. And yet, clearly, we would hardly recognize ourselves if we hadn't also developed systems of trust and care and nurture. So why do these more constructive resources go unrecognized?"

SoA asked artists, makers, and communicators to question the tools of creativity—reason, sensing, feeling—in an apocalyptic world: how does creativity engage possibility; how is communication related to survival; and what roles do cultural forms—music, dance, storytelling, image-making—play in the transmission of knowledge and the creation of society. SoA presented these questions as "a way of asking about our own

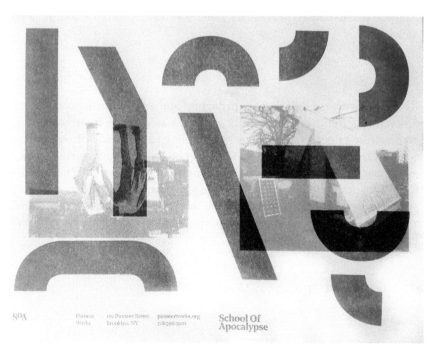

FIGURE 2.21   School of the Apocalypse (SoA) pamphlet. Image by SoA, 2016.

orientation to society/reality/creativity as a process of ongoing inquiry, rather than a fixed set of information or skills."

Approach to Education

SoA was a multi-course educational program at Pioneer Works through June 2016, and at Sunview Luncheonette through April 2018. It had around two hundred participants and produced more than a dozen different projects. The school examined connections between creative practice and notions of survival through courses and programming that applied theoretical and practical experience to intellectual investigation. It took the position that "[w]hen learning is seen as a primary activity of experience rather than an institutional practice; it can take many different forms." They took it one step further, "When other people's experience is recognized as a valuable resource for understanding the learning space... '[s]chool' becomes a way to create time for ideas and practice that might not otherwise find a place in daily activity. It enables risk by creating support, and by transforming failure into a tool for reflection."

The SoA was a space for slowing down, for simplifying, but also for thinking more broadly. For them, the idea of art education was not just about learning a set of techniques, but about finding a community of collaborators who will help to think critically about their work. SoA's vision of a school was one in which the intensity of people's commitment depended on their own interest and not according to their institutional definition. In that way, structure, and order were required, but SoA avoided establishing themselves as experts with answers, as well as presenting themselves as judges controlling other people's investigations. And finally, SoA wanted the school to be free of cost.

Approach to Organizing

Its Organization

"The core structure of SoA is based on the meeting structures of the Quaker Church with its set of tools for joint decision-making in everything from business questions to interpersonal disputes." In this, the SoA's primary format was the "monthly meeting." It met at the same time every month and had presentations and discussions on themes decided by the administration group. Anyone could join at any time. Once every three months, they had a "quarterly meeting"—platforms for suggesting subjects of research, as well as presenting work that had been done. Anyone could suggest a research topic or project at these meetings; there was no requirement for prior attendance. This proposal process was the only way that subjects were determined. A subject of research moved forward and became a "working group" as long as the person who presented the idea could find two other people to become collaborators. "Working group" topics were posted online on the SoA webpage and Facebook group, completely open to the public. People suggesting topics gave a five- to ten-minute presentation at the quarterly meeting and then had one month to convene a meeting with potential collaborators to confirm a project. The groups had three months to develop their project, and each defined their own way of working. They presented the results of their work at the following "quarterly meeting" and also online on the SoA website. All working groups could continue working for as long as they liked and there was no limit to the number of working groups that could form.

The SoA was discontinued in April 2018.

Its Organizing

In modeling its gatherings on Quaker meetings, the SoA was practicing and modeling communal decision making and consensus for change. Just as everyone in a Quaker meeting is invited to talk, and the moments of silence between speakers insist on listening and respect, the groundwork is made for collective identification.

The school did not teach organizing as much as recognize that, in developing a network of artists concerned with survival, they were building a community for everyone.

Notes

1 CASE STUDY write-up was developed via and quotes come from exchanges with Bennett between Nov. 18–26, 2023. https://samiamido.com/Clever-Slice.
2 Bennett, "Clever/Slice."
3 Bennet made clear that the aim of the school was an enactment of academic resistance, not an analysis/history of the critique. She and her colleague Ari Elefterin created "Re-imagining the Critique" where they do test alternative feedback methods and explore workshops with faculty and students. Bennett and Elefterin, "Re-Imagining the Critique."
4 Bennett and Fryer, "Taking Back the Crit: Contextualizing through Feedback."
5 ibid
6 Lerman, "Critical Response Process."
7 CASE STUDY write-up was developed via and quotes come from exchanges with RIOT between Nov. 18–26, 2023. https://riot.today/.
8 RIOT, "RIOT."
9 ibid
10 ibid
11 CASE STUDY write-up was developed via and quotes come from exchanges with Despont between Nov. 18–26, 2023. https://www.catherinedespont.com/school-of-apocalypse.

FEMINISM/GENDER

(XL) Parlour

Raison d'Etre

Parlour[1] is a feminist organization that aims to increase equity in the built-environment professions. The organization's work encompasses a comprehensive, intersectional approach (Figure 2.22). As they write:

> Parlour is a research-based advocacy organization working to improve gender equity in architecture and the built environment professions. As

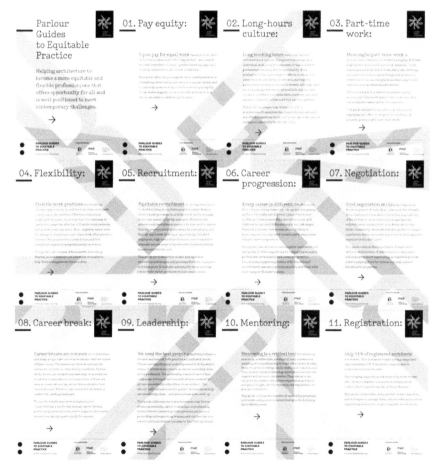

FIGURE 2.22 Parlour guides to equitable practice. Image courtesy of Parlour, 2014.

activists and advocates, we aim to generate debate and discussion. As researchers and scholars, we provide serious analysis and a firm evidence base for change. As active participants in Australian architecture, we seek to open opportunities and broaden definitions of what architectural activity might be.

Based in Australia, Parlour's influence is global. As an organization that offers innumerable strategies for people to gather, to fight institutional bias, to transform the profession, and to change education, it is a source of significant information about the biases in architectural practice, more so than a traditional academic school.

Approach to Education

Parlour's essential activism puts organizing front and center in a way not possible in a traditional "school."

It undertakes research producing both quantitative and qualitative findings. Their emphasis on research and data has been a major aspect of its success and ability to institute change, with data analysis led by Gill Matthewson. Parlour has an extensive editorial program and a huge editorial archive and repository. The programs bring people together in various forms—symposia, exhibitions, workshops, publications, lectures, and social media—but those that are specifically educational are listed here:

Parlour LIVE!

1 Deadly Djurumin Yarns was a Parlour event grounded in the experiences of First Nations women in the built-environment professions. The yarns understand storytelling as an important mode of knowledge exchange.
2 Stepping Up is an extensive editorial and event program directly aimed at changing and improving workplaces. It includes developing and implementing workplace policies and protocols and reshaping organizational cultures and habits to better support equity. Each month's meeting explores a specific topic through a set of articles and an online conversation.
3 Light at the End of the Tunnel ran weekly throughout the pandemic, aiming to equip people to make the profession architects want and need. It offered mutual support, solidarity, and camaraderie to isolated architects as they navigated the world of online work. (The 2021 sessions were presented in partnership with the University of Melbourne. The 2020 sessions were in partnership with Monash University.)

Marion's List

Marion's List, dedicated to the legacy of Marion Mahony Griffin, a prominent Chicago architect who made significant contributions to Australian architecture, is a compilation designed to help organizations and individuals find a broader range of people to participate in opportunities such as talks, panels, juries, sessional teaching, critiques, writing, and criticism. This compilation provides a platform for them to showcase their profiles and connects them to a guide to Wikipedia editing, aimed at increasing the representation of women as leaders in the built environment.

University of Melbourne Convenings

"Transform: Altering the Futures of Architecture" were convenings held at the University of Melbourne in 2013. The series asked, among other things: How is gender equity reshaping and reinvigorating our professions and disciplines? What action is underway? What demands are being made? Where do we each find agency? With what complexities must we engage? What do we need to better understand? How do we each find agency? What are the effects of transforming practice and the professions? This event was influential in kicking off many subsequent events and inquiries.

"Transformations: Action in Equity" was a two-day exchange organized collaboratively by Parlour and the University of Melbourne in 2019. It was organized as a series of discussions investigating key modes of action—organizing from the grassroots, leadership through policy, reshaping the workplace, and rewriting history. It also presented conversations about mental wellbeing, non-binary gender identities and gendered indigeneity.

Parlour Reading Room

Parlour's take on the book club, the Reading Room, invites the Parlour community to organize their own groups around six themes: intersectional feminism; the profession through a feminist lens; considering collective access; intersectional urban environments; "still possible worlds;" and intersectional practice. Each theme includes a set of facilitation guides to prompt discussion and a recording of the Parlour Reading Room Conversation.

Parlour Repository

Parlour has collected the videos and audio recordings from their Live! events programs. The repository is a library of all Parlour events and an accessible library of feminist knowledge production.

Approach to Organizing

Its Organization

Parlour began in 2012 as a website developed by Justine Clark, as part of a research grant funded by the Australian Research Council through the Linkage scheme—which aims to facilitate research connections between academia and industry. Led by Dr Naomi Stead (who, at that time, was at the University of Queensland), the larger project was called *Equity and Diversity in the Australian Architecture Profession: Women, Work and Leadership*. Researchers included Justine Clark, Gill Matthewson, Professor Julie Willis, Dr. Karen Burns, Professor Sandra Kaji-O'Grady, Dr. Amanda Roan, and Professor Gillian Whitehouse. Research partners included the Australian Institute of Architects, Architecture Media and three large architectural practices. When the research funding ended in 2015, Parlour became a non-profit organization—Parlour Inc.—to enable the work to continue. Since then, Parlour's work has been supported through donations and sponsors (Parlour Partners). In 2022, Parlour launched the Parlour Collective, a supporter program with institutional partners including the Australian Institute of Architects, the Association of Architecture Schools of Australasia and universities—including the University of Melbourne, the University of Queensland, Monash University, the University of Newcastle, and the University of Tasmania.

Current office holders are Justine Clark, Naomi Stead, Susie Ashworth, Gill Matthewson, Alison McFadyen, Sarah Lynn Rees, and Alison Cleary.

Its Organizing

Enough said! Parlour walks the walk. Many organizers, including those in the Lobby's Academia Working Group are learning their organizational skills from Parlour.

Note

1 CASE STUDY write-up was developed via and quotes come from exchanges with Parlour between Nov. 18–26, 2023. https://parlour.org.au/.

PLURAL WORLDMAKING

(L) Loudreaders

Raison d'Etre

Loudreaders[1] is an anticapitalist, anticolonial, antipatriarchal platform for reimagining architecture education as a critical spatial practice. It explores alternative frameworks for architectural knowledge through afroqueer, diasporic, anti-racist, indigenous, transfeminist, and other antihegemonic worldviews. Inspired by the practice of "loud-reading," a tactic started by Puerto Rican tabacalera workers at the turn of the twentieth century— wherein a literate worker was hired to read to, or teach, the rest of the workers throughout long days of cigar rolling,[2] Loudreaders views the world through a Caribbean lens. It appreciates the Caribbean as the origin point for the plantation blueprint, and thereby a locus for the revolution blueprint; at the same time, it defines the Caribbean less as a geographic specificity and more as a system of relationships mediated by landscapes and peoples, water, and oceanic trade (Figure 2.23).

Loudreaders is the evolution of a series of antidisciplinary collaborations involving Puerto Rican architect, artist, curator, educator, author, and

FIGURE 2.23   Nicole Cecilia Delgado presents during the summer program Loudreaders Trade School in Rio Piedras, Puerto Rico. Photograph by Jason Mena, 2023.

theorist, Cruz Garcia, and French architect, artist, curator, educator, author, and poet, Nathalie Frankowsi, otherwise known as WAI Architecture Think Tank. Its intellectual roots are connected to a series of projects, including a 2017 collaboration with a member of Garcia's and Frankowski's Beijing-based Intelligentsia Gallery network; poet Christopher Rey Pérez invited Garcia and Frankowski to contribute to the "Tropical Opacity" edition of the *Dolce Stil Criollo* magazine in which they pondered questions of the "post-colonial," or as it was later articulated: "What happens when, like in Puerto Rico, the colony never ends, when it is everywhere?"[3] Garcia and Frankowski pooled their connections and formalized their practices as Loudreaders as a way of providing for students where universities were failing. COVID presented an opportunity to realize an architecture anti-school—to, just as the tabacalera workers had once done, use the tools of academia to reclaim power. As they say, "Everyone deserves access to the tools and knowledge they need to create a more just and equitable world… Loudreaders is committed to providing a space where people from all backgrounds can come together to learn, share, and create."[4]

Approach to Education

Loudreaders seeks to re-wire architecture education. It is a platform of platforms with several expressions: planetaries, an online and itinerant library/archive, a trade school, and a publisher. Each platform, then, has multiple points of entry—virtual and asynchronous (via Zoom, Facebook, Vimeo, and download), material and live (via print and event). In other words, it operates as a fluid and open system of knowledge production.

Planetaries are Loudreaders short-form productions. They are, as their name implies, inherently global in reach. They center on full-day or multi-day events that bring together designers, filmmakers, philosophers, poets, and unlimited others to encourage networks of solidarity across fields, cultures, lands, territories, and ecologies. Planetaries are thematic, focused on a specific idea, project, or text. They involve presentations, discussions, and how-to workshops.

The Loudreaders Trade School is an expanded planetary, multiplying similar activities over prolonged periods of time, including ten-day antidisciplinary learning occurrences in which everyone is a student. Launched as virtual during the 2020 pandemic lockdown, it offered its first in-person iteration in Puerto Rico in the summer of 2023. In the latter version, Loudreaders brought together, in collaboration with the University of Puerto Rico, international participants to contribute to Caribbean-informed loudreading, small group discussions (or destemming), and speculative worldmaking workshops.

The output and records of the planetaries and trade school are consolidated in the Loudreaders archive, an open-source library of alternative architectural knowledge that serves all, particularly those who could not otherwise afford the education. This library/archive also takes the form of traveling installations where workshops and loudreading sessions are offered. The Loudreaders archive and publications, then, provide content for future loudreading. Loudreaders has, at the time of this writing, provided over one hundred lectures and workshops and its publications have been downloaded tens of thousands of times in locations around the world.

Approach to Organizing

Its Organization

Loudreaders, for funding purposes, is registered as a 501c3 non-profit. Its supports include individual donations, publication sales, and grants from the Mellon Foundation, the re:arc institute, the Graham Foundation, and the ACSA.

   Loudreaders is stewarded by Cruz Garcia and Nathalie Frankowski but is a project of their Post-Novis[5] collective. It understands itself as a nonhierarchical, open-access platform in which belonging, and content creation are inclusive. It works internally through collaborative practices and actively seeks external alliances with individuals and organizations. It prioritizes building solidarity in global efforts toward a just and equitable built environment.

Its Organizing

Through Loudreaders, the organizing tactic of loudreading has become an organizing strategy, a systemic approach to forwarding missing appreciations in architecture education. Its planetaries and trade school sessions conflate education and organizing, drawing together those with shared interests and cultivating collective understanding and intention. Its publications are tools for more widely disseminating planetary and trade school knowledge. As a public pedagogy for the built and destroyed environment, it is mobilizing change by building a community of and resources for anticolonial architects. Additionally, Loudreaders engages in direct action, by joining in protest, lending its voice, and making room for sympathetic liberation struggles.[6]

(XL) African Futures Institute (AFI)

Raison d'Etre

The African Futures Institute (AFI)[7] is a physical, digital, and conceptual "laboratory of the future" that focuses on Africa and the African Diaspora as a form of "World Making." It offers a new model of education

FIGURE 2.24   African Futures Institute (AFI) Workshop in Accra. Photograph by Festus Jackson-Davis, 2022.

"that breaks down inherited disciplinary boundaries and brings together the arts, humanities and sciences (Figure 2.24)."[8]

The AFI came into existence at a very specific time in global history, following Black Lives Matter protests worldwide and the escalation in awareness of climate change. It recognizes that a school of architecture ought to prepare students for life beyond both the profession and the academy. It also is interested in a model of architecture education that goes beyond national boundaries and borders, envisioning a post-nation-state disciplinary model that operates at a global, rather than national or regional level.

AFI asks numerous what-if's: What if Africa and the African Diaspora held the key to overcoming so many contemporary challenges of race, environmental justice, new forms of urbanism?"[9] What if a new school of architecture suddenly emerged from a new and unexpected place? What if Africa and the African diaspora held the key to overcoming so many contemporary challenges of race, environmental justice, and new forms of urbanism? What if a new African school could teach the Global North how to embed diversity, equity, and inclusion at the heart of built environment pedagogy? What if a constellation of progressive global voices could find the space and freedom to pursue a truly transformative agenda? What if a new and progressive school could produce a generation of truly innovative African and diaspora architects, unafraid to tackle some of the world's thorniest issues? What if we reversed almost a thousand years of exploitative practices, giving Africa's dynamism and creative energy a space in which to flourish? What if Africa was truly understood as the laboratory of the future?[10]

Approach to Education

Not all XL case studies are schools in the proper sense; AFI is. Its mission is to:

> Transform Africa's built environments by offering a new generation of African architects, urban designers, and policymakers an opportunity to lead the conversation around social and environmental equity, particularly on the African continent. It aims to transform African architectural education by placing climate change, diversity, and access at the centre of architectural pedagogy, not at its margins.[11]

Its aim is to teach people to handle complexity and diversity, "specifically using the wisdom and experiences of marginalized or oppressed groups to renovate architectural education and discourse."

Pedagogically, its aim, on the one hand, is to offer design excellence while opening education to the formerly oppressed: "Rather than choosing between Princeton or a pedagogy of the oppressed, what is the marriage between the two?" And on the other, its aim is to link decolonization to decarbonization. Together, the goal is to "train future citizens, [meant] in the broadest possible sense of the word citizen." Theory and practice are combined, and design is understood in the broadest possible sense, not merely the design of the built environment but the design of information and events. Its initial cohort of students will not join an accredited program, but rather join the AFI's annual Nomadic African Studios—a fully funded program that runs four times a year for a four-week period each time.

Administratively, the school emphasizes African students and architecture proper, but accepts students with no architectural background and not just from Africa. As Lokko, says, "Architecture operates a bit like a nation-state, always protecting its boundaries. Nine times out of ten, the protection of the discipline is about the exclusion of "others." ...This is about African futures not shaped by geographical boundaries."[12] The Nomadic African Studios operate in different locations each year—Accra, Dakar, Kigali, Praia, Cotonou, and Johannesburg in the initial three-year cycle—offering fully funded places to twenty-four graduate students, early-career academics, and early-career practitioners in each studio who "wish to learn more about the issues it will specialize in: diversity, equity, and inclusion in the built environment." Academic faculty are drawn from the AFI's network of academic advisors, who are seconded from their home institutions to teach during the month-long studio four times a year. An international cohort of critics provides feedback, mentoring, and academic insights at each studio, chosen specifically for the intersection of their interests and expertise and the aims of each Nomadic African Studio.

Approach to Organizing

Its Organization

Lesley Lokko founded the AFI in Accra, Ghana, in the spring of 2021. In November of the same year, Lokko was appointed curator of the Venice Architecture Biennale. The demands of running two projects simultaneously meant that the AFI's academic plans were put on hold until after the Biennale ended in November 2023. Instead, it ran a lively program of public events, discussions, workshops, seminars, and symposia in Accra as plans for the academic offerings took shape in the background. With the Biennale successfully delivered, the school anticipates a next cohort of fifty percent students from Ghana, twenty-five percent from other African countries, and the remaining twenty-five percent from beyond—but again, no quotas, and open to all invested in the issue of African Diaspora. In its initial three-year cycle, the AFI is funded entirely through philanthropic means, supported by a consortium of funders including the Ford and Mellon Foundations.

The multiple scales of organizing required to run the AFI is a lesson in and of itself. It is constantly seeking ways to mitigate against the risk posed by its reliance on a single person's vision. Administrative and logistical competencies in Ghana tend to be low; mentorship, exposure, support, and ongoing training are required across all levels of the organization, including finance, compliance, legal, and communications.

The organizational framework is modeled on the ways the various stakeholders (students, teachers, followers, and researchers) interact with each other and the officials in Accra, Ghana. The school itself models the positive outcomes of organizing, stakeholder investment, engagement, and career growth opportunities.

Its Organizing

When AFI says that the school teaches new tools, new languages, and new mechanisms for change, among these tools are organizational skills. Seeing itself as not just a school but as an institute, AFI's reach goes beyond the students and teachers to policymakers, particularly those currently operating in cities across Africa. Each year, one iteration of the Nomadic African Studio is devoted to policymakers and mayoral officers, drawing on existing networks of expertise in city-making such as the Council on Urban Innovation and the African Centre for Cities at the University of Cape Town.

Notes

1 CASE STUDY write-up was developed via and quotes come from exchanges with Garcia and Frankowski between Nov. 18–26, 2023. https://loudreaders. com/.
2 The books that these *lectores* read for the workers were mostly books of philosophy or literature that shared an emancipatory imagination.
3 Dolce Stil Criollo, "Dolce Stil Criollo, Border Theatrics."
4 "Support Loudreaders."
5 "Post-Novis with WAI Think Tank: A Great LOUDREADING Is in the Making. But No One Has Noticed."
6 Text based on a Nov. 3, 2023 interview between Andrea Dietz and Cruz Garcia.
7 CASE STUDY write-up was developed via and quotes come from exchanges with Lokko between Nov. 18–26, 2023. https://www.africanfuturesinstitute.com/.
8 African Futures Institute, "African Futures Institute."
9 Cephas, Marjanović, and Miljački, "This Is for Everyone."
10 Africa Futures Institute, "About the Africa Futures Institute."
11 African Futures Institute, "AFI FAQ."
12 Stathaki, "Venice Architecture Biennale 2023 curator Lesley Lokko on decolonisation, decarbonisation, and diversity."

PART 3
Toward the Planetary

Introduction

Through a scalar study of institutional typologies, Part 2 explores how architecture education—and the discipline of architecture—can be rethought and restructured through the framework of organizing in order to contend with the global crises confronting contemporary society. From the studio to the nation-state, Part 2 details the constraints of, and fallouts from, existing norms, and puts forward "sites of possibility," preliminary approaches for bridging gaps between the status quo and rapidly evolving needs within the built and natural environments. Part 3 takes a further step back, viewing the knowledges and practices of architecture with a planetary conscientiousness. While the planetary can also be considered a scale, its characteristics transcend those of previous scales and impact all of them. Part 3, in turn, takes a simultaneously more speculative and more methodological approach than Part 2. It asks and suggests how architecture might get to a place where it is not simply reactive to burgeoning pressures, but active in a greater effort to work through what it means to live in community with one another and to steward a common planet.

In recognizing the Earth's thriving as the ultimate goal of organizing, Part 3 situates architecture within the vast, interconnected web of influences that shape the inhabitation of the planet. Part 2 starts this process, revealing interdependencies across the scales of architecture education, and demonstrating, as architecture historian Molly Wright Steenson posits, "the notion [that] architecture provides a means for relating elements of a problem that are at different scales to one another."[1] Part 3 picks up

DOI: 10.4324/9781003411284-11

where Part 2 leaves off, advancing transcalarity as vital to global healing and, therefore, to architecture's reconstitution.

Part 3 forwards an internationalist and extranational vision (beyond the nation-state) for architecture as an expanded and decentered field. It presupposes the "building" as interwoven with, and inseparable from, life and power, material and immaterial production, and reproduction. It suggests multiplying the interests, means, methods, roles, and responsibilities of architecture, and speaks to an architecture cognizant and considerate of its ecological, infrastructural, and social impacts. At the same time, it challenges architecture as an isolated, self-referential, and independent domain, and instead develops an understanding of architecture as distributed across wider systems—a shared knowledge and practice held among many human and other-than-human elements within intertwined built and natural environments.

Part 3 has three sections. The first section situates architecture in relation to other worldviews, positing new influences for its dynamics and references. It shares two contrasting frameworks for understanding the planetary—systems thinking and indigenous knowledges—that each offer alternate paradigms for worldbuilding and introduce key concepts for expanding and decentering architecture. The second reflects on the discipline's present and past involvement—or lack thereof—in movements for change in the built and natural environments. It seeks insight for overcoming architecture's insularity in the lessons of these realities and histories. Finally, it sets up a springboard from the writings of this book to its application, positing two practical emphases—language and technology—and visioning a renewed purpose for architectural work to jumpstart and orient the organizing efforts ahead.

Note

1 Steenson, *Architectural Intelligence.*

EXPANDING AND DECENTERING ARCHITECTURE

The magnitude of planetary challenges dwarfs the current capabilities of architecture knowledge and practice. These pressures compel architecture, among other disciplines charged with the livability of the Earth, to expand. This chapter re-envisions architecture, positioned within an interconnected web of disciplines and worldviews—as and in an expanded field—as having the agency to play a vital role in healing, caring for, and maintaining the world. Architecture as an expanded field multiplies the interests, projects, means, methods, roles, and responsibilities of the discipline, opens up its alliances and associations, and necessitates a conscientiousness for global impact. Situating architecture in an expanded, interdisciplinary field requires embracing trailblazing perspectives, interdisciplinary approaches, and inclusive relationships that recognize architecture as one knowledge system among many operating in and serving the built and natural worlds.

The notion of the expanded field in architecture is not new. Architecture adopted the "expanded field" term from Rosalind Krauss's seminal 1979 essay, "Sculpture in the Expanded Field."[1] Krauss's essay inspired a rich body of observational and speculative scholarship on the substance of architecture and its territory. Texts by Anthony Vidler,[2] Louis Rice and David Littlefield,[3] Jane Rendell,[4] and Cidália Silva,[5] for example, all debate architecture's definition and encourage a variety of options for its purview and directions for its ways of working. The main ideas from these precursor expanded field models—disciplinary interdependency and intellectual fluidity—carry over today. Today's expanded field continues to be motivated by questions of universal concern. It is compelled to consider complex interdependencies more deeply, adapt to constant change, and

DOI: 10.4324/9781003411284-12

develop continuously through and in response to collaborative efforts that are accountable to both human and other-than-human wellbeing.

To realize such an expanded field is to decenter architecture. Decentering, or the deprivileging of hegemonic understandings of, and roles in, the built and natural environments, takes two forms: (1) it creates a plural understanding of architectural expertise, and (2) it distributes architectural practices among other communities and fields. In other words, a decentered architecture can no longer be described by a singular canon, nor a singular professional criterium. And a decentered architecture is shared, accessible, inclusive, a porous domain for work in the built and natural environments. Both decenterings open architecture to and reposition it in service to disparate worldviews.

Worldviews

To break away from its existing model, architecture needs new conceptual frameworks. In its expanded, decentered field, architecture is called—through the vanguard of organizing—to reimagine its practices for the pluriverse, or, as Arturo Escobar explains in *Designs for the Pluriverse,* "a world where many worlds fit."[6] Critical to navigating the many worldviews that populate the pluriverse is understanding two versions of subjectivity, one conceived around positionality, the idea that subjectivity stems from one's situated perspective, and the other around the commons, the shared resources accessible to and preserved for all.

Positionality refers to the cultural, social, and historical factors that shape an individual's existential perspective. It is an awareness that experience and identity—including class, race, gender, and sexual orientation—influence the way information is constructed, perceived, and interpreted. In the words of faculty and fellows from the California Institute of Integral Studies, an educational initiative uniquely focused on intersectional[7] philosophies of self, society, and the planet:

> Positionality acknowledges complex differentials of power and privilege while simultaneously identifying the value of multiple ways of knowing and being that arise from our multiple identities. The goal of revealing individual and relative positionality is to de-center dominant ways of thinking and expose multiple ways of thinking as diverse assets for self-knowing and collective-knowing.[8]

Recognizing positionality lays the groundwork to counteract the erasure of diversity propagated by colonial and capitalist powers that benefit only the privileged. Countering this invisibility requires not only acceptance of diverse positionalities, but active elevation of marginalized voices, dismantling of oppressive systems, and redistribution of influence and resources to repair lasting harms.

The commons refers to the natural and cultural resources available to all members of a given society, which contrast to resources privately owned or controlled. The term is frequently used to describe shared natural resources such as air and water—the conditions for a habitable Earth— but it encompasses a much broader set of domains such as public spaces and goods that all members of a society can access and use (parks, streets, town squares, and public transportation), culturally shared knowledges and systems (languages, open-source software, and ethically accessible literature and music), or the "collaborative commons" (principles of collective stewardship, governance, and mutual care). The Earth is the ultimate commons for human and other-than-human life; it encompasses and connects the many interlocking and neighboring commons within and across terrestrial matter. The commons implicates the always-already state of community with others. In the words of Michael Hardt and Antonio Negri, political philosophers and the coauthors of *Empire*, an acclaimed book and critique of globalization:

> We share bodies with two eyes, ten fingers, ten toes; we share life on this Earth; we share capitalist regimes of production and exploitation; we share common dreams of a better future. Our communication, collaboration, and cooperation, furthermore, not only are based on the common that exists but also in turn produce the common. We make and remake the common we share every day.[9]

In organizing, positionality is key to recognizing and supporting the unique contributions of everyone involved in collective action; for practice in the pluriverse, it is a framework for similarly contextualizing architectural expertise. When architects conceptualize their craft as intrinsically bound to shared common spaces and resources, they acknowledge their mutual dependence on and duty of care to wider communities. By situating their practice within an interconnected commons, rather than an isolated domain, designers recognize that they both shape and are shaped by the collective welfare of multiple worldviews.

Together, the notions of positionality and the commons enable architecture to support and be in dialogue with others working for planetary health and interconnectedness. They are entry points into working through and with the worldviews that inform the Earth's many advocates. In the writing that follows, architecture is decentered by two worldviews—one of the sciences and the other of indigenous knowledge—representing groups already active in efforts to address the global climate crisis. Both scientists and indigenous peoples have unique ways of conceptualizing and acting in the environment—through analytical frameworks and ontological understandings, respectively. These distinct approaches do not necessarily align with each other. They are presented, in turn, as introductions to positionalities with which architecture must engage if it is to join the movement to design and shape a just world in a thriving planet. They also provide examples in holding space for difference in the commons of the pluriverse.

Social-Ecological-Technological Systems (SETS)

Systems thinking is a field of study that analyzes how systems shape behavior within a complex world, identifying wholes and mapping relationships between parts. Social-ecological-technological systems (SETS) are a transdisciplinary approach to analyzing the complex interactions between the many systems that traditional sciences—natural and social—have separated. The social systems of SETS encapsulate the behavior, values, decisions, policies, and economies of individuals and groups.[10] The ecological systems instantiate the natural environment, including the wildlife, water, and natural resources that comprise ecosystems and biodiversity.[11] The technological systems refer to the infrastructures, instruments, tools, machines, processes, and techniques used to develop the environment.[12] By structuring measures for considering the layers of relatedness between all three components, SETS offer evidence-based approaches to situating people and the environment across different scales, interconnected throughout the planetary field.

In operational terms, SETS are a mapping technique informed by many sources of information. They chart interactivity and exchange between human interventions in the environment (the social-technological) and complex temporal impacts that a given intervention has on the other-than-human (ecological) world that surrounds it. A step-by-step strategy to SETS mapping begins with identifying the spatial instabilities, conflicts, or resources at stake in a given situation,[13] and contextualizing them with relevant social, ecological, and technological forces.[14] One interaction at a time, SETS mapping analyzes how these systems mutually relate, influence each other, and contribute to the issues identified.[15] SETS follows up by evaluating how changes in one system affect other systems over time,[16] considering insights from diverse disciplines to gain a holistic understanding.[17] There are multiple methods for these analyses and evaluations, each measuring performance according to a specific lens—including innovation, life-cycle, perspective, and risk.[18] A concluding step involves recommending solutions that take into account integrated SETS.[19]

SETS are an evolution of social ecological systems (SES), one of the assessment frameworks developed by political scientist Elinor Ostrom which led to her 2009 Nobel Prize in Economic Sciences, "for her analysis of economic governance, especially the commons."[20] Studying the relationships between communities and resources, Ostrom discovered that, "human beings have tended to formulate sensible rules to help maintain resources that are used on an everyday basis."[21] She synthesized those rules into descriptive methodologies for tracking, predicting, and managing interdependencies between people and the world around them. Ostrom's frameworks are today the go-to tools for science and government to engage quantifiably with the complexity of the environment.

SETS, in particular, are used in environmental science, political science, and urban planning research, including in academic, public, and private settings. Many of the insights generated through the application of SETS increasingly support municipalities and oversight agencies in the development of large-scale and long-term construction projects. In these applications, SETS are posited as, "an undertaking to reflexively bring sustained adaptation, anticipatory futures, loose-fit design, and cogovernance into organizational decision-making."[22] Specifically, SETS are the means by which built environment projects are determined to have negative, neutral/zero, or positive impact on the world[23]—and are, therein, tools that an expanded, decentered field of architecture might use to design in greater harmony with nature and the planetary commons.

Accounting for the layered relationships of cause and effect with SETS constitutes a breakthrough compared to the limited grasp of ecological dynamics characteristic of Western environmental development paradigms. Incorporating SETS into architecture education could enhance learning by embedding traditional architectural practices within a holistic approach, one that anticipates transdisciplinary collaboration informed by social engagement practices necessary for cultivating environmental resilience. Conjoining SETS methodologies to architecture education expands the bounds of architectural design and produces systems-oriented, socially-engaged, technologically-savvy, and environmentally conscious architect-citizens, and places the field of architecture within the landscape of planetary interconnectedness.

SETS also allows organizers to map the interactions and dynamics between how people understand the world, and their material manifestation in built infrastructures and ecological systems. This mapping is essential for strategic organizing that ties grassroots environmental efforts to large-scale movements of capital; it offers a path connecting small-scale interventions with large-scale systems. SETS are not, in and of themselves, a framework for justice. When deployed as frameworks for analysis and action, they can empower organizers to practice within more expansive contexts to bring about change. Organizing is essential to the mobilization of the SETS framework in the pursuit of environmental justice and climate action.

Indigenous Knowledge

Recently, climate abuses and catastrophes have drawn increasing societal attention to indigenous knowledge as a beacon for environmentalism. Indigenous knowledge[24] broadly refers to the distinctive wisdom and practices of people with deep perennial connections to specific lands. It is embodied and intergenerational; it encompasses knowledge based on relational practices among humans, animals, plants, land, water, and other-than-humans. Indigenous knowledge questions positions of spatial and temporal relationality within a larger environmental framework.

Indigenous knowledge, similarly, is gaining momentum in architecture education. Universities are opening schools and departments oriented to indigenous understandings of building as sympathetic with ecology. Huri Te Ao—School of Future Environments, a transdisciplinary school within the Auckland University of Technology, relies on indigenous ways of knowing to work through place-based action.[25] One of the more established of these programs, the Indigenous Design and Planning Institute (iD+Pi) at the University of New Mexico, started in 2011 with the goal of educating and engaging students, faculty, professionals, and community leadership in "culturally appropriate design and planning practices."[26]

The emphases of the iD+Pi, as described in an overview talk on the institute's work, by Theodore Jojola, affiliated faculty and member of the Pueblo of Isleta,[27] demonstrate an application of indigenous knowledge specific to the nineteen indigenous communities that share the lands of contemporary New Mexico's high plains region. According to Jojola, iD+Pi teachings rely on two premises: (1) a conceptualization of knowledge as spiral and (2) a framing of time in increments of seven generations. In the former, all knowing is "place-knowing" that originates in a person's or community's homeland, expands through "migratory-knowing," an appreciation of travel as a seeking of unfamiliar wisdoms, and evolves through mergers of place- and migratory-knowing. "Place-knowing" consists of deep familiarity with both the environmental systems and human traditions, the ceremonies, and responsibilities, into which a person is born or adopted. In the latter, awareness spans seven generations; every person is situated as the middle generation, with conscientiousness for three generations prior and three generations after.

The iD+Pi, Jojola says, recognizes inhabitation as an embodiment of spiral knowledge and an expression of seven generations time. The built form is a simultaneous accommodation of everyday living, ceremonial event, and relations with unseen worlds—conversant with celestial bodies and acknowledging the duality of life and death. Non-temporary building is planned in seven phases, adapting every twenty years to generational insight for one hundred and forty years before settling as a landmark in the community fabric. To guide inhabitation toward these ideals, the iD+Pi works through a design toolkit.

Jojola ascribes three purposes to the iD+Pi toolkit; it steers the setting of aspirations, structures research, and redefines engagement for indigenous-informed community action. Indigenous-informed design aspires to supporting individual community members through their lifecycle of receiving, learning, providing, and teaching; to cultivating demographic balance in the feminine and the masculine, the young and the old; and to managing human and natural resources by prioritizing "land tenure," the notion that inherited space, the collective space of the environment, has the most value. There are three tools for indigenous-informed research in the constructed environment, each an iteration of mapping—one that compares agricultural, water, and ecological systems; one that draws out "place-knowing;" and one that locates cultural assets.

The most comprehensive of the tools that Jojola introduces is a participatory process titled with a descriptive acronym, PUEBLO. A means of eliciting community feedback, PUEBLO relies on six prompts. "Painting" asks community members for visual narratives, images that depict individual perceptions of place. "Underneath" is a speculative exercise, an inquiry into the origins of place and its evolution over time. The notion of "East," the cardinal direction of the rising of the Sun, inspires discussion about individual and community nurturing, the resources that are needed to start and sustain the human lifecycle. "Balance" is a consensus building process for defining the qualities of a healthy community. The work of "Love," a word linked with matriarchal tradition, affirms, and orders the community around the role of the mother. And, the final step, "Offerings," directs the community through ceremony, situating it in contribution to a larger context and attendant to the Creator.

Indigenous knowledge is intrinsically local, embedded in the particularities of place. The practices of the iD+Pi are unique to it and, necessarily, cannot be copied directly anywhere else. Because this guide is not anchored in a single, specific locale, its elevation of indigenous knowledge, also, can be only general, open-ended. It forwards, simply, that, when organizing, indigenous knowledge is sited and belongs to local people. To organize for climate change according to indigenous practices means mobilizing locally in solidarity with multiple and diverse other localities, each honoring specificities in individual circumstance, while also recognizing the interconnectedness of unique struggles. And, indigenous knowledge, in the context of worldbuilding, means acting with responsibility and care for the environment so that the Earth can be left in better condition for successive generations.

In an expanded, decentered field of architecture, then, it is important not to co-opt indigenous knowledge for ecocentric building practices. Rather, the work is to open space for and support indigenous people in the stewardship of the environment. Over time, architects have dodged responsibility for the impacts of building, dispersing, and relinquishing it to owners, developers, and contractors through a parceling of property, contracts, and tasks. The building industry, then, has entrusted sustainability certifications, which increasingly are proving spurious[28] and, regardless, are enforceable only until a construction contract closes out, to check its damages. Architecture in service to indigenous knowledge reassumes responsibility and care for the planet. Organizing to rewrite architecture's contractual structures, or developing lifetime maintenance strategies for the environment, for example, are pathways to both supporting indigenous people and honoring indigenous sovereignty. Architects are called to limit the impact of new and existing construction and to work to do so in consultation with indigenous peoples. Architects, herein, become barriers to consumptive and extractive processes and facilitators of more balanced approaches.

Architecture made relational to a worldview informed by indigenous knowledge is called to identify and dismantle deleterious practices of power. Its architects must know when and how to share the work with others. Indigenous knowledge models for architecture the transcendence of disciplinary boundaries in the environment toward the ushering in of localized, holistic practices that prioritize human and non-human life and material and immaterial balance.

SETS and Indigenous Knowledge

At the same time, the mainstream is turning to indigenous knowledge in the search for addresses to the climate crisis, ongoing resistance movements, and calls for sovereignty within indigenous communities and nation-states are reminders that navigating worldviews requires respect, sensitivity, and understanding. Here, the importance of appreciating positionality is made clear. An expanded, decentered architecture may not work in the same way with SETS as with indigenous knowledge. While it is possible for architecture to transgress either, to transgress systems thinking is profoundly different than to transgress indigenous knowledge. Because architecture, currently, has no interrelational practices for connecting its knowledges with others, it is not prepared to do complex outreach; without the sophistication to discern and meet circumstantial boundaries and outlooks, it is likely to transgress. To meaningfully engage the worldviews of "missing others," architecture must cultivate adaptive methods that enable collaborative interdisciplinarity, equitable cultural collaborations, and the capacity to contribute substantively toward collective impact in shaping both constructed and natural environments.

Similarly, architecture is in need of frameworks for upholding the commons, for accommodating disparate worldviews. SETS and indigenous knowledge, as worldviews that both share interests and are at odds, demonstrate this need. On the one hand, both are rooted in an acceptance of the bonds between the material and the living. SETS is tied closely to the ideas of new materialism, "a range of contemporary perspectives in the arts, humanities and social sciences that have in common a theoretical and practical 'turn to matter.'"[29] New materialism expands on the ideas of Marxist materialism, or ideas of interdependence between material conditions and social relations, by recognizing the profound significance of life other-than-human, the environment, and nature in shaping all things human.[30] It argues for the fundamental interconnectedness of the social, technological, and ecological world, positing that power, life, production, and reproduction are inseparable from planetary ecosystems. In comparison, as evidenced by a consensus survey of indigenous peoples around the world, the idea that human, other-than-human, and planetary health are inextricably reflexive of each other, are one and the same, is a widely held tenet of indigenous knowledge.[31]

On the other hand, SETS, as systems thinking, as an extension of the sciences, is an uncomfortable pairing with indigenous knowledge. The sciences, in general, meet indigenous knowledge with friction; for many indigenous peoples, the sciences are associated with expeditions that paved the way for colonizing movements,[32] with human medical experiments,[33] with repetitive dismissals of traditional wisdom,[34] and as logics used to structure ecological harm.[35] Regarding new materialism specifically, Alison Ravenscroft, a scholar of Australian neocolonialism, draws out an indigenous critique of the subject, noting its insular reliance on self-referential arguments:

> [Colonialism's] elision of Indigenous intellectual labors…brings new materialism itself into an unwitting alliance with the very imperialism of the Western sovereign subject that it avowedly strives to undo. So deep is the Western subject's sense of itself as original and self-made that other knowledges, including ones that arose prior to the Western ones, can disappear from view.[36]

In other words, despite alignments, SETS and indigenous knowledge may not always work well together. But, in frameworks that uphold the planetary commons, there is room for such disjuncture.

Frameworks that uphold the planetary commons also encourage the development of mutualities between differing worldviews. Bridging and mending work that is beginning between the natural sciences and indigenous knowledge is such a development. This work is happening through indigenous leaders in the natural sciences like Melanie Goodchild, an Anishinaabe (Ojibway) systems thinking and complexity scholar, whose research focuses on decolonizing systems thinking and whose professional endeavors weave the natural sciences and indigenous knowledge to address climate change.[37] It is happening in natural science and indigenous knowledge collaborations like the prescribed burn partnership between Yosemite National Park and the Southern Sierra Miwuk Nation and the Tuolumne Band of Me-Wuk.[38] And it is prompted by the calls to action issued in the wake of Canada's 2015 Truth and Reconciliation Commission, in which indigenous environmentalists and allies implored natural scientists to redress destructive and racist practices in the sciences.[39]

Tensions in the planetary commons between contrasting worldviews like those of SETS and indigenous knowledge may never fully resolve. However, rather than invalidating one another, their differences contribute to the variety, outreach, debate, and negotiation that describe the pluriverse. Overlaps in divergent perspectives, then, reinforce the interconnectedness binding terrestrial matter, human and other-than-human life, and highlight the grounds for solidarity in the fight for social and ecological justice. As for the cases of SETS and indigenous knowledge, neither one alone can bring about the change needed in the built and natural environments. Yet in both the agreements and differences between these worldviews, there is hope for driving the change so desperately needed. Their dialectic, while marked by opposition, yields new possibilities for collective action to foster the common good.

Notes

1 Krauss's expanded field description builds from a quaternary mapping of disciplines adjacent to sculpture. The map is posited as a diagrammatic tool for making sense of the development in the 1960's of artforms that defied conventional expectations for sculpture and yet were called sculpture. It creates space for these unfamiliar expressions by locating sculpture and its adjacencies, of which architecture is one, as words tied to points in an abstract terrain. It establishes a spectrum whereby works are situated closer in the terrain to what they are and further from what they are not. And it sets up the potential for designations that either are negations or compounds of existing terms. In other words, Krauss's expanded field places disciplines and their works alike in conceptual and material relations. For more, see Krauss, "Sculpture in the Expanded Field."

2 In Anthony Vidler's expanded field, architecture is expanded through new possibilities for form and program inspired by landscape, biology, and the humanities. Conventions are challenged through the introduction of an external influence. For more, see Vidler, "Architecture's Expanded Field."

3 In Louis Rice's and David Littlefield's edited text, architecture's expanded field is transgressive and combinatory. It is made up of instances in which architecture's boundaries are reconsidered, its norms violated, its places resituated, and it practices muddied for experimental and generative purposes. For more, see Rice and Littlefield, *Transgression.*

4 For Jane Rendell, architecture's field is expanded through conditions shared with other fields that have the same or share similar means and methods of production. For more, see Rendell, *Art and Architecture.*

5 For Cidália Silva, architecture is expanded as the understanding of the city grows to encompass the entire urban settlement and by contending with the impermanence and uncertainty of time. For more, see Ferreira Silva, "Architecture as Expanded Field."

6 Escobar, *Designs for the Pluriverse*, xvi.

7 Kimberlé Williams Crenshaw, a leading scholar of critical race theory, in her early positing of the concept of intersectionality, states: "I consider intersectionality a provisional concept linking contemporary politics with postmodern theory. In mapping the intersections of race and gender, the concept does engage dominant assumptions that race and gender are essentially separate categories. By tracing the categories to their intersections, I hope to suggest a methodology that will ultimately disrupt the tendencies to see race and gender as exclusive or separable. While the primary intersections that I explore here are between race and gender, the concept can and should be expanded by factoring in issues such as class, sexual orientation, age, and color." Crenshaw, "Mapping the Margins." Positionality is a consideration of identity—where intersectionality describes compound identities—as it relates to social orders and systems of power.

8 Acevedo et al., "Positionality as Knowledge."

9 Hardt and Negri, *Multitude*, 128.

10 Ostrom, "A General Framework for Analyzing Sustainability of Social-Ecological Systems."

11 Berkes, Colding, and Folke, *Navigating Social-Ecological Systems.*

12 Liu et al., "Complexity of Coupled Human and Natural Systems."

13 Ostrom, "A General Framework for Analyzing Sustainability of Social-Ecological Systems."

14 Waltner-Toews et al., "Perspective Changes Everything."

15 Collins et al., "An Integrated Conceptual Framework for Long-term Social–Ecological Research."

16 Glaser et al., *Human-Nature Interactions in the Anthropocene.*

17 Schlüter et al., "Capturing Emergent Phenomena in Social-Ecological Systems."

18 McConville, "Socio-Technical System Analysis."

19 Bojórquez-Tapia et al., "Addressing Complex, Political and Intransient Sustainability Challenges of Transdisciplinarity: The Case of the MEGADAPT Project in Mexico City."

20 Indiana University, "Honoring Elinor Ostrom, the First Woman to Win a Nobel in Economic Sciences."

21 National Academy of Sciences, "Elinor Ostrom."

22 Chester et al., "Sensemaking for Entangled Urban Social, Ecological, and Technological Systems in the Anthropocene."

23 Gebler et al., "Defining the "Positive Impact" of Socio-Technical Systems for Absolute Sustainability."

24 Indigenous knowledge is an excessively broad category, and a fundamentally colonial construct. It attempts to group the expansive diversity of knowledge from equally diverse peoples and places into one concept by establishing global positional binaries between "indigenous" and "non-indigenous." These monolithic groupings exclude the diverse ways in which groups, clans, tribes, nations, bands, *oyates*, *tiospayes*,* etc., make relations with humans and other-than-humans through intergenerational connections, economies, and modes of governance. In reality, the indigenous condition transcends race, genetic code, and self-identity. It is about acknowledged social connections and collective recognition of belonging to a place or people. This may arise through enrolment, citizenship, and membership, as well as non-status, or honorary, recognition. The term also implies a point of origin that often fails to address deeply localized spatial and temporal knowledge developed over extended time spans. (*The words "oyates" and "tiospayes" come from Dakota, Lakota, and Nakota languages. Oyate refers to "the people." Tiospaye refers to family, extended families, and kin. Both are inclusionary terms not bound by nation-state borders.)
25 See CASE STUDY.
26 The University of New Mexico, "Indigenous Design and Planning Institute: About iD+Pi."
27 Jojola, "iD+Pi Concepts."
28 Clay, Severnini, and Sun, "Does LEED Certification Save Energy? Evidence from Retrofitted Federal Buildings"; Barth, "Is LEED Tough Enough for the Climate-Change Era?"
29 Global Social Theory, "New Materialism."
30 Morton, *Humankind*.
31 Redvers et al., "The Determinants of Planetary Health."
32 Pratt, *Imperial Eyes*.
33 Owens, "Canada Used Hungry Indigenous Children to Study Malnutrition"; Sovereign Union, "'Lab Rats'—Medical Experiments on Aboriginal Children in Care'.
34 Nicholas, "It's Taken Thousands of Years, but Western Science Is Finally Catching up to Traditional Knowledge."
35 Hernandez, *Fresh Banana Leaves*.
36 Ravenscroft, "Strange Weather."
37 Goodchild, "About Me."
38 National Park Service, "Yosemite National Park Fire Managers Partner with Indian Tribes for Prescribed Fire Project."
39 Wong et al., "Towards Reconciliation."

MOVEMENTS TOWARD CHANGE

As the impacts of the climate crisis grow, alongside escalating civic and so-cial upheaval, uncertainty permeates the global environment. This chapter examines the proliferating attempts to counter ecological instability, both present and historical. Across these efforts at all scales, from grassroots to worldwide, architecture frequently plays a marginal or altogether absent role. This holds true whether initiatives are community-driven or institu-tional, employing localized or sweeping interventions.

Architects don't typically have seats at the tables at which environmen-tal policy is written. If they do, they are there as subject matter experts or special issues advocates, and their expertise is fixed to how the overseeing nation-state defines the profession. In 2022, for instance, the American In-stitute of Architects (AIA) claimed credit for specific provisions of the US Inflation Reduction Act[1]—the country's most sweeping built environment legislation in decades. These included expanded building energy codes, funding energy efficiency and emissions reduction, and tax incentives for building reuse and improvement.[2] Though substantial, the AIA's contribu-tions were limited to corrective adjustments within an agenda controlled by more embedded interests. The AIA's work, herein, was that of a latecomer to an infrastructural policy conversation that, by the time the AIA joined, already spanned multiple years and two presidencies.[3] The AIA's own advo-cacy campaign banner, "Buildings Are Infrastructure,"[4] evidences architec-ture's overlooked role and limited scope within public awareness.

Architecture's accessory role in the space of governance reflects the profession's reticence to risk its tenuous position within the capitalist workings of the Architecture/Engineering/Construction (AEC) industry.

DOI: 10.4324/9781003411284-13

In safeguarding its familiar holdings, the profession has fallen behind in developing—much less championing—bold ideas for the future of architectural practice. With the exception of a handful of outlier initiatives like Architecture 2030,[5] truly projective thinking for the environment is coming not from within the profession, but instead from outside voices: agricultural and environmental think tanks, social service organizations, artists and community groups, labor unions, degrowth economists, youth activists, and indigenous peoples.

It is in non-architecture groups that the models for collective action in the built and natural environments are located. In 1990, for example, the Southwest Organizing Project (SWOP), based in New Mexico, wrote a letter to the "Big Ten" environmental organizations naming their racist policies and practices.[6] In the letter, organizers state that people of color had for centuries, "been subjected to racist and genocidal practices including the theft of lands and water, the murder of innocent people, and the degradation of our environment..."[7] It describes six examples of how environmental organizations "continue to support and promote policies which emphasize the clean-up and preservation of the environment on the backs of working people in general and people of color in particular,"[8] while ignoring cultural survival. The letter emphasizes that, "We suffer from the end results of these actions but are never full participants in the decision-making which leads to them."[9] SWOP exposes how powerful institutions oppress those most impacted by hazardous environmental practices. In opposition to these practices, SWOP calls for the full involvement in environmental decision-making of those who historically have been without power. The letter, which took the mainstream environmental community by surprise, led to the organizing of the first People of Color Environmental Leadership Summit in Washington DC in 1991 at which seventeen principles for environmental justice jumpstarted the now prevalent environmental justice movement.[10]

Recent organizing movements, such as The Red Nation, refer to this as "people power." Defined as the power of the collective, people power is practiced through the redistribution of material resources to meet an entire community's needs.[11] In their climate-based action plan, "Red Deal: Indigenous Action to Save the Earth," The Red Nation proposes to extend the Green New Deal,[12] the more progressive and wide sweeping policy proposal that informed the Inflation Reduction Act, by organizing around both explicit environmental protections, as well as free and accessible housing, public transportation, and infrastructure.[13] While these issues are within the purview of architecture, there is no mention of architects in the "Red Deal." Not only is architecture not included in their solution, it is perceived as part of the problem, largely accountable for the current environmental crisis through its complicity with the ruling class and its exploitative capitalist and colonialist practices. The Red Deal implies this complicity, calling for divestment from carceral institutions specifically and development forces generally, in the section, "What Creates Crisis Cannot Solve It."[14] In contrast, movements like #Landback[15] and organizations such as the NDN Collective,[16] have displayed a more nuanced understanding in their calls for land sovereignty and decision-making authority. Their positions recognize the interdependent relationship between built environments and the natural world as multifaceted and complex, rather than mutually exclusive. This awareness creates opportunities for architects allied with these people power movements to act not as power brokers, but as partners invested in environmental stewardship.

Though there are numerous architecture-adjacent standout individuals and groups—including Coleman Coker and Sarah Gamble, authors of *Environmental Activism by Design*,[17] Architects Climate Action Network,[18] and Design Justice Network[19]—architecture is not a go-to motivator of the global environmental movement. With increasing awareness that architecture's status quo is damaging, however, architects in larger numbers are starting to reach out and join the conversation. As the field of architecture opens up, it must not forget the lessons of its own past. After all, architecture has a long tradition of expanding and contracting the breadth of its expertise to meet its own ends.

Past Expansions

Architecture has attempted to be more than it is, more than the sculpture of inhabitable form, more than the management of capital development and construction processes, multiple times in its history. These movements have been as short lived as a couple of decades and lasted as long as half a century. Each time, they are motivated by societal shift; each time, they are overcome by centripetal forces. If architecture finally is to break out of its insularity, it must work beyond the arguments that keep drawing it inward. Each of the following three cases reviews a period of architectural expansion and identifies the reasons for its ultimate contraction. These reasons remain barriers to architecture's expanded, decentered field and are touchpoints for today's organizing.

* * *

Post World War I, the Congrès Internationaux d'Architecture Moderne (International Congress of Modern Architecture or CIAM) organized as a coalition of professional architects to assert their views on urban reconstruction. In semi-regular convenings, architects from around Europe gathered with the purpose of "plac[ing] the new architecture into its 'true economic and social environment.'"[20] Between its founding in 1928 and its dissolution in 1959, CIAM's ideas transformed cities and landscapes around the globe. They also did real harm to local communities, through wrongheaded approaches to urbanism. As a result, CIAM contributed to a loss of standing for the profession. Its heavy-handed approach to building, and the widespread public distrust of architects that it caused, is a cautionary tale for today's organizers.

CIAM's signature document, the Athens Charter, was composed during the fourth meeting of the Congress in 1933. The Charter issued a series of demands: that housing districts should occupy a region's best sites, that all dwellings require a minimum amount of solar exposure, that communities should not be built along transportation routes, that modern techniques should be used to construct high-rise apartment towers spaced widely apart, and that as much land as possible should be set aside for large, green parks. By the 1950s it became clear that the policies CIAM had pursued for the previous two decades were deficient. A group of its younger members argued that the "four functions" of the Athens Charter—living, working, recreation, and transportation—corresponded neither to the ways in which urban problems presented themselves, nor to the means of solving them. In 1953, these younger members, identifying themselves as CIAM 10 or Team 10,[21] went public with their rejection of the Athens Charter and began working toward a new mission statement. They advocated for unique solutions within each of the cities their members represented.[22] As the result of this mutiny, CIAM split into two factions: the older architects against the younger. Not long after, at its 1956 convening, the Congress as a consolidated body disbanded. While splinter groups continued to exist into the 1980s, international cooperation and advocacy between architects regarding the goals of architecture ceased. In not allowing space for multiple perspectives or unique contextual solutions, by not accepting new understandings of the environment, CIAM was unable to course correct, and imploded.

CIAM's history reveals the magnitude of change that is possible when architects work together, across borders, for the future of the planet. Its demise also reveals the fragility of a collective that does not accommodate difference or change. Both CIAM's successes and failures highlight the skill set—inclusivity, curiosity, and adaptability—necessary for organizing successfully beyond the nation-state.

* * *

The United States has been home to multiple movements to expand the field of architecture over the past one hundred years. The origins of these movements trace to the New Deal, circa 1933–1939, when architects were put to work with landscape architects, artists, urbanists, engineers, and scientists to address the material, infrastructural, and environmental needs of the country.[23] The interdisciplinarity required of New Deal projects prompted architects to broaden their interests and reconceptualize their roles, knowledges, and practices. These endeavors in disciplinary fluidity have primarily taken two directions: environmentalism and architecture-citizenship. The former coalesced around the environmental awakening and back-to-the-earth thinking that defined the West Coast hippy era of the 1960s. The latter was fueled by the upending of the socio-cultural order preceding the end of the twentieth century due to globalization and technological advancements.

While the notion of architecture as environmental design can be traced to the 1930s, a result of architectural contributions to large-scale territorial planning under the New Deal,[24] environmentalism as a cause did not organize until mid-century. The environmental movement and its DIY mentality reframed what habitation and the constructed environment could and should look like. Spurred by counterculture authors like Jack Kerouac, whose 1957 text *On the Road* inspired a mass rejection of capitalist workerism and consumerism, or Rachael Carson, whose 1962 book *Silent Spring* exposed the degradations of the environment caused by rampant pesticide use, the public at large came to question the standards by which they were living. From young people who called the Vietnam War the "war against nature,"[25] to urbanites who uprooted to live simply in rural settings, concern for the environment permeated popular culture.

The environmental movement gained traction in architecture at the University of California, Berkeley—not only due to its epicenter status within many anti-war protests, but because a concentration of back-to-the-earth thinkers taught there. Under the direction of William Wurster, Berkeley's College of Environmental Design was structured around two emphases, one environmental, at the scale of landscape or urbanism, and another social, considering architecture as small acts of personal space-making.[26] T.J. "Jack" Kent, a founding member of Telesis, a group that brought together architects, academics, and planners to reconsider equitable and sustainable urban growth, was the founding professor of the urban planning department at UC Berkeley. Sim van der Ryn, a founder of the Outlaw Builder Studio,[27] an experimental and educational building practice that sought more ecologically balanced ways of living with the planet, also was faculty.

Environmentalism propelled architecture at UC Berkeley into the public arena. In May 1969, tensions erupted when a semi-abandoned lot near the university sustained as a public park by local residents was seized through eminent domain for a university sports field and student housing.[28] The subsequent protests over what came to be known as People's Park drew environmental design faculty and students out of the classroom and into a fight against the city and university[29]—a fight that culminated in "Bloody Thursday," one of the more violent campus clashes of the era.[30] This resistance, and the recoil from the shock of its major events, ultimately succeeded in holding off the university's plans for the site.[31] The energy surrounding People's Park, then, propelled community and environmental activism in Berkeley's architecture school for another ten years. Additionally, it ended up drawing Sim van der Ryn, who took a leading role in advocating for the designation of People's Park as a permanent community-led space, into the role of State Architect in Governor Jerry Brown's administration. In that position, he organized the Office of Appropriate Technology (OAT), an initiative tasked with developing and implementing sustainable practices at the state level that is recognized as a catalyst for California's current status as a governmental leader in the environmental movement.[32]

Like much of the expansive progress of its era, the engagement of architecture schools in community and environment in the 1960s declined over the next decade due to confrontation with two cultural forces, one liberal and one conservative. On the one hand, such outreach, which too commonly consisted of nonconsensual or short lived investigations of underprivileged communities, came—via civil rights, feminist, and literary criticism—to be associated with othering and social engineering.[33] On the other hand, the pro-developer, pro-profit backlash surrounding Ronald Reagan's tenures, first as the governor of California, then as the president of the United States, led to restrictions, immediately on the University of California, and eventually on higher education in general; Reagan enforced cuts in governmental funding to universities and enabled the policing of activism on college campuses.[34] Environmentalism, marked as an inflammatory subject, came to be seen as a threat to the discipline of architecture. A contingent of influential East Coast architecture schools closed ranks, working to ensure that the principles of modernism and continental theory were considered more essential to architecture's *raison d'être* than civic involvement or sustainability. At the epicenter of this inward thrust, the Institute for Architecture and Urban Studies (IAUS), under the direction of Peter Eisenman, produced texts establishing the "deep structure" of architectural language and arguing for architecture as an apolitical and autonomous discipline.[35] Architecture, in many ways, has not moved past this shutdown.

The history of the environmental design movement provides valuable insights for any future expanding and decentering of architecture. In many ways, it represents an ideal—an involved architecture, critical of the systems of power and active in its projection of alternatives. At the same time, its failings must be processed and addressed. Though the movement theoretically allowed for plurality—connecting the ecological and the social, aligning architecture to landscape architecture and urban planning, allowing for both systems thinking and design—the volatility of the times pitted interest areas against one another. An inability to perceive and uphold the commons created a sense of competition between intellectual camps and positionalities. The resulting tensions left the expanded field of architecture vulnerable both to dismantling from the outside and welcoming of the neutrality that the architecture-as-pure-design route offered.

* * *

For a brief period at the turn of the twenty-first century, the field of architecture in the United States appeared to be expanding once again. The approximately twenty-year-long phase was a reaction to two realizations: (1) the promise of the well-designed city that had captivated architects for much of the twentieth century had not delivered, and (2) architects had to completely redesign their work-flow due to the rapid advancement of computer aided drafting (CAD) and digital fabrication. By force of circumstance, architecture was starting over, and looking outside itself.

Lars Lerup, Dean of the Rice School of Architecture in Houston, Texas, from 1993 to 2009 (and former faculty at the University of California, Berkeley), explained the work of that era: "The task at hand is to rescue architecture, no more, no less."[36] Lerup's vision for the reinvigoration of architecture fell largely into the realm of higher education. His approach to the rethinking of architecture and the architectural profession is described in the post-graduation goal that he established for his students, namely, that they eschew the architect's traditional career path and pursue more impactful alternatives. Lerup called on his students to "defy the various suburban machineries and insert the missing link because they already know that the abyss between technology and nature must be bridged."[37] Lerup worked toward his goal by freeing his school's curriculum from strict adherence to accreditation criteria, enabling open inquiry of the constructed environment, and positioning students in the community as citizen ambassadors for the field.

Rice was not alone in redirecting architecture education toward the outside world. This was the moment when Samuel Mockbee founded Auburn's Rural Studio, in 1993, relocating architecture to a rural setting, charging it to perform civil service, upending its material palette, and entrusting its construction to students. This was when William McDonough, Dean of the University of Virginia School of Architecture from 1994–1999,

wrote *Cradle to Cradle: Remaking the Way We Make Things*,[38] push-
ing architecture toward a new phase of environmentalism. This era saw
the launch of the Master of Science in City Design and Social Science at
the London School of Economics, in 1998, a ground-breaking program
at the intersection of commerce, design, and politics in the environment.
This was also the heyday of the Southern California Institute of Architecture's reimagination of spatial representation, and redirection of architecture as a form of communications media. Each of these examples speaks to
a notion of architects as citizens, dissolving the boundaries between architecture and everyday places and practice, and celebrating all experiences
as those shaped by the environment. From the vantage of institutions of
higher education throughout the world, architecture in the late 1990s and
early 2000s was on the precipice of a thorough transformation.

At Rice, however, architecture's "rescue" mission would not withstand
the developments of the late 2000s. In the mid-2000s, when the school's
accreditation status—and thereby the university's tolerance for its experi-
mentalism—was in jeopardy, Lerup's project abruptly ended. The neoliberal reforms that Reagan championed in the 1980s had, by that time,
curtailed the flexibility of universities to develop their own teaching agen-
das. The movement to expand architecture by bringing it into communities then shifted to the development of independent platforms and schools
for the advancement of architecture and the constructed environment. A
few landmark examples include projects like Archeworks, Beta-Local, the
Center for Land Use Interpretation, and the Center for Urban Pedagogy.[39]
In the early 2010s, the growing density of these alternative models for
cultivating architectural production indicated that there was a future for
the expanded field outside of the establishment. This momentum slowed
when both academic and independent platforms for activating architect-
citizens collided with economic crises. For academia, the death blow came
with the 2008 recession. Architecture school graduates could not find traditional architecture jobs, jobs for which there was a known line of ascent,
and the prospect of aspiring to speculative jobs, jobs that did not yet exist
or that typically were filled by those with different training, did not and
could not bear out. The architect-citizen had nowhere beyond the campus
to go. Independent platforms met a similar fate during the 2020 pandemic
shutdowns and corresponding civil unrest. Economic pressures made it
impossible for organizations without privilege to continue operations[40]
and a widespread awakening to exploitative labor practices,[41] meritocratic
discrimination,[42] and racism as systemic to the non-profit model[43] revealed
independent platforms as part of the problem.

The shortcomings in the most recent bursts of disciplinary fluidity have
pushed the field of architecture back into its shell; they also have revealed
that the structures to develop a new kind of architect do not yet exist.

Academic initiatives and independent platforms have proven to be exceptions to, not changes in, overarching governing systems. Efforts to widen architecture's relevance cannot succeed by relying solely on academic initiatives, nor can the independent project be a primary force for change. Realizing a broadened conception of architectural practice demands simultaneous innovation across education and practice. The development of the architect-citizen can only arise by coordinately developing the ladders to their education, practice, and societal roles. Academia and practice must work cooperatively with one another and other fields through new frameworks and methods to forge these supportive structures.

Notes

1 US Government, "H.R.5376 — Inflation Reduction Act of 2022."
2 AIA, "Architects Celebrate Climate Action and Community Investment in the Inflation Reduction Act."
3 Cook and Restuccia, "Trump Aides Try to Quash Tax Hike Rumors amid Infrastructure Talks."
4 Rogers, "Buildings Are Infrastructure."
5 "Architecture 2030."
6 The Big Ten includes the Sierra Club, Sierra Club Legal Defense Fund, National Audubon Society, National Wildlife Federation, Environmental Defense Fund, Environmental Policy Institute/Friends of the Earth, Izaak Walton League, The Wilderness Society, National Parks and Conservation Association, Natural Resources Defense Council Southwest Organising Project, "Southwest Organizing Project Letter to Big 10 Environmental Groups," 16 March 1990.
7 Southwest Organising Project.
8 ibid
9 Córdova, Bravo, and Acosta-Córdova, "Environmental Justice and The Alliance for a Just Transition."
10 Durlin, "The Shot Heard Round the West."
11 The Red Nation, *The Red Deal — Indigenous Action to Save Our Earth*, 34.
12 The Green Party of the United States, "Green New Deal."
13 ibid
14 ibid
15 #Landback is a generational movement with a long legacy of organizing and sacrifice to get indigenous lands back into indigenous hands. For more information, see https://landback.org/.
16 NDN Collective (pronounced "Indian Collective") is an indigenous-led organization dedicated to creating sustainable solutions on indigenous terms by building indigenous power through organizing, activism, philanthropy, grant-making, capacity-building, and narrative change. For more information, see https://ndncollective.org/.
17 In their monograph focused on the Gulf Coast Design Lab at the University of Texas, Coleman Coker and Sarah Gamble articulate the means for pursuing community good and environmental justice through design and activism. For more information, see Coker et al., *Environmental Activism by Design*.
18 The Architects Climate Action network has published a manifesto explaining their aims for addressing global climate change and environmental degradation and the means for achieving them. For more, see https://www.architectscan.org/.

19 The Design Justice Network is an internationalist community of people committed to upholding ten principles for practicing in the constructed environment. For more, see https://designjustice.org/.
20 Mumford, *The CIAM Discourse on Urbanism, 1928–1960*, 9.
21 Risselada et al., *Team 10*.
22 Alison and Peter Smithson (England), Aldo van Eyck (Netherlands), Jaap Bakema (Netherlands), Georges Candilis (France), Shadrack Woods (France), John Voelcker (England), and William and Jill Howell (England) were the founding members of Team 10.
23 In the 1920s United States, the New Deal was a set of federal programs and policies implemented by President Franklin D. Roosevelt in response to the Great Depression. It aimed to provide relief, recovery, and reform, addressing the economic and social challenges faced by the US during the 1930s. The New Deal served as precedent for the Green New Deal, introduced in the US House of Representatives in 2019. For more on the New Deal, see: Rauchway, *The Great Depression & the New Deal*.
24 Sachs, *Environmental Design*.
25 Zierler, *The Invention of Ecocide*.
26 For further readings on this era, see Rome, "Give Earth a Chance." And Barber, *Modern Architecture and Climate*.
27 Stott, "Ludic Pedagogies at the College of Environmental Design, UC Berkeley, 1966 to 1972."
28 Brenneman, "The Bloody Beginnings of People's Park. Category: Features from The Berkeley Daily Planet."
29 Allen, "The End of Modernism?"
30 Vignet, "The Decades-Long People's Park Battle: A Brief Video History."
31 In September 2023, Governor of California, Gavin Newsom, signed a bill greenlighting UC Berkeley's development plan for People's Park KQED News Staff, "Newsom Signs Bill Paving Way to Build New Student Housing at People's Park in Berkeley."
32 Hersey, "The Scout: Sim Van Der Ryn & the Outlaw Builders."
33 Sachs, *Environmental Design*.
34 Bady and Konczal, "From Master Plan to No Plan: The Slow Death of Public Higher Education."
35 Till, *Architecture Depends*, 21–22.
36 Lerup, *After the City*, 86.
37 Lerup, 174.
38 McDonough and Braungart, *Cradle to Cradle*.
39 Archeworks (1993–2018) was a non-profit alternative design school in Chicago at which students worked in multidisciplinary teams with nonprofit partners to create design solutions for social and environmental concerns. Beta-Local (2009–) is a non-profit organization dedicated to supporting and promoting cultural practices and transdisciplinary knowledge exchange in San Juan, Puerto Rico. The Center for Land Use Interpretation (1994–) is a nonprofit research and education organization based in Los Angeles involved in exploring, examining, and understanding contemporary landscape issues in the United States. The Center for Urban Pedagogy (1997–) is a nonprofit organization based in Brooklyn that uses the power of design and art to improve the quality of public participation in urban planning and community design.
40 The 2020 pandemic exacerbated the precarity of small and medium-sized non-profit and private art, design, and public service entities. Though focused on the collapse of a commercial art gallery, Patton Hindle's essay explains the

stresses shared by similar organizations "A Month After I Published a Book About How to Run an Art Gallery, I Closed Mine. Here's Why."

41 Kohomban and Collins, "The Systematic Starvation of Those Who Do Good."

42 This resource from the Harvard Gender Action Portal describes inequities generated by meritocratic environments Castilla and Benard, "The Paradox of Meritocracy in Organizations."

43 Grim, "ELEPHANT IN THE ZOOM: Meltdowns Have Brought Progressive Advocacy Groups to a Standstill at a Critical Moment in World History." describes the reckoning taking place in progressive circles regarding the lack of representation of people of color in their own ranks.

LOOKING FORWARD

This chapter bridges ongoing and preceding movements for change in architecture to the realization of architecture as a valued participant in the stewardship of the planetary commons. Aligned with effective organizing principles, it grounds collective action in the present while instigating visioning to motivate the future. It describes two steps critical to reconstituting architecture, multiplying its expertise as and desegregating its efforts in an expanded, decentered field. First, for the here and now, the tools of language and digital technology are introduced as the means for developing connections with those imbued with different worldviews, and those who have decision-making power in the built environment—from community to institutional and governmental leaders. Second, looking forward, a focus on the purpose of the architectural project offers an aspirational beacon and a springboard for imaginings yet to unfold.

Preparations for Organizing

An expanded, decentered architecture requires participation from diverse communities, both within and outside the field. These collaborative efforts require the development of effective approaches to exchange and outreach. More pointedly, architects are called to reevaluate their familiar modes of relating and to cultivate new technological capabilities in preparation and support for vitalizing their role in the stewardship of the planetary commons.

DOI: 10.4324/9781003411284-14

Language

Architecture has a language problem. Its discourse is notoriously opaque, even off-putting, to broader audiences. The inability to communicate effectively is central to public perception of architecture's irrelevance. One reason for the communications barrier is internal to the discipline, a byproduct of the valorization of countless hours spent in studio isolated from diverse interactions; the long-term isolation compounds linguistic barriers. Another reason is mass unfamiliarity with architectural thinking. Because spatial and environmental processes are not taught in primary and secondary education, architectural ideas are generally foreign to those who do not attend architecture school. Frustrated with repeat struggles to explain the gist of what the field is about, architects too often approach their linguistic failings with arrogance and condescension, thereby alienating the public and perpetuating the divide.

If architecture is to become more inclusive and accessible, architects need to re-examine the opaque, specialized language, or "architecture-speak," that pervades the field. Architecture-speak traces principally to the vocabularies of formalism and theory. The language of architectural form, so vital to the discipline's frameworks and values, sounds cryptic and alien to those without training. Terms like "datum," "layering," "additive," "subtractive," "program," or "section" may be meaningful to architects, but do not confer expertise in the way legal and medical terminology does. Unlike law and medicine, architecture has not succeeded in conveying the urgency and relevance of its mission to the public. As the late architecture educator Marco Frascari explains, architects tend "to discuss [their work] as an art or science overlooking the fact that architecture is above all a profession"[1] entrusted with serving people's needs and interests. To become more accessible, architects need to communicate in plainer language how their work impacts communities.

Making architecture relatable involves turning to extra-disciplinary practices for building understanding, for moving from the abstract and complex to the straightforward. Three such practices are: the science of learning, undeveloped directions in kinaesthetic knowing, and storytelling.

Research in the science of learning demonstrates that the process by which humans learn is relatively consistent. James Lang, emeritus professor of English and former director of the D'Amour Center for Teaching Excellence, explains in *Small Teaching*, a go-to handbook for new teachers, that learning progresses from a build-up of knowledge, to a build-up of understanding, to a build-up of inspiration. Each build-up is a prerequisite for the next. "We have to know things…to think critically about them," he writes, and ultimately, to create new things.[2] Because architects are not taught to teach, it is not uncommon for architecture faculty to skip steps in the classroom, to ask for creativity prior to understanding or even knowledge. The same is true when architects address the public. If architecture is to achieve public understanding, much less drive public inspiration—and action— architects must contribute to the build-up of public knowledge of their work. Architects and educators must look to the science of learning for guidance, breaking down the knowledge of architecture into digestible pieces for popular appreciation and advancement.

Architecture's language, in many ways, is more visual than textual or verbal. This is both a hindrance and a site of possibility. It is problematic insofar as the visualization bias emphasizes images and models that demand specialized training to comprehend. Visualization becomes a compelling mode of relating if it is reconsidered through the lens of kinaesthetic knowing. Kinaesthetic knowing is a knowledge model from the nineteenth century during which, according to architecture historian Zeynep Çelik Alexander, there was a moment of questioning whether or not "the body's physical exchanges with the world produce reliable knowledge without recourse to language, concepts, propositions, or representations?"[3] This model sought to recognize an intelligence not restricted to linguistic, mathematical, scientific, or similar intellectual frameworks, but tied instead to sensory appreciation. Now abandoned, this line of inquiry developed a methodology for testing visuals and other sensory products in conversation with broad publics. This process for drawing out human responses to material conditions remains a pathway for improving the relatability of architecture today. By rethinking architecture's representations as discursive instead of demonstrative, responsive instead of deterministic, by emphasizing architecture's kinaesthetic nature, architecture multiplies its means both for making connections and for bettering its understanding of others.

Humans have evolved physiologically to comprehend information through narrative formats.[4] Paul Emmons and Luc Phinney, both colleagues of the aforementioned Marco Frascari, wrote in a book tribute to their friend's pedagogical legacy about the importance of storytelling to architecture's expanded field:

> Confabulation is one of the most essential, least acknowledged, skills of the architect. Confabulation finds connections, proposes questions, and offers an expanded field for architectural insights... [T]he convergence of architecture and storytelling is not just a question of "painting a picture with words" to better visualize or persuade us of an already-extant architectural idea. Stories are constitutive and offer ways of seeing unavailable to other creative modes.[5]

Storytelling, in other words, is an artform that has the potential to elevate architectural ideas. For example, Parlour,[6] a membership organization for advancing gender equity in the built environment, sees storytelling as pivotal in the popularization of underrepresented voices in the built environment. Storytelling similarly creates a premise for community outreach, for building and aligning coalitions and mobilizing causes. It provides a format for developing conceptual bridges between architecture and other disciplines—from commerce to technology to the sciences. It offers a coherent outlet for advocacy to centers of influence like humanitarian, philanthropic, and regulating agencies.

Whether informed by the science of learning, kinaesthetic knowing, or storytelling, language is an established knowledge area of organizing. Studies in the language of organizing reveal it to contain a mix of approaches rearranged from many sources. The language of organizing combines tactics used in informal discourse, formal discourse, performance, public speaking, and writing. It is informed by a wide range of ideas from identity and cultural studies, psychology and sociology, resource mobilization and political process theory, mediation, leadership and organization models, journalism, and marketing. It is realized through multimedia—static and kinetic—in print, digital, and technological forms. Because its references and expressions are constantly shifting, organizing language coheres only temporarily.[7] Organizing language, like organizing itself, is characterized by its awareness of circumstance and its engagement with, and openness to, diverse perspectives. It requires prioritizing the audience alongside the message. It involves knowing when to step forward and when to step back. Above all, it depends on the recognition that organizing language is shared, collective speech, in which everyone has a space and a voice. As architecture prepares for, and engages in, shifts in the discipline and the world, the language of organizing in all its forms must be understood as the means of connecting with the diverse groups working toward the wellbeing of humans and other-than-humans on an interconnected planet.

Digital Technology

Communication and language, through digitization, are now inextricably interwoven with technology. In addition, digital technologies play a pivotal role in shaping and articulating architecture, serving not only as the medium through which ideas are conceived and communicated but as essential facilitators of fabrication and construction processes. Architecture's active interest in the capabilities and directions of digital technology is necessary for the realization of an expanded, decentered field. Both a critical focus for organizing and an arena in which architecture organizers can and must cultivate more agility and dexterity, digital technology is explored here as a means for addressing challenges in both architecture and the planetary commons.

The technological acceleration of recent decades—marked by the advent of personal computers, iPhones, and the digital economy—not only has heightened global inequities but, paradoxically, also has exacerbated domestic disparities within the very nations proliferating the ostensibly "revolutionary" technologies.[8] Technology and its modes of development are non-neutral, deeply interconnected with evolutions in the global political economy—and, in turn, with enabling or disabling the stewarding of the planetary commons. It is embedded in economic and social control structures and incentives, each reciprocally shaping the other's forms and functions.

In a condition referred to as "digital colonialism,"[9] the use of digital technologies by privileged nation-states to maintain economic, political, and social domination over less privileged nation-states perpetuates longstanding inequities. Exploitative dynamics—in which less privileged communities bear the health burdens of resource extraction processes, are targeted in experimental surveillance or data accumulation projects, while tech giants achieve exorbitant wealth—is designed to be self-reinforcing. The innovation economy serves to concentrate, rather than decentralize, power and wealth. Under the capitalist model that guides what technology is and does, innovation is motivated by profit—leveraging cultural hegemony, consumerism, and data extraction to accumulate more and more—rather than cultural or environmental priorities.

Several forms of resistance have emerged to counter the socioeconomic inequities exacerbated by the innovation economy. They entail efforts such as open-source platforms and protocols; user consent requirements and privacy agreements; algorithm accountability and transparency regulations; Corporate Social Responsibility (CSR) programs, including social impact and ethical supply chain initiatives; partnerships with nonprofits; community-centered innovation sponsorships; and activist 'Venture Capitalist' firms (VCs). These measures, however, struggle to transform underlying profit motives and power imbalances. They lack adequate funding and are themselves subject to the technology development system's competitive pressures. Technology should emerge from democratically determined values rather than determine those values. Approaches like community data governance, cooperative platforms, and public interest technology boards are needed to distribute agency in technology.

Architecture has been complicit in digitization's inequitable extraction and centralization of power. It has handed over the reins of design and production to tech innovation, subjecting the livelihoods of its communities to the whims of the startup economy. The technology and innovation sectors, having already caused significant disruptions in the field, wield considerable influence and power over architecture. Computer-aided design (CAD), for example, originally developed for the aerospace, automation, and electronics industries, when first adopted into architecture, startled the discipline, upsetting its workflows and forcing a massive restructuring of professional practices. A product designed without direct or meaningful input from architects, CAD indentured architecture to digital processes in which it had little influence. CAD's proliferation as a product of Autodesk[10] and dominance over two-dimensional representation, then, paved the way for Autodesk Revit and similar Building Information Modeling (BIM) software to facilitate the standardization of three-dimensional architectural representation and building assembly logics, as well as ossify the ways that architecture coordinates with allied fields.[11]

From the perspective of the technology innovation sector, architecture is a client. In the best of cases, digital product professionals consult architects through qualitative and quantitative User Experience Research (UXR). User testing is structured as a means for tweaking earlier conceptualizations and design decisions. And the cycle continues. Architecture is asked to adapt repeatedly to external assessments of its work. While technology promises to increase efficiency, its recurring upgrade cycles extract both time and resources from those beholden to it. CAD, BIM, and other innovation economy products, then, create barriers to the work of architecture, excluding those who cannot afford costly licenses, and bolster those with preexisting privilege, promoting false equivalencies between technological capacity and value to the constructed environment.

Architects must recognize their ethical duties in mediating the exploitative and unjust dynamics of digitization, rather than uncritically participating in and facilitating further disempowerment. Architecture, too, can only benefit from organizing to encourage technology's democratization. This is especially true as swift advancements in Artificial Intelligence (AI) technologies implicate yet another phase of substantial reordering for architecture—and the world. Projections regarding the global impacts of AI range from apocalyptic to neoliberal-utopian. Projections specifically regarding the impact of AI on architecture—predicting either the discipline's demise or its liberation—are similarly extreme. The rapid content generation capabilities of AI, encompassing photorealistic imagery to design schematics and environmental analyses, pose the dual threat of rendering architects obsolete or revolutionizing the scope and methodology of architecture. Unlike CAD and BIM, architects are more actively engaged in the development of AI platforms and are serving as early adopters of its capabilities. Notably, XKool, an AI company dedicated to advancing the architecture industry, is led by former employees of the Office for Metropolitan Architecture (OMA).[12] The increasing open accessibility of AI tools like Dall-E, Midjourney, Stable Diffusion, and others for text-to-image and image-to-image generation has led to a growing use of AI in design conceptualization and representation within academia and practice. These involvements create openings for architecture both to shape the trajectory of AI, but also proactively position the field to navigate and harness the transformative potential of AI as it relates to a holistic set of questions.

Many look to AI for the transformative potential of its unparalleled computational capacities, as compared to technological evolutions seen in the recent past.[13] AI's facility with data analysis and interpretation is suggestive of opportunities for an expanded, decentered architecture. By relieving the architectural workload of time-consuming visualization activities, it positions the labor of design to be more humane and leaves room for more meaningful efforts. Tasks that once were impossible, such as incorporating research critical to addressing the environmental crisis into design solutions, AI makes them possible. But do those benefits balance out with the harm caused by the economic models that bear them?

The narratives tied to the conveniences of AI must be confronted alongside the power structures they enable. Amidst the AI transition, architects must confront critical questions: How can AI be implemented to overcome the widening global and domestic inequities the technology economy has otherwise created? Who bears the burdens, and who reaps the rewards of this transformation? How is AI regulated? What will be the impacts of AI on the planetary commons? Despite bold assertions from some techno-oligarchs prophesying the eventual obsolescence of work through AI,[14] it is imperative to discern that such proclamations never imply the demise of capitalism or the eradication of global subjugation under late neoliberal power—quite the opposite.

Organizations like the Algorithmic Justice League (AJL)[15] offer vital guidance for architecture organizers navigating AI's dangers and ethical challenges while understanding where its potential for good lies. With goals to raise public awareness of AI impacts, equip advocates with resources, amplify affected groups, orient and influence policymakers, and motivate responsible innovation, the AJL serves as an important precedent and model for catalyzing change at the intersection of technology and social justice. They remind architects that where technology comes from matters. Technology's origins dictate the terms of its use. How it is deployed matters. Technology is a channel for both constructive and destructive forces in society and the environment. How it is perceived matters. It can be leveraged for connection, or for isolation. To organize today is to recognize technology's development, mechanics, and machinations as ever-present catalysts for and within any progressive movement.

Beyond AI, digital technology underlines the development of a spatial frontier with which architecture flirts but largely has considered other— that of digital and virtual reality. Digital and virtual reality already have slipped, via augmented reality, into architectural space. In gaming design, architecture plus storytelling are key components of resource management simulations that both teach environmental stewardship and inform real-world project planning from within virtual space.[16] Digital technology provides a multitude of entries for engaging with other worldviews. Technologies for collaborative working are touchpoints for relating to distinct ways of perceiving and acting in the environment. They record environmental behaviors and spatial conditions, translate information between sectors, encourage creative exchange, and facilitate complex assembly and construction challenges. Rather than eschewing these developments, what if architecture understood them as what they are—options in the arsenal of tools for articulating the environment of the commons?

At the same time, digital technologies distance architecture from the material realities of its designed decisions. As the connection of architecture to the world increasingly is processed through technological exchanges, so too increases the amount of calculation required to anticipate interplays between digital and physical reactions; and the amount of organizing needed to channel technology for the good increases as well. Alternatively, there is also growing interest in digital technology as a complement to natural regeneration. The Regenerative Architecture Lab[17] at Cornell University, for example, allies data collection, material and waste research, and science and technology in a drive to reorganize the construction industry. A center of collaboration for biologists, engineers, architects, economists, and industry partners, it looks to digital technology's analytical and computational capabilities to support the advancement of cyclical building practices and products.

Organizing and architecture, in a collective effort to engender planetary wellbeing, are bound inescapably to digital technologies. Digitization either can power the expansion and decentering of architecture, or it can further entrap the field in the compromising dynamics of the innovation economy. This reality is far from being reflected in today's architecture curriculum. Architecture education, instead, can help foster the necessary progressive movements by teaching organizing alongside knowledge and skill sets required of deeper engagement with digital technologies. In many ways, this proposition is little more than an acknowledgement and bolstering of patterns already happening. Architecture's training is easily transferable to product design, user experience, and user research. Recent architecture graduates are moving, due to the pressure of student loans and life's general unaffordability,[18] in significant numbers to the technology sector to access its comparatively inflated salaries. Instead of detachment from this trend, however, architecture education can work to influence it. By explicitly integrating digital technology know-how and critical insight into its societal and disciplinary impacts, architecture education can become a center for change. Teaching students about the history of architecture's digitization, highlighting the beneficiaries and victims, empowers architecture graduates to examine the promises and perils of technology's innovation economy and to confront its difficulties through actions.

A Vision for Organizing

Organizing, in part, is a means of situating progressive efforts within present conditions, of identifying shared interests and struggles, mobilizing collective action, and consensus building. Organizing, overall, is a means of situating in time, of looking both backwards and forwards to witness the interdependencies of momentary causes and effects. Organizing is incomplete without proposals for alternate approaches to its motivating challenges, without ambitions for what it will look like on the other side of having organized. Futuring, then, requires both planning: laying out the ingredients and increments of progress, and imagining: describing the qualities of the goal and its impacts. Imagining provides an encouraging vision to accompany the work of organizing, and it acts as a guide and a metric, a way of charting a course and keeping organizing on track.

If cultivating modes of relating—through language and technology—is a first step in the planning for multifaceted field of architecture accessible enough to make a difference in the world, what follows is a first step in a parallel process of imagining. Organizing for the wellbeing of the Earth, and for architecture's valued role therein is, of course, a vast and variable effort; many visions must describe it. Indeed, many visions must describe the expanded, decentered field of architecture itself. If architecture is to work alongside other worldviews in service to stewarding the environment, the architectural project, in particular, stands out as a locus for aspirational thinking.

The gap between an expanded, decentered field of architecture and the status-quo reveals the architectural project—the subject of architecture's work—as critical to change. The architectural project is opened to questioning. What is it? Who is it for? How does it materialize? What methods does it employ? Architecture may always be buildings, but what a building is may shift. Or perhaps, architecture really is everything that makes up the experiential, spatial, and temporal world. Certainly architecture can no longer be the privileged territory of those with the means to commission work. It cannot even be for humans alone. Architecture could be organic, digital, conceptual, and any mix thereof. Regardless, the possibilities upend the architectural workflow, its delivery processes, and its labor practices.

Rethinking the architectural project need not be disruptive; the changes may, in fact, be radically simple. Vital to the process of changing architecture, its practices and projects alike, is building in conditions of care and upholding the principles of organizing: championing inclusivity, operating in context, anticipating impacts, and embracing adaptability. In other words, as architecture moves to expand and decenter, it must structure a "just transition." Looking to the guidelines of the Just Transition Alliance, an organization working to support workers in getting away from unhealthy treatments and conditions, architecture is reminded that "[t]he process for achieving [a] vision should be a fair one that should not cost workers or community residents their health, environment, jobs, or economic assets."[19]

To imagine the architectural project in an expanded, decentered field, then, is to return to fundamentals. It is led by two basic inquiries. First, what does it mean to shelter when sheltering is destroying the habitat on which shelter relies? If architecture, at its core, is the art of providing refuge, of nurturing habitat, its projects, intrinsically, are acts of access to comfort and wellbeing and works of ecological balance. Second, what, then, does it mean to gather—to bring together humans with different worldviews, to bring together humans with other-than-humans—in ways that ease and transform today's troubled relations? The expanded, decentered architectural project appreciates that to provide true refuge, to really nurture habitat, is to create community: to draw out and build up the interconnectedness of living in the world.

Lastly, the vision of the architectural project, as well as of an expanded, decentered architecture and of planetary stewardship, must be collective. Those who are most vulnerable must lead this imagining. Here, then, this guide turns to the ideas and contributions of others. It has aimed to start a conversation, to inspire solidarity among, and provide support to, movements for change in architecture education, and to link architecture's knowledge and practices to the needs of and solutions for the global environment. It now entrusts the organizing thereof to ongoing and yet-to-be-organized movements—and to its readers.[20]

Notes

1 Frascari, "Professional Use of Signs in Architecture," 16.
2 Lang, *Small Teaching*, 15.
3 Alexander, *Kinaesthetic Knowing*, 8.
4 Cron, *Wired for Story*.

5 Emmons et al., *Confabulations*, 4.
6 See CASE STUDY.
7 Alexander, Jarratt, and Welch, *Unruly Rhetorics*, 13.
8 Qureshi, "Technology, Growth, and Inequality: Changing Dynamics in the Digital Era."
9 Kwet, "Digital Colonialism: The Evolution of US Empire."
10 While CAD technology dates to 1957, an invention of Dr. Patrick J. Hanratty, a computer scientist and businessperson whose Arizona company focused on manufacturing and consulting, Autodesk was founded by a team of programmers in 1982, after acquiring a preexisting CAD program.
11 To learn more about how BIM and IPS have transformed architectural workflow, see: Deamer, "Marx, BIM, and Contemporary Labor."
12 Wainwright, "'It's Already Way beyond What Humans Can Do": Will AI Wipe out Architects?'
13 Suleyman, "How the AI Revolution Will Reshape the World."
14 Kleinman and Seddon, "Elon Musk Tells Rishi Sunak AI Will Put an End to Work."
15 It should be mentioned that the Algorithmic Justice League is an initiative supported by the Massachusetts Institute of Technology (MIT) Media Lab, a university group with deep ties to the innovation economy and its capital investments. Algorithmic Justice League, "Algorithmic Justice League."
16 Bianco, "What If Video Games Could Help Fight Climate Change? No, Really."
17 https://labs.aap.cornell.edu/real
18 Landmark communities facilitating these transitions are Architechie, "Architechie" and Out of Architecture OOA, "O/A."
19 Just Transition Alliance, "Just Transition Principles."
20 Find organizations in which to get involved by visiting The Architecture Lobby's ABCHub: https://architecture-beyond-capitalism.github.io/abc-hub/.

CODA

Coauthoring: An Experimental Endeavor

Coauthoring is a cornerstone practice for organizers in The Architecture Lobby (TAL) and within TAL's Academia Working Group (AWG). In these contexts, organizing often entails collaboratively creating time-bound campaigns, such as the annual iterations of the ABC school. TAL's commitment to coproduction steered the organized, structured, and grounded approach that we, the coauthors of this guide, followed when undertaking the experimental task of collectively writing this book.

Early efforts of the AWG involved a collaborative piece titled "Not as Easy as ABC" reflecting on the first iteration of the Architecture Beyond Capitalism (ABC) School in 2021, published in *Log* journal as part of a thematic issue on coauthoring. Understanding coauthorship as "both a tool for, and theory of, capitalist critique,"[1] the text explored how the tension between individual and collective authorship could disrupt and possibly reform the capitalist enforcement of individual authorship and authority. It continued the ABC School's counter model for synthesizing organizing and education, fostering the collaborative creation of academic endeavors. *The Organizer's Guide to Architecture Education* serves as a reflection on and a continuation of these initiatives.

Initially, this project was contemplated as an edited volume where each author singularly contributed their expertise. A compiled collection of essays captures individual expertise, but is confined to aggregating monological viewpoints, without opportunities for response, conversation, or long-term engagement. In our internal conversations, we wondered

DOI: 10.4324/9781003411284-15

about the value of scholarly work and depth of understanding that can be achieved without authentic dialogue. We pondered whether we might be overlooking the art of active listening in pursuit of efficiency. Although coauthoring academic writing may not be the easiest or most efficient approach, we made a conscientious choice to model our ideals, a decision that substantially enhanced both the process behind and outcome of this book, hopefully providing a model for resisting standard academic protocols. Ultimately, coming together as coauthors enabled the creation of a comprehensive and purposeful guide that neither coauthor could have produced individually. Or, as described by Dark Matter U,[2] an anti-racist design education initiative:

> Coauthorship prioritizes the space that two or more people hold together and acknowledges that the relationship itself "births" something different and better than what either individual could contribute by themselves. Ultimately, coauthorship challenges the view that success results from individual action and merit! And it certainly makes the business of getting things done more fun.[3]

In the end, the text represents the culmination of 18 months of structured consensus building between coauthors. Each coauthor contributed and let go of ideas along the way. The detailed discussions during the planning and drafting of this guide, along with opportunities for each coauthor to reflect on their individual experiences, led to a more nuanced understanding of the systems and practices that define architecture education in distinct contexts, including Australia, Aotearoa New Zealand, and the United States. Much of the book's research was shaped by holding space for insights inherent to the positionality of multiple constituencies. This included perspectives of "missing others" in the field of architecture and diverse worldviews in the constructed environment. The bonds and relational understanding forged through this collective craft exemplify coauthoring's fundamental goals, giving momentum to its promise of kinship and mutualism.

* * *

The backbone of the coauthorship process was weekly videoconference calls attended by all coauthors for close to a year and a half. In retrospect, six collaborative phases emerged: planning, brainstorming, research, round robin, development, and editing. The first six months of conversation focused on developing both the outline of the book and the collaborative strategies, culminating in the negotiation and validation of a publishing contract. During the ensuing three-month brainstorming phase, open-ended ideas were considered and argued, resulting in a mutually agreed upon outline. Research was then distributed, with each coauthor exploring and synthesizing topical findings. Close to nine months into the collaboration, writing began as a round robin rotation of the text in outline form first, and then in fleshing text format. Each coauthor focused on one chapter for a week, before passing the writing along to the next coauthor in the chain. There was an ebullience and intensity to this routine that imbued each week's hand off with relief. Once the chapters were back where they started, each coauthor developed the text they inherited into a first draft. During the editing process, which included a review by an external editor, everyone had a role stitching together concepts and unifying the text's voice.

Collaborative work is often perceived as untenable due to the potential for disagreement. While there were moments of tension within this coauthoring effort, the overall experience was resoundingly positive for all involved, owing largely to the coworking approaches that we adopted. We endeavored with collective agreements, equitable communications tactics, and cooperative administrative structures. Before beginning the writing, at each phase shift, and as needed, we developed community contracts. To compose these collective agreements, coauthors shared individual preferences and concerns while working together to reach consensus. For example, acknowledging that writing a book takes time and exposes vulnerabilities, we developed a statement of empathy and care; we gave each other grace to come and go as our schedules allowed, and we committed, no matter what, to recognizing everyone as a valued contributor. Already accustomed, through our involvement with TAL, to conversation facilitation protocol[4] and facilitation methods that foster hearing from all present participants evenhandedly in a group meeting setting, we upheld these practices in our weekly gatherings and extended their logics to the writing process itself. For example, the idea for the round robin writing phase was inspired by the "popcorn" meeting tactic, in which everyone in a virtual room checks in with everyone else by sharing and then "popcorning" to someone who has not yet shared.

We also set up cooperative administrative structures, thoroughly documenting our processes, organizing our materials for inclusive access, and distributing labor through conversational processes. We were able to co-research, co-write, and co-edit by using digital platforms such as Zoom, Google Docs, Google Drive, Dropbox, Zotero, Zoom, Miro, and Notion. These platforms enabled multimedia idea exchange, the creation of a collective resource archive, and real-time text feedback. Translating between them, however, led to some unique challenges— from misidentifying the most recent version of a file to broken citation links to incompatibilities that developed due to software updates. Given our coauthors' varying levels of proficiency with and confidence in these tools, we developed collective agreements for navigating any document handling issues that arose. In other words, over time, our collective agreements, equitable communications tactics, and cooperative administrative structures all came to influence each other. They constituted an adaptable framework for guiding both the writing process and the writing relations.

* * *

We acknowledge that every decision made in this guide is ultimately political. One of our bigger internal debates centered on how best to disseminate the material. Collaboration with a large, corporate publisher would necessitate adhering to their templates and deadlines, but would offer advantages such as marketing and extensive distribution. Working with a smaller independent press or nonprofit publisher, or self-publishing, lacked these benefits, but would allow flexibility in visualization, formatting, timing, etc. We considered our options through the lens of distribution, factoring criteria such as the book's purchasing cost, its availability in libraries and university catalogs, and its relevance to a global audience. Routledge, an imprint under the global publishing giant Taylor & Francis and our chosen publisher, accommodated these considerations. However, their invitation also required a strategic market analysis: identifying a "target audience," understanding competitors, and distinguishing our work—a process that provoked questions about how to challenge and transcend the capitalist publishing system while using its tools. After a few negotiations, we concluded that the contract with Routledge provided a secure framework for crafting the book. We appreciated that having this text would empower us, the coauthors, to raise awareness about our concerns and we prioritized the work of cohering our arguments and mobilizing them in a timely fashion.

It was crucial for us that the book take the form of a guide, striking a very different tone and affordance than many academic texts. While scholarly research and discourse can offer a certain depth, quality, and autonomy to a body of knowledge, the standard format and style of scholarly writing conflicted with the subject matter of organizing. After all, academia is often stereotyped for its tendency toward virtue signaling, as opposed to laying the ground for genuine action, and many who must be brought into the movement for reform in the building sector find themselves alienated by academia and academic writing. Within the constraints of the academic book, we oriented the composition toward more inclusive and purposeful writing. To that end, we attempted to define terms whenever possible, even those that might appear obvious to those familiar with the world of architecture, we included the HOW-TO series that guides our readers through specific organizing practices, and we curated a CASE STUDY series that exemplifies the practices introduced in our main text.

Our coauthoring decisions are biased, as they reflect our unique positionalities. As coauthors, we brought our own perspectives and experiences, which influenced the ultimate shape of the material, direction, and presentation within these pages. In navigating our subjectivities, we have made every effort to land in the space that is the most inclusive, the most generous, and the most just. Indeed, we are coauthoring precisely because coauthoring aspires to representative ideation. While we hope that we have made room for all perspectives in our writing, we understand that we may not have succeeded. We opted, for example, to write in American (US) English, even though, for a few of our coauthors, English is a second language, or British English is native. We were persuaded that American English is the publishing standard, with the broadest reach at this moment in time. We know, however, that the reach is not comprehensive. The language in which this book is written speaks to our overwhelming identification as Western educated. Our personal demographics, those of primarily white cisgendered people, mostly women, implicate a limited worldview. We have been able, through one coauthor, to include first-person indigenous perspectives, and through a few others, to consider the global reception of the content's dominantly Western focus. More broadly, we have worked to uplift the efforts and thinking of communities and cultures to which we may not belong but strive to build coalitions with. But we accept that this specific project falls short. Nonetheless, we see our work as only a beginning and are committed to ongoing efforts to magnify diverse voices and movements for equity in architecture education and the constructed environment.

* * *

This guide is not intended as a definitive document, but rather as a support for a conversation encouraging and informing a collective blueprint for action. To continue organizing for solidarity and justice, we are fundamentally interested in readers' organizing:

- Readers of this guide are invited to look for existing kinship efforts, both academic and community-based, local to them, and to stand in solidarity with those alienated by dominant systems of power in architecture education and beyond.
- Readers of this guide are invited to become members of TAL, which supports and welcomes members from all over the world and orients

them in joining and, when relevant, founding a local chapter or work-ing group. Being a member of TAL allows one to join the AWG, which organizes the ABC School and maintains the ABC Hub, an open-source digital platform for asynchronous resource sharing and solidarity building.
- Readers are invited to fill in, correct, or redirect the histories, analyses, and/or observations that we have made. We are not experts in many of the areas that matter to us, and any reactions or readjustments will help make more precise and poignant the positions put forward in this book.
- Finally, readers of this guide are invited to keep in touch with this guide's coauthors through our Substack (https://togae.substack.com/) and our email (togae2023@gmail.com).

What we advocate for in this guide is grounded in practicality—none of it is radical. These motions for change in architecture are already unfold-ing, embedded in communities seeking mutualism. It can continue to be pursued, and it can be actualized, by connecting with one another in soli-darity. This book is a stone thrown into the future which we all construct collectively. Together, we will shape an expanded, decentered architecture and a more equitable, interconnected, and thriving planet.

Notes

1 The Architects Lobby et al., "Not as Easy as ABC."
2 "Creating New Forms of Knowledge, Institutions, Collectivity, Community, and Design_."
3 Log 54, p. 29.
4 See HOW-TO.

BIBLIOGRAPHY

ABC Architecture Beyond Capitalism School. '2021 A-B-O-U-T'. ABC Architecture Beyond Capitalism School, 2021. https://abc.architecture-lobby.org/architecture-beyond-capitalism-2021.

ABC Architecture Lobby. 'ABC Architecture Beyond Capitalism'. The Architecture Lobby, 2023. https://abc.architecture-lobby.org/.

Acevedo, Sara Maria, Michael Aho, Eri Cela, Juei-Chen Chao, Isabel Garcia-Gonzales, Alec MacLeod, Claudia Moutray, and Christina Olague. 'Positionality as Knowledge: From Pedagogy to Praxis'. *Integral Review* 11, no. 1 (1 February 2015): 28–46. http://integral-review.org/pdf-template-issue.php?pdfName=vol_11_no_1_acevedo_et_al_positionality_as_knowledge.pdf.

ACSA. 'Convening'. ACSA, 2023. https://www.acsa-arch.org/conference/convening/.

Africa Futures Institute. 'About the Africa Futures Institute'. Africa Futures Institute, 2023. https://www.africanfuturesinstitute.com/about-the-afi.

AIA. '2020 Code of Ethics and Professional Conduct'. The American Institute of Architects, August 2020. https://content.aia.org/sites/default/files/2020-08/2020_Code_of_Ethics.pdf.

AIA. 'Architects Celebrate Climate Action and Community Investment in the Inflation Reduction Act'. American Institute of Architects, 12 August 2022. https://www.aia.org/press-releases/6534285-architects-celebrate-climate-action-and-co.

AIAS. 'AIAS and NAAB Partner to Promote Healthy Studio Culture'. The American Institute of Architecture Students, 11 April 2018. https://www.aias.org/aias-and-naab-partner-to-promote-healthy-studio-culture/.

Alexander, Jonathan, Susan Carole Funderburgh Jarratt, and Nancy Welch, eds. *Unruly Rhetorics: Protest, Persuasion, and Publics*. Composition, Literacy, and Culture. Pittsburgh, PA: University of Pittsburgh Press, 2018.

Alexander, Zeynep Çelik. *Kinaesthetic Knowing: Aesthetics, Epistemology, Modern Design*. Chicago, IL; London: The University of Chicago Press, 2017.

Algorithmic Justice League. 'Algorithmic Justice League'. Algorithmic Justice League, 2023. https://www.ajl.org/.

Allen, Peter. 'The End of Modernism?' *Journal of the Society of Architectural Historians* 70, no. 3 (1 September 2011): 354–74. https://doi.org/10.1525/jsah.2011.70.3.354.

Amereida contributors. 'Open City'. cc amereida, 2023. http://amereida.cl/Ciudad_ Abierta.

Angélil, Marc and Dirk Hebel. *Deviations: Designing Architecture – A Manual.* Basel: Birkhäuser Architecture, 2008.

Angélil, Marc, Liat Uziyel, and Eidgenössische Technische Hochschule Zürich, eds. *Inchoate: An Experiment in Architectural Education.* Zürich: ETH Zürich, 2003.

Architechie. 'Architechie'. Architechie, 2023. https://architechie.org/.

Architecture 2030. 'Architecture 2030', 2023. https://www.architecture2030.org/.

Aria Strategies LLC. 'Facilitation as an Equity Strategy'. Aria Strategies LLC, 6 May 2020. https://ariastrategiesllc.com/amplify-good/facilitation-as-an-equity-strategy.

AUT. 'Accreditation for MArch (Prof)'. AUT New Zealand, 22 November 2022. https://www.aut.ac.nz/news/stories/accreditation-for-march-prof.

Avelino, Flor. 'Theories of Power and Social Change. Power Contestations and Their Implications for Research on Social Change and Innovation'. *Journal of Political Power* 14, no. 3 (2 September 2021): 425–48. https://doi.org/10.1080/ 2158379X.2021.1875307.

Bady, Aaron, and Mike Konczal. 'From Master Plan to No Plan: The Slow Death of Public Higher Education'. Dissent, Fall 2012. https://www.dissent magazine.org/article/from-master-plan-to-no-plan-the-slow-death-of-public-higher-education/.

Banham, Reyner, Sutherland Lyall, Cedric Price, and Peter Hall. *A Critic Writes: Essays by Reyner Banham.* Edited by Mary Banham and Paul Barker. First paperback printing. Acentennial Book. Berkeley, Los Angeles, CA; London: University of California Press, 1999.

Barber, Daniel A. *Modern Architecture and Climate: Design before Air Conditioning.* Princeton, NJ: Princeton University Press, 2020.

Barth, Brian. 'Is LEED Tough Enough for the Climate-Change Era?' *Bloomberg*, 5 June 2018, sec. CityLab Environment. https://www.bloomberg.com/ news/articles/2018-06-05/reconsidering-leed-buildings-in-the-era-of-climate-change.

Berkes, Fikret, Johan Colding, and Carl Folke, eds. *Navigating Social-Ecological Systems: Building Resilience for Complexity and Change.* 1st ed. Cambridge, London: Cambridge University Press, 2001.

Bernstein, Ethan, and Ben Waber. 'The Truth About Open Offices'. Harvard Business Review, December 2019. https://hbr.org/2019/11/the-truth-about-open-offices.

Bianco, Karn. 'What If Video Games Could Help Fight Climate Change? No, Really'. Wired, 6 August 2018. https://www.wired.co.uk/article/climate-change-game-design-simcity-civilisation.

Bojórquez-Tapia, Luis A., Hallie Eakin, Bertha Hernández-Aguilar, and Rebecca Shelton. 'Addressing Complex, Political and Intransient Sustainability Challenges of Transdisciplinarity: The Case of the MEGADAPT Project in Mexico City'. *Bridging Science and Policy through Collaborative, Interdisciplinary Global Change Research in the Americas* 38 (1 June 2021): 100604. https:// doi.org/10.1016/j.envdev.2020.100604.

Brenneman, Richard. 'The Bloody Beginnings of People's Park. Category: Features from The Berkeley Daily Planet', 20 April 2004. https://www.berkeleydaily planet.com/issue/2004-04-20/article/18700.

Brillon, James. 'Instagram Account Dank.Lloyd.Wright Aims to "Amplify Narratives That Are Excluded from Architecture's Official Consensus"'. Dezeen, 30 August 2022. https://www.dezeen.com/2022/08/30/instagram-dank-lloyd-wright-interview.

Brown, Deidre. *Māori Architecture: From Fale to Wharenui and Beyond*. Auckland: Raupo, 2009.

Buchanan, Peter. 'The Big Rethink: Architectural Education'. *The Architectural Review* 232, no. 1388 (October 2012): 91–101,4. https://www.proquest.com/trade-journals/big-rethink-architectural-education/docview/1114483329/se-2?accountid=12372.

Burridge, Frank, Aaron Cayer, Kirsten Day, Peggy Deamer, Andrea Dietz, Jessica Garcia Fritz, Palmyra Geraki, Daniel Jacobs, Valérie Lechêne, and Natalie Leonard. 'Beyond Capitalism?: Organizing Architecture Education'. *Journal of Architectural Education* 76, no. 2 (3 July 2022): 34–42. https://doi.org/10.1080/10464883.2022.2097501.

Carey, Adam. 'Three Victorian Vice Chancellors Paid $1 Million-plus, despite Uni Deficits'. *The Age*, 11 May 2023, sec. Education. https://www-theage-com-au.eu1.proxy.openathens.net/national/victoria/three-victorian-vice-chancellors-paid-1-million-plus-despite-uni-deficits-20230510-p5d75z.html.

Castilla, Emilio J., and Stephen Benard. 'The Paradox of Meritocracy in Organizations'. *Administrative Science Quarterly* 55, no. 4 (December 2010): 543–676. https://doi.org/10.2189/asqu.2010.55.4.543.

Chester, Mikhail V., Thaddeus R. Miller, Tischa A. Muñoz-Erickson, Alysha M. Helmrich, David M. Iwaniec, Timon McPhearson, Elizabeth M. Cook, Nancy B. Grimm, and Samuel A. Markolf. 'Sensemaking for Entangled Urban Social, Ecological, and Technological Systems in the Anthropocene'. *Npj Urban Sustainability* 3, no. 1 (26 June 2023): 39. https://doi.org/10.1038/s42949-023-00120-1.

Chomsky, Noam, Peter R. Mitchell, and John Schoeffel. *Understanding Power: The Indispensable Chomsky*. New York, NY: New Press, 2002.

Clay, Karen, Edson Severnini, and Xiaochen Sun. 'Does LEED Certification Save Energy? Evidence from Retrofitted Federal Buildings'. *Journal of Environmental Economics and Management* 121 (1 September 2023): 102866. https://doi.org/10.1016/j.jeem.2023.102866.

Coker, Coleman, Sarah Gamble, Thomas Fisher, and Katie Swenson. *Environmental Activism by Design*. Novato, CA: Applied Research & Design, an imprint of ORO Editions, 2022.

Collins, Scott L, Stephen R Carpenter, Scott M Swinton, Daniel E Orenstein, Daniel L Childers, Ted L Gragson, Nancy B Grimm, et al. 'An Integrated Conceptual Framework for Long-term Social–Ecological Research'. *Frontiers in Ecology and the Environment* 9, no. 6 (August 2011): 351–57. https://doi.org/10.1890/100068.

Colomina, Beatriz. *Privacy and Publicity: Modern Architecture as Mass Media*. Cambridge, MA: MIT Press, 1996.

Cook, Nancy, and Andrew Restuccia. Trump Aides Try to Quash Tax Hike Rumors amid Infrastructure Talks'. Politico, 17 May 2019. https://www.politico.com/story/2019/05/17/trump-tax-hike-rumors-infrastructure-1331703.

Córdova, Teresa, José Bravo, and José Miguel Acosta-Córdova. 'Environmental Justice and The Alliance for a Just Transition: Grist for Climate Justice Planning'. *Journal of Planning Literature* 38, no. 3 (August 2023): 408–15. https://doi.org/10.1177/08854122221121120.

Cortright, Marisa. *'Can This Be? Surely This Cannot Be?': Architectural Workers Organizing in Europe*, 2021.

Cranbrook Academy of Art. 'Architecture'. Cranbrook Academy of Art. Accessed 14 October 2023. https://cranbrookart.edu/departments/architecture/.

Crenshaw, Kimberle. 'Mapping the Margins: Intersectionality, Identity Politics, and Violence against Women of Color'. *Stanford Law Review* 43, no. 6 (July 1991): 1241. https://doi.org/10.2307/1229039.

Cret, Paul P. 'The Ecole Des Beaux-Arts and Architectural Education'. *Journal of the American Society of Architectural Historians* 1, no. 2 (1 April 1941): 3–15. https://doi.org/10.2307/901128.

Cron, Lisa. *Wired for Story: The Writer's Guide to Using Brain Science to Hook Readers from the Very First Sentence.* 1st ed. New York, NY: Ten Speed Press, 2012.

Cuff, Dana. *Architecture: The Story of Practice.* 1. paperback ed. Cambridge, MA: The MIT Press, 1992.

Curedale, Robert. *Design Methods 1: 200 Ways to Apply Design Thinking.* Cambridge, MA: MIT Press, 2012.

Dark Matter U_. 'Creating New Forms of Knowledge, Institutions, Collectivity, Community, and Design_'. Accessed 4 December 2023. https://darkmatteru.org/.

Deamer, Peggy. 'Practicing Practice'. Perspecta 44: Domain, September 2011. 160–167.

Deamer, Peggy. 'Marx, BIM, and Contemporary Labor'. In *Building Information Modeling,* edited by Karen M. Kensek and Douglas Noble, 1st ed., 313–19. Wiley: Hoboken, NJ, 2015a. https://doi.org/10.1002/9781119174752.ch23.

Deamer, Peggy, ed. *The Architect as Worker: Immaterial Labor, the Creative Class, and the Politics of Design.* London, New York: Bloomsbury Academic, 2015b.

Deamer, Peggy. *Architecture and Labor.* 1st ed. New York, NY: Routledge, 2020a. https://doi.org/10.4324/9780429325182.

Deamer, Peggy. 'Deprofessionalisation'. In *Architects after Architecture: Alternative Pathways for Practice,* edited by Harriet Harriss, Rory Hyde, and Roberta Marcaccio, 184–90. New York, NY: Routledge, 2020.b

Deleuze, Gilles, and Félix Guattari. *A Thousand Plateaus : Capitalism and Schizophrenia.* Minneapolis: University of Minnesota Press, 1987.

Design Justice Network. 'Home.' https://designjustice.org/.

Design Studio for Social Intervention. 'What Does it Mean to Live in a Neighborhood?'. https://www.ds4si.org/design-gym-classes

DMU. 'Creating New Forms of Knowledge, Institutions, Collectivity, Community, and Design_'. Dark Matter U_, 2023. https://darkmatteru.org/.

Durlin, Marty. 'The Shot Heard Round the West'. High Country News, 1 February 2010. https://www.hcn.org/issues/42.2/the-shot-heard-round-the-west?b_start:int=1#body.

Emmons, Paul, Marcia F. Feuerstein, Carolina Dayer, and Luc Phinney, eds. *Confabulations: Storytelling in Architecture.* Abingdon, Oxfordshire: Routledge, 2018.

ERI. 'Architect Salary in Sweden'. Economic Research Institute, December 2023. https://www.erieri.com/salary/job/architect/sweden.

Escobar, Arturo. *Designs for the Pluriverse: Radical Interdependence, Autonomy, and the Making of Worlds.* New Ecologies for the Twenty-First Century. Durham: Duke University Press, 2018.

'Eugene Emmanuel Viollet-Le-Duc'. In *Architectural Theory: From the Renaissance to the Present,* 214–25. Köln: Taschen, 2006.

Federal Aviation Administration. 'Office of International Affairs'. United States Department of Transportation, n.d. https://www.faa.gov/international_affairs.

Fennema, Meindert, and Eelke M. Heemskerk. 'When Theory Meets Methods: The Naissance of Computer Assisted Corporate Interlock Research'. *Global Networks* 18, no. 1 (January 2018): 81–104. https://doi.org/10.1111/glob.12178.

Ferreira Silva, Cidália. 'Architecture as Expanded Field'. *The International Journal of the Constructed Environment* 1, no. 3 (2011): 55–70. https://doi.org/10.18848/2154-8587/CGP/v01i03/37491.

Flynn, Katherine. 'How Is Student Debt Shaping Architecture?' Architect, 1 March 2023. https://www.architectmagazine.com/aia-architect/aiafeature/how-is-student-debt-shaping-architecture_o.

Forde, Tessa. 'Starting a Free School of Architecture'. *Charrette* 6, no. 1 (2020): 121–43.

Foucault, Michel. *Power*. Edited by James D. Faubion. Translated by Robert J. Hurley. Essential Works of Foucault 3. New York, NY: Penguin Books, 2020.

Frascari, Marco. 'Professional Use of Signs in Architecture'. *Journal of Architectural Education* 36, no. 2 (2023).

Freire, Paulo, Donaldo P. Macedo, and Ira Shor. *Pedagogy of the Oppressed*. Translated by Myra Bergman Ramos. 50th anniversary edition. New York, NY: Bloomsbury Academic, 2018.

FSA Organizers. 'ABOUT'. Free School of Architecture, 2018. https://www.freeschoolofarchitecture.org/.

Gebler, Malte, Max Juraschek, Sebastian Thiede, Felipe Cerdas, and Christoph Herrmann. 'Defining the "Positive Impact" of Socio-Technical Systems for Absolute Sustainability: A Literature Review Based on the Identification of System Design Principles and Management Functions'. *Sustainability Science* 17, no. 6 (November 2022): 2597–2613. https://doi.org/10.1007/s11625-022-01168-1.

Glaser, Marion, Gesche Krause, Beate M. W. Ratter, Martin Welp, and Andrew Halliday, eds. *Human-Nature Interactions in the Anthropocene: Potentials of Social-Ecological Systems Analysis*. Routledge Studies in Environment, Culture, and Society 1. New York, NY; London: Routledge, 2012.

Global Social Theory. 'New Materialism'. Global Social Theory, n.d. https://globalsocialtheory.org/topics/new-materialism/.

Gogol, Frank. 'What Are Credit Hours?' stilt, 24 November 2023. https://www.stilt.com/education/what-are-credit-hours.

Goodchild, Melanie. 'About Me'. Melanie Goodchild, 2023. https://www.melaniegoodchild.com.

Griffin, Alexander. *Rise of Academic Architectural Education: The Origins and Enduring Influence of the Academie... d'architecture*. S.l.: Routledge, 2021.

Grim, Ryan. 'ELEPHANT IN THE ZOOM: Meltdowns Have Brought Progressive Advocacy Groups to a Standstill at a Critical Moment in World History'. The Intercept_, 13 June 2022. https://theintercept.com/2022/06/13/progressive-organizing-infighting-callout-culture/.

Grozdanic, Lidija. 'Which Countries Pay the Highest Salaries for Architects?' arch daily, 15 November 2017. https://www.archdaily.com/883722/which-countries-pay-the-highest-salaries-for-architects.

Gutman, Robert, Dana Cuff, John Wriedt, and Bryan Bell. *Architecture from the Outside in: Selected Essays*. 1st ed. New York, NY: Princeton Architectural Press, 2010.

Hardt, Michael, and Antonio Negri. *Multitude: War and Democracy in the Age of Empire*. Reprint edition. New York, NY: Penguin Books, 2005.

Henrich, Joseph. *The Secret of Our Success: How Culture Is Driving Human Evolution, Domesticating Our Species, and Making Us Smarter*. NJ and Oxford: Princeton University Press, 2016.

Hernandez, Jessica. *Fresh Banana Leaves: Healing Indigenous Landscapes through Indigenous Science*. Huichin, unceded Ohloe land, aka Berkeley, CA: North Atlantic Books, 2022.

Hersey, Cole. 'The Scout: Sim Van Der Ryn & the Outlaw Builders'. Dispatches, 21 June 2021. https://dispatchesmag.com/reappraisal-outlaw-builders/.

Hickman, Matt. 'Dark Matter University Brings a New Model of Architectural Education to Light'. *The Architect's Newspaper*, 29 September 2020. https://www.archpaper.com/2020/09/storied-hbcu-dark-matter-university-brings-new-model-of-architectural-education-to-light/.

Hindle, Patton. 'A Month After I Published a Book About How to Run an Art Gallery, I Closed Mine. Here's Why'. Artnet news, 10 January 2019. https://news.artnet.com/news/a-month-after-i-published-a-book-about-how-to-run-a-gallery-i-closed-mine-heres-why-1435756.

hooks, bell. *Teaching to Transgress: Education as the Practice of Freedom.* New York, NY: Routledge, 1994.

'How Much Are Private-College Presidents Paid?', n.d.

Indiana University. 'Honoring Elinor Ostrom, the First Woman to Win a Nobel in Economic Sciences'. Indiana University, 2023. https://ostromworkshop.indiana.edu/about/ostroms-history/nobel-prize/index.html.

Jackson, Philip W. *Life in Classrooms.* New York, NY: Teachers College Press, 1990.

Jojola, Ted. 'iD+Pi Concepts'. YouTube, 15 July 2021. https://www.youtube.com/watch?v=-bXA0BFw7Rw.

Jones Jr, La Mont. 'One Culprit in Rising College Costs: Administrative Expenses'. US News, 1 June 2023. https://www.usnews.com/education/articles/one-culprit-in-rising-college-costs.

Just Transition Alliance. 'Just Transition Principles'. Just Transition Alliance, 2022. https://jtalliance.org/what-is-just-transition/.

Kleinman, Zoe, and Sean Seddon. 'Elon Musk Tells Rishi Sunak AI Will Put an End to Work'. BBC.com, 3 November 2023. https://www.bbc.com/news/uk-67302048.

KNOW. 'KNOW: Knowledge in Action for Urban Equity'. Urban Know, 2021. https://www.urban-know.com/.

Kohomban, Jeremy, and David Collins. 'The Systematic Starvation of Those Who Do Good', 2017. https://doi.org/10.48558/9WEW-Z846.

Koolhaas, Rem, Bruce Mau, and Hans Werlemann. *S, M, L, XL.* 2nd edition. New-York, NY: The Monacelli Press, 1995.

Kostof, Spiro. *A History of Architecture: Settings and Rituals.* Edited by Greg Castillo. 2nd ed. New York, NY; Oxford: Oxford University Press, 1995.

KQED News Staff. 'Newsom Signs Bill Paving Way to Build New Student Housing at People's Park in Berkeley'. KQED, 8 September 2023. https://www.kqed.org/news/11959483/legislation-that-could-push-peoples-park-student-housing-project-forward-heads-to-newsom.

Krauss, Rosalind. 'Sculpture in the Expanded Field'. *October* 8, no. Spring (1979): 30–44. https://doi.org/10.2307/778224.

Kruft, Hanno-Walter. *A history of architectural theory: From Vitruvius to the present.* London, New York: Zwemmer; Princeton Architectural Press, 1994.

Kvan, Thomas, Bingkun Liu, and Yunyan Jia. 'The Emergence of a Profession: Development of the Profession of Architecture in China'. *Journal of Architectural and Planning Research* 25, no. 3 (Autumn 2023). https://www.jstor.org/stable/43030836.

Kwet, Michael. 'Digital Colonialism: The Evolution of US Empire'. tni Longreads, 4 March 2021. https://longreads.tni.org/digital-colonialism-the-evolution-of-us-empire.

Lang, James M. *Small Teaching: Everyday Lessons from the Science of Learning.* Second edition. San Francisco, CA: Jossey-Bass, 2021.

Larson, Magali Sarfatti. 'Professionalism: Rise and Fall.' *International Journal of Health Services*, Vol. 9, No. 4, 1979. 607–627.

Larson, Magali Sarfatti. *The Rise of Professionalism: Monopolies of Competence and Sheltered Markets*. Piscataway, NJ: Transaction Publishers, 2013. xiii.

Last, Nana. 'Of.' Assemblage 39, August 2000: 106–117.

Lerup, Lars. *After the City*. First MIT Press paperback ed. Cambridge: MIT Press, 2001.

Levantovskaya, Maggie. 'Organizing Against Precarity in Higher Education'. Current Affairs, 6 April 2022. https://www.currentaffairs.org/2022/04/organizing-against-precarity-in-higher-education.

Liu, Jianguo, Thomas Dietz, Stephen R. Carpenter, Marina Alberti, Carl Folke, Emilio Moran, Alice N. Pell, et al. 'Complexity of Coupled Human and Natural Systems'. *Science* 317, no. 5844 (14 September 2007): 1513–16. https://doi.org/10.1126/science.1144004.

Maldonado, Camilo. 'Price Of College Increasing Almost 8 Times Faster Than Wages'. Forbes, 24 July 2018. https://www.forbes.com/sites/camilomaldonado/2018/07/24/price-of-college-increasing-almost-8-times-faster-than-wages/?sh=79e45ea366c1.

Martin Brown, and Carlo Battisti, eds. 'RESTORD 2030: A Regenerative Guides for Educators Students and Practitioners'. Eurac Research, 2021. https://www.eurestore.eu/wp-content/uploads/2021/11/FAD_Restord-2030_ok.pdf.

Martin, Reinhold, Jacob Moore, and Jordan Steingard, eds. *Green Reconstruction: A Curricular Toolkit for the Built Environment*. New York, NY: Temple Hoyne Buell Center for the Study of American Architecture, Columbia University, 2021.

McAulay, Scott. 'A New Education for Climate Change'. The RIBA Journal. Accessed 13 August 2023. https://www.ribaj.com/intelligence/anthropocene-architecture-schoolscott-mcaulay-climate-emergency.

McConville, Jennifer. 'Socio-Technical System Analysis'. Swedish University of Agricultural Sciences, 5 November 2021. https://www.slu.se/en/departments/energy-technology/research/environmental-engineering/socioteknisk-systemanalys/.

McDonald, Joseph P. *The Power of Protocols: An Educator's Guide to Better Practice*. 3rd Edition. The Series on School Reform. New York, NY: Teachers College Press, 2013.

McDonough, William, and Michael Braungart. *Cradle to Cradle: Remaking the Way We Make Things*. 1st ed. New York, NY: North Point Press, 2002.

McGurran, Brianna, and Alicia Hahn. 'College Tuition Inflation: Compare The Cost Of College Over Time'. Forbes Advisor, 9 May 2023. https://www.forbes.com/advisor/student-loans/college-tuition-inflation/.

McKinley, Jess. 'A Town-Gown Clash Over the Costs of Public Services'. *The New York Times*, 16 September 2013. https://www.nytimes.com/2013/09/17/nyregion/a-town-gown-clash-over-the-costs-of-public-services.html.

McKinsey & Company. 'Enduring Ideas: The Three Horizons of Growth', 1 December 2009. https://www.mckinsey.com/capabilities/strategy-and-corporate-finance/our-insights/enduring-ideas-the-three-horizons-of-growth.

Mertz, August (Sandy). 'Teaching Secrets: Arranging Optimal Classroom Seating'. Education Week, 31 July 2012. https://www.edweek.org/teaching-learning/opinion-teaching-secrets-arranging-optimal-classroom-seating/2012/07.

Ministry of Education and New Zealand Qualifications Authority. 'New Zealand and the Bologna Process'. New Zealand Government, 2008.

Morton, Timothy. *Humankind: Solidarity with Nonhuman People*. London; New York, NY: Verso, 2017.

Mumford, Eric Paul. *The CIAM Discourse on Urbanism, 1928-1960*. 1. MIT Press paperback ed. Cambridge, MA: MIT Press, 2000.

Murawski, Michał, and Jane Rendell. 'The Social Condenser: A Century of Revolution through Architecture, 1917–2017'. *The Journal of Architecture* 22, no. 3 (3 April 2017): 369–71. https://doi.org/10.1080/13602365.2017.1326680.

NAAB. 'Conditions for Accreditation 2020 Edition'. National Architectural Accrediting Board Inc, 10 February 2020. https://www.naab.org/wp-content/uploads/2020-NAAB-Conditions-for-Accreditation.pdf.

NAAB. 'History'. National Architectureal Accrediting Board, 2023. https://www.naab.org/about/history/.

National Academy of Sciences. 'Elinor Ostrom'. National Academy of Sciences, 2023. https://www.nasonline.org/member-directory/deceased-members/45787.html.

National Council of Architectural Registration Boards. 'Licensing Requirements Tool'. NCARB, 2023. https://www.ncarb.org/get-licensed/licensing-requirements-tool.

National Park Service. 'Yosemite National Park Fire Managers Partner with Indian Tribes for Prescribed Fire Project'. National Park Service, 15 November 2021. https://www.nps.gov/articles/000/yosemite-national-park-fire-managers-partner-with-indian-tribes-for-prescribed-fire-project.htm.

Neuckermans, Herman. 'European Architectural Education in Motion', 2005.

New York State Licensed Professions, Office of the Professions. 'New York State Licensed Professions.' https://www.op.nysed.gov/professions-index.

Ng, Rashida. 'Breaking the Chains'. In *Rethinking the Crit*, edited by Patrick Flynn, Maureen O'Connor, Mark Price, and Miriam Dunn, 185–93, 1st ed. London: Routledge, 2022. https://doi.org/10.4324/9781003289432-17.

Ngā Aho. 'Takenga Mai'. Ngā Aho, 2023. https://ngaaho.maori.nz/page.php?m=155.

Nicholas, George. 'It's Taken Thousands of Years, but Western Science Is Finally Catching up to Traditional Knowledge'. The Conversation, 15 February 2018. https://theconversation.com/its-taken-thousands-of-years-but-western-science-is-finally-catching-up-to-traditional-knowledge-90291?xid=PS_smithsonian.

Ockman, Joan, and Rebecca Williamson, eds. *Architecture School: Three Centuries of Educating Architects in North America*. Cambridge, MA; Washington, DC: MIT Press; Association of Collegiate Schools of Architecture, 2012.

OOA. 'O/A'. Out of Architecture, n.d. https://www.outofarchitecture.com/.

Ostrom, Elinor. 'A General Framework for Analyzing Sustainability of Social-Ecological Systems'. *Science* 325, no. 5939 (24 July 2009): 419–22. https://doi.org/10.1126/science.1172133.

Outer Coast. 'Outer Coast', n.d.

Owens, Brian. 'Canada Used Hungry Indigenous Children to Study Malnutrition'. *Nature*, 23 July 2013, nature.2013.13425. https://doi.org/10.1038/nature.2013.13425.

OXMAN. 'Nature x Humanity', 2023. https://oxman.com/.

P2PU. 'Welcome to Peer 2 Peer University, the Home of Learning Circles'. Peer 2 Peer University, 2023. https://www.p2pu.org/en/.

Padan, Yael. 'Researching Architecture and Urban Inequality: Toward Engaged Ethics'. *Architecture and Culture* 8, no. 3–4 (1 October 2020): 484–97. https://doi.org/10.1080/20507828.2020.1792109.

Padan, Yael, Vanesa Castán Broto, Jane Rendell, and David Roberts. 'A "minifest" as the Promise of Collective Voice'. *Axon: Creative Explorations* 10, no. 2 (December 2020): 1–17. https://axonjournal.com.au/issue-vol-10-no-2-dec-2020/minifesta-promise-collective-voice.

Penta, Leo J. 'Hannah Arendt: On Power'. *The Journal of Speculative Philosophy* 10, no. 3 (1996): 210–29. https://www.jstor.org/stable/25670190.

Pratt, Mary Louise. *Imperial Eyes: Travel Writing and Transculturation*. 2nd ed. London; New York, NY: Routledge, 2008.

Prospero, Michele. 'Gramsci: Political Scientist'. In *A Companion to Antonio Gramsci: Essays on History and Theories of History, Politics and Historiography*, edited by Davide Cadeddu, 93–104. Studies in Critical Social Sciences, volume 164. Leiden; Boston: Brill, 2020.

Qureshi, Zia. 'Technology, Growth, and Inequality: Changing Dynamics in the Digital Era'. Global Working Paper. Washington, D.C, USA: Global Economy and Development at Brookings, February 2021. https://www.brookings.edu/wp-content/uploads/2021/02/Technology-growth-inequality_final.pdf.

Rauchway, Eric. *The Great Depression & the New Deal: A Very Short Introduction*. Very Short Introductions 166. Oxford; New York, NY: Oxford University Press, 2008.

Ravenscroft, Alison. 'Strange Weather: Indigenous Materialisms, New Materialism, and Colonialism'. *The Cambridge Journal of Postcolonial Literary Inquiry* 5, no. 3 (September 2018): 353–70. https://doi.org/10.1017/pli.2018.9.

Readings, Bill. *The University in Ruins*. Cambridge, MA: Harvard University Press, 1996.

Redvers, Nicole, Yuria Celidwen, Clinton Schultz, Ojistoh Horn, Cicilia Githaiga, Melissa Vera, Marlikka Perdrisat, et al. 'The Determinants of Planetary Health: An Indigenous Consensus Perspective'. *The Lancet Planetary Health* 6, no. 2 (February 2022): e156–63. https://doi.org/10.1016/S2542-5196(21)00354-5.

Reich, Robert. 'The Myth of the "Free Market" and How to Make the Economy Work for Us', 16 September 2013. https://robertreich.org/post/61406074983.

Rendell, Jane. *Art and Architecture: A Place Between*. London: I. B. Tauris, 2006.

Rendell, Jane. 'Critical Spatial Practice as Parrhesia'. *MaHKUscript: Journal of Fine Art Research* 1, no. 2 (13 December 2016a): 16. https://doi.org/10.5334/mjfar.13.

Rendell, Jane. 'Critical Spatial Practice as Parrhesia'. *MaHKUscript: Journal of Fine Art Research* 1, no. 2 (13 December 2016b): 16. https://doi.org/10.5334/mjfar.13.

Rendell, Jane. 'Giving an Account of Oneself: Architecturally'. *Journal of Visual Culture* 15, no. 3 (December 2016c): 334–48. https://doi.org/10.1177/1470412916665143.

Rendell, Jane. 'Configuring Critique (or "the Art of Not Being Governed Quite so Much")'. In *The Routledge Companion to Criticality in Art, Architecture, and Design*, edited by Chris Brisbin and Myra Thiessen, 1st ed. Milton Park, Abingdon, Oxon; New York, NY : Routledge, 2018.: Routledge, 2018. https://doi.org/10.4324/9781315623412.

Rendell, Jane. 'Silver: A Courthouse Drama'. In *Building Critique: Architecture and Its Discontent*, edited by Gabu Heindl, Michael Klein, Christina Linortner, and Österreichische Gesellschaft für Architektur, 1st edition. Leipzig: Spector Books, 2019.

Rendell, Jane. 'Home-Work Displacements'. In *Non-Standard Architectural Productions: Between Aesthetic Experience and Social Action*, edited by Sandra Karina Löschke, 117–41. London; New York: Routledge, 2020a.

Rendell, Jane. 'Hotspots and Touchstones: From Critical to Ethical Spatial Practice'. *Architecture and Culture* 8, no. 3–4 (1 October 2020b): 407–19. https://doi.org/10.1080/20507828.2020.1792107.

Rendell, Jane. 'Seven Studies for "A Holding"'. In *Remote Practices: Architecture at a Distance*, edited by Matthew Mindrup and Lilian Chee, 93–99. London, UK: Lund Humphries Publishers, 2022a.

Rendell, Jane. 'Site-Writing as Holding'. Edited by Igor Marjanovik, Jay Cephas, and Miljački. *JAE*, Pedagogies for a Broken World, 78, no. 2 (Fall 2022b): 201–2022.

Rendell, Jane. 'Silver'. A Published Event, 21 November 2023. https://lostrocks. net/books/silver.

Rendell, Jane, Enrique Cavelier, Sophie Chamberlain, Sean Cham, Yuxiao Chen, Rachael Docherty, Abdulrahman El-Taliawi, et al. 'Selvedges/Self-Edges'. In *Slow Spatial Reader: Chronicles of Radical Affection*, edited by Carolyn F. Strauss, 144–57. Amsterdam: Valiz, 2021.

RepRisk. 'ESG with a Risk Lens and Transparency'. RepRisk, n.d. https://www. reprisk.com/approach.

Rice, Louis, and David Littlefield, eds. *Transgression: Towards an Expanded Field of Architecture*. Critiques: Critical Studies in Architectural Humanities, Volume 10. London; New York: Routledge, Taylor & Francis Group, 2015.

Risselada, Max, Dirk van den Heuvel, Victor Joseph, Nederlands Architectu-urinstituut, and Team 10, eds. *Team 10: 1953 - 81; in Search of a Utopia of the Present; [This Publication … Accompanied the Exhibition 'Team 10 - a Utopia of the Present' Held at the Netherlands Architecture Institute, Rotterdam from September 24th 2005 to January 8th 2006, after Which It Traveled to Milan, Paris an Other Cities]*. Rotterdam: NAi Publishers, 2005.

Roberts, David. 'Reflect Critically and Act Fearlessly: A Survey of Ethical Codes, Guidance and Access in Built Environment Practice'. Bartlett Ethics Commission, 2018. https://static1.squarespace.com/static/5f296e79b9afb21109987448/t/61af97a609c 72d7ceb4da9b3/1638897586685/Built+Environment+Codes+Review_Roberts.pdf.

Roberts, David. 'Why Now: The Ethical Act of Architectural Declaration'. *Architecture and Culture* 9, no. 4 (2 October 2021): 587–605. https://doi.org/10.1080/20507828. 2020.1792110.

Roberts, David, Jane Rendell, Yael Padan, Ariana Markowitz, and Emmanuel Os-uteye. 'Practising Ethics: Guides for Built Environment Research'. *The Journal of Architecture* 27, no. 5–6 (18 August 2022): 673–707. https://doi.org/10. 1080/13602365.2022.2143395.

Rogers, Jocelyn. 'Buildings Are Infrastructure'. American Institute of Architects, 18 June 2021. https://www.aia.org/articles/6410108-buildings-are-infrastructure.

Rome, Adam. '"Give Earth a Chance": The Environmental Movement and the Sixties'. *Journal of American History* 90, no. 2 (1 September 2003): 525. https:// doi.org/10.2307/3659443.

Rudin, Jake, and Erin Pellegrino. *Out of Architecture: The Value of Architects Beyond Traditional Practice*. 1st ed. London: Routledge, 2022. https://doi. org/10.4324/9781003300922.

Sachs, Avigail. *Environmental Design: Architecture, Politics, and Science in Post-war America*. Charlottesville, VA: University of Virginia Press, 2018. https:// doi.org/10.2307/j.ctv3f8rr0.

Schlüter, Maja, L. Jamila Haider, Steven J. Lade, Emilie Lindkvist, Romina Martin, Kirill Orach, Nanda Wijermans, and Carl Folke. 'Capturing Emergent Phenomena in Social-Ecological Systems: An Analytical Framework'. *Ecology and Society* 24, no. 3 (2019): art11. https://doi.org/10.5751/ES-11012-240311.

Sharpe, Bill, Anthony Hodgson, Graham Leicester, Andrew Lyon, and Ioan Fazey. 'Three Horizons: A Pathways Practice for Transformation'. *Ecology and Society* 21, no. 2 (2016): art47. https://doi.org/10.5751/ES-08388-210247.

Shaw, Danny. 'Revealed: One in Three Russell Group University Bosses Received Pay Rises Last Year'. The Tab, 22 April 2022. https://thetab.com/ uk/2022/04/22/revealed-one-in-three-russell-group-university-bosses-received-pay-rises-last-year-247978.

Simon, Caroline. 'Bureaucrats And Buildings: The Case For Why College Is So Expensive'. Forbes, 5 September 2017. https://www.forbes.com/sites/caroline-simon/2017/09/05/bureaucrats-and-buildings-the-case-for-why-college-is-so-expensive/?sh=d0ae524456a4.

Slaughter, Sheila, and Gary Rhoades. 'The Neo-Liberal University'. *New Labor Forum* 6, no. Spring-Summer (2000): 73–79. https://www.jstor.org/stable/40342886.

Smiley, Erica, and Sarita Gupta. 'The Future We Need: Organizing for a Better Democracy in the Twenty-First Century'. In *The Future We Need*. Ithaca, New York: Cornell University Press, 2022. https://doi.org/10.1515/9781501764844.

Southwest Organising Project. 'Southwest Organizing Project Letter to Big 10 Environmental Groups', 16 March 1990. https://www.ejnet.org/ej/swop.pdf.

Sovereign Union. '"Lab Rats" - Medical Experiments on Aboriginal Children in Care'. Sovereign Union - First Nations Asserting Sovereignty, 2022. http://nationalunitygovernment.org/content/lab-rats-medical-experiments-aboriginal-children-care.

SRI. 'Protocols'. CLEE. Accessed 7 December 2023. https://www.schoolreformini tiative.org/protocols/.

Staff writer. 'Brazil Authorities Expect Mariana Dam Disaster Deal to Close in December'. Mining.com, 29 November 2023. https://www.mining.com/brazil-authorities-expect-mariana-dam-disaster-deal-to-close-in-december/.

State Higher Education Finance. 'In the News', 2023. https://shef.sheeo.org/in-the-news/.

Stathaki, Ellie. 'Venice Architecture Biennale 2023 curator Lesley Lokko on decolonisation, decarbonisation and diversity'. Wallpaper*, 6 October 2022. https://www.wallpaper.com/architecture/lesley-lokko-is-africa-the-laboratory-of-the-future

Stead, Naomi, Maryam Gusheh, and Julia Rodwell. 'Well-Being in Architectural Education: Theory-Building, Reflexive Methodology, and the "Hidden Curriculum"'. *Journal of Architectural Education* 76, no. 1 (2 January 2022): 85–97. https://doi.org/10.1080/10464883.2022.2017699.

Steenson, Molly Wright. *Architectural Intelligence: How Designers, Tinkerers, and Architects Created the Digital Landscape*. London, England: The MIT Press, 2017.

Stevens, Garry. 'Struggle in the Studio: A Bourdivin Look at Architectural Pedagogy', 2023.

Stott, Timothy. 'Ludic Pedagogies at the College of Environmental Design, UC Berkeley, 1966 to 1972'. In *The Culture of Nature in the History of Design*, edited by Kjetil Fallan, 1st ed., 58–71. Abingdon, Oxon; New York, NY: Routledge is an imprint of the Taylor & Francis Group, an Informa Business, 2019, Routledge, 2019. https://doi.org/10.4324/9780429469848-5.

Student Organizing Across Syllabi and Project Briefs. YouTube. ABC School 2022, 2022. https://www.youtube.com/watch?v=vH6LN0O6fy4.

Sudjic, Deyan. *The Edifice Complex: How the Rich and Powerful Shape the World*. London: Allen Lane, 2005.

Suleyman, Mustafa. 'How the AI Revolution Will Reshape the World'. TIME, 1 September 2023. https://time.com/6310115/ai-revolution-reshape-the-world/.

Suntrup, Edward L. 'NLRB v. Yeshiva University and Unionization in Higher Education'. *Industrial Relations Law Journal* 4, no. 2 (1981): 287–307. https://www.jstor.org/stable/24049573.

The Architects Lobby, Aaron Cayer, Albert Chao, Kirsten Day, Peggy Deamer, Andrea Dietz, Jessica Garcia Fritz, et al. 'Not as Easy as ABC'. *Log Journal* 54, no. Co-authoring (Winter/Spring 2022): 45–57.

The Architecture Lobby. 'The Architecture Lobby'. The Architecture Lobby, 2023. https://architecture-lobby.org/.

The Architecture Lobby Academia Working Group. 'S-T-U-D-I-O'. ABC Architecture Beyond Capitalism School, 2022. https://abc.architecture-lobby.org/architecture-beyond-capitalism-2022.

The Architecture Lobby Academia Working Group. 'Future Belonging: Organizing for Global Change'. ABC Architecture Beyong Capitalism, 2023. https://abc.architecture-lobby.org/.

The Bartlett Development Planning Unity. 'Speech Extractions Witness, Testimony, Evidence in Response to the Mining Industry'. UCL, October 2016. https://www.ucl.ac.uk/bartlett/development/events/2016/oct/speech-extractions-witness-testimony-evidence-response-mining-industry.

The Business of Architecture. 'Architects Registration Changes 2024'. Accessed 18 November 2023. https://aca.org.au/architects-registration-changes-2024/.

The Green Party of the United States. 'Green New Deal'. Green Party US, n.d. https://www.gp.org/green_new_deal.

The Red Nation. *The Red Deal — Indigenous Action to Save Our Earth*. Common Notions, 2021.

Temple Hoyne Buell Center for the Study of American Architecture. 'Green Reconstruction: A Curricular Toolkit for the Built Environment'. Columbia University. Accessed 13 December 2023. https://power.buellcenter.columbia.edu/initiatives/green-reconstruction-curricular-toolkit-built-environment.

The University of New Mexico. 'Indigenous Design and Planning Institute: About iD+Pi'. The University of New Mexico. Accessed 6 December 2023. https://idpi.unm.edu/about-idpi.html.

Till, Jeremy. *Architecture Depends*. Cambridge, MA: MIT Press, 2009.

TILT Higher Ed. 'Transparency in Learning and Teaching', 2023. https://tilthighered.com/.

Toward a More Just Design Studio: Analyzing Power Dynamics in Studio Spaces, 2022. https://www.youtube.com/watch?v=8Qu5Va3fDxo.

Trimboli, Oscar. *How to Listen: Discover the Hidden Key to Better Communication*. Vancouver, BC: Page Two, 2022.

Trust for London. 'It's All about Power', 2022. https://trustforlondon.org.uk/research/its-all-about-power/.

UCL. 'Ethics in the Built Environment'. UCL, July 2023. https://www.ucl.ac.uk/bartlett/research/ethics-built-environment.

UCL News. 'BHP Billiton and UCL Launch Natural Resources Initiative'. UCL, 10 June 2011. https://www.ucl.ac.uk/news/2011/jun/bhp-billiton-and-ucl-launch-natural-resources-initiative.

UNESCO. 'What You Need to Know about Education for Sustainable Development'. UNESCO, 17 November 2023. https://www.unesco.org/en/education-sustainable-development/need-know.

United States Supreme Court. 'NLRB v. YESHIVA UNIVERSITY, 444 U.S. 672 (1980)'. FindLaw, February 1980. https://caselaw.findlaw.com/court/us-supreme-court/444/672.html.

University of Melbourne. 'iDARE: Innovation, Design, Art, Ethics'. University of Melbourne, n.d. https://idare.vca.unimelb.edu.au/.

US Government. 'H.R.5376 - Inflation Reduction Act of 2022'. Congress.gov, 2022. https://www.congress.gov/bill/117th-congress/house-bill/5376/text/rh.

Veblen, Thorstein. 'The Higher Learning in America: A Memorandum on the Conduct of Universities by Business Men', n.d.

VeneKlasen, Lisa, and Valerie Miller. *A New Weave of Power, People, and Politics: The Action Guide for Advocacy and Citizen Participation*. Bourton-on-Dunsmore, Warwickshire: Practical Action Pub, c2007.

Vidler, Anthony. 'Architecture's Expanded Field'. *Artforum International*, April 2004.

Vignet, Anna. 'The Decades-Long People's Park Battle: A Brief Video History'. KQED, 10 March 2023. https://www.kqed.org/news/11942975/peoples-park-battle.

Wainwright, Oliver 'Snubbed, Cheated, Erased: The Scandal of Architecture's Invisible Women'. *The Guardian*, 17 October 2018. https://www.theguardian.com/artanddesign/2018/oct/16/the-scandal-of-architecture-invisible-women-denise-scott-brown.

Wainwright, Oliver. '"It's Already Way beyond What Humans Can Do": Will AI Wipe out Architects?' The Guardian, 7 August 2023. https://www.theguardian.com/artanddesign/2023/aug/07/ai-architects-revolutionising-corbusier-architecture.

Waltner-Toews, David, James J. Kay, Cynthia Neudoerffer, and Thomas Gitau. 'Perspective Changes Everything: Managing Ecosystems from the inside Out'. *Frontiers in Ecology and the Environment* 1, no. 1 (February 2003): 23–30. https://doi.org/10.1890/1540-9295(2003)001[0023:PCEMEF]2.0.CO;2.

Walton, Chris. 'Graduate Students at the University of Michigan's Taubman College Are on Strike for Better Pay'. The Architect's Newspaper, 30 May 2023. https://www.archpaper.com/2023/05/graduate-students-at-the-university-of-michigans-taubman-college-are-on-strike-for-better-pay/#:~:text=Labored%20Relations-,Graduate%20students%20at%20the%20University%20of%20Michigan's%20Taubman,on%20strike%20for%20better%20pay&text=On%20March%2029%2C%20over%202%2C000,of%20Architecture%20and%20Urban%20Planning.

Waterloo School fo Architecture. 'Architecture: Co-Op'. University of Waterloo, 2023. https://uwaterloo.ca/architecture/academic-programs/co-op.

Weber, Max, Guenther Roth, and Claus Wittich. *Economy and Society: An Outline of Interpretive Sociology*. Berkeley, CA: University of California Press, 1978.

Wikipedia. 'Progressive Stack'. Wikipedia, April 2023. https://en.wikipedia.org/wiki/Progressive_stack.

Willis, Daniel. 'Are Charettes Old School?' *Harvard Design Magazine*, Winter/Fall -2011 2010. https://www.harvarddesignmagazine.org/articles/are-charrettes-old-school/.

Wong, Carmen, Kate Ballegooyen, Lawrence Ignace, Mary Jane (Gùdia) Johnson, and Heidi Swanson. 'Towards Reconciliation: 10 Calls to Action to Natural Scientists Working in Canada'. Edited by Idil Boran. FACETS 5, no. 1 (1 January 2020): 769–83. https://doi.org/10.1139/facets-2020-0005.

Woolard, Caroline. 'The Meeting'. Self-published, 2020. https://book.caroline-woolard.com/chapter-1-the-meeting.

Yang, K. Wayne. *A Third University Is Possible*. Forerunners: Ideas First from the University of Minnesota Press. Minneapolis, MN: University of Minnesota Press, 2017.

Yates-Francis, Matangireia. '*TŪHONONGA: Architecture Co-Occupying with Earth and Sky*'. Master's Thesis, Auckland University of Technology, 2022. Tuwhera Open Access Repository.

Zierler, David. *The Invention of Ecocide: Agent Orange, Vietnam, and the Scientists Who Changed the Way We Think About the Environment*. Illustrated edition. Athens: University of Georgia Press, 2011.

INDEX

T - #0214 - 021224 - C0 - 229/152/12 - PB - 9781032532813 - Matt Lamination